Pierre L. van den Berghe

Man in Society

A BIOSOCIAL VIEW

In *Man in Society,* Pierre van den Berghe, the well-known sociologist, avoids what most books in the field say, and he says much that they should, perhaps, say. Many texts claim that sociology is a science of society, using a heavy arsenal of jargon, and, in fact, presenting the student with a bad ethnography of North American society — couched in pompous platitudes and indigestible prose. Van den Berghe makes no claim that sociology is a science; he minimizes jargon; he refuses to talk down to the student; and he tries to raise the basic problems of human behavior by examining the *entire* range of that behavior — instead of a single time and place.

Generally, textbooks ignore the biological aspects of human behavior, focussing overwhelmingly on industrial and Western societies to the nearly complete neglect of agrarian and stateless societies. *Man in Society* takes a look at the nature of human nature by comparing *Homo sapiens* with other species, and it treats Western industrial societies as simply one special type of a social system among many. Thus, this text is heavily comparative, both in a cross-species and in a cross-cultural way. The author is also concerned with problems of biological and social evolution, drawing on the past, as well as the present, to determine what the range of human behavior is.

The content of the book is at least as much anthropological as sociological, as van den Berghe refuses to believe that there is a meaningful distinction between the two disciplines. He maintains that the two disciplines separated mainly because of the racism in the intellectual milieu of late 19th century Europe. The study of whites became sociology, while the exotic dark savages beyond the pale were relegated to anthropology.

The biosocial approach adopted here is explicitly anti-racist, since it defines the entire human species as the scope of sociology, holding that fundamental aspects of human behavior are remarkably uniform throughout the species.

Pierre L. van den Berghe is Professor of Sociology at the University of Washington, Seattle. His many books include *Age and Sex in Human Societies, A Biosocial Perspective* (1973); *Academic Gamesmanship* (1970); *Race and Racism, A Comparative Perspective* (1967, 1969); and *South Africa, A Study in Conflict* (1965, 1967). Professor van den Berghe attended Stanford University, the Sorbonne, and Harvard University where he earned his Ph.D. He has taught at Harvard, University of Natal, South Africa, the Sorbonne, Wesleyan University, State University of New York at Buffalo, University of Nairobi in Kenya, and the University of Ibadan, Nigeria. His experience includes field work in Mexico, South Africa, Guatemala, Kenya, Nigeria, and Peru.

ELSEVIER

52 Vanderbilt Avenue
New York, N.Y. 10017

Jacket Design by Loretta Li

ISBN 0-444-99000-3

MAN
IN
SOCIETY

A BIOSOCIAL VIEW

Pierre L. van den Berghe

ELSEVIER

New York/Oxford/Amsterdam

ELSEVIER SCIENTIFIC PUBLISHING COMPANY, INC.
52 Vanderbilt Avenue, New York, N.Y. 10017

ELSEVIER SCIENTIFIC PUBLISHING COMPANY
335 Jan Van Galenstraat, P.O. Box 211
Amsterdam, The Netherlands

ISBN 0-444-99000-3 (Hardbound Edition)
ISBN 0-444-99010-0 (Paperbound Edition)

Library of Congress Cataloging in Publication Data

Van den Berghe, Pierre L
  Man in society.

  Bibliography: p.
  Includes index.
  1. Sociology.   2. Social sciences.   I. Title.
HM51.V33   301   74-32422
ISBN 0-444-99000-3 (Hardbound Edition)
ISBN 0-444-99010-0 (Paperbound Edition)

Manufactured in the United States of America

DESIGNED BY LORETTA LI

"As soon as those who are considered the promoters of science become persuaded of their infallibility, they naturally proclaim as indubitable things that are not only unnecessary but often absurd, and having proclaimed them they cannot repudiate them."

LEO TOLSTOY

"Unfettered thought is the most essential of research methods."

STANISLAV ANDRESKI

Contents

Preface

Another introductory sociology text calls for an apology since there are scores in existence. The main reasons why so many get written are to be found in their authors' egotism and greed (not necessarily in that order). The captive undergraduate clientele seeking enlightenment, amusement, utopia, or simply credits in introductory sociology, is immense, and the share of the market captured by any text seems to bear precious little relationship to quality. So, why not another one?

My motivation, however, is not purely mercenary and narcissistic. I have a profound and growing dissatisfaction with the fare offered to introductory sociology students, especially in the United States. We sociologists offer students neither solid technical training in a scientific discipline nor a humanistic education, but rather a pretentious and inchoate mixture of fact and ideology, the intellectual poverty of which is hidden behind a smokescreen of jargon and quantitative methodology. All too often, the end product is enough of a crashing bore to deter the more creative students from entering the field, thereby closing the cycle of mediocrity. This is a pity because sociology can be an exciting intellectual adventure, which I hope to convey here.

Most American sociology texts start with the premise that their task is to impart a certain technical baggage to the student: a hundred words or so of basic jargon (often collected in a glossary at the end); a score or two of "basic ideas" reverently attributed to a handful of founding fathers; and a tedious mixture of empirical description, statistical tables and graphs, and thinly disguised ideological cant—all of which passes for a general theory of society. Some of the more successful texts spare both students and instructors the trouble of thinking by packaging these pretentious trivia and pompous verities into ambiguous multiple-choice questions. The critical and inquisitive student, who often rightly concludes that several alternative answers are plausible or that all are nonsense, is penalized, but that matters little. A freshly baked undergraduate batch gets its five credits toward that travesty of education known as a B.A. The few who survive this ordeal by tedium, who get into some of the more advanced courses, and who are lucky enough to encounter competent teachers, may get a glimpse of what sociology can be—most certainly do not.

This book is an attempt to expose the student to a subversive kind of antisociology sociology. My basic premise is that a student should leave an introductory sociology class with many more questions and far more dissatisfaction about his society than when he entered it. Good sociology should begin with the application of radical skepticism and criticism to one's own society, to one's place in it, and by extension to all social behavior. Sociology should, in short, be *alienating*. As Socrates put it some 2400 years ago, the choice is between being a satisfied pig wallowing in complacency or a dissatisfied human intellectually coming to grips with himself and his fellows. If lucidity is the crowning achievement of the human condition, its inevitable corollary is mental discomfort: what Balzac called the human comedy is seldom edifying.

What distinguishes the sociologist from the layman is not a technical baggage attested to by a sheepskin. A far more significant criterion is whether a person is naive or is a critically informed member of his society. My indictment of professional sociologists as a group is based on my belief that they show little less social naiveté than people whom they call laymen. I am not repeating here the frequent charge that sociology is common sense expressed in jargon. Rather, I am saying that every society in every epoch has produced a few wise and lucid persons who were perceptive observers and analysts of their own or other societies. Very few of them have been formally trained sociologists and, conversely, the vast majority of the latter do far worse than the inspired amateurs. Few social science monographs, for example, approach the quality of data found in the works of the European social novelists Jane Austen, Dickens, Tolstoy, Turgenev, Gogol, Maupassant, Balzac or Zola, to name a few. Plato, Ibn Khaldun, Thomas Aquinas, Machiavelli, Montesquieu, Rousseau, Hobbes, John Stuart Mill, Tocqueville, and Marx easily dwarf in sociological accomplishments the last 25 years of printed output of professional sociologists.

If most of my strictures seem to be aimed at "mainstream" or "establishment" sociology, it does not follow that I am endorsing "radical" or "new left" sociology either. There is a kind of philistinism and antiintellectualism of the left that is as stultifying as that of the right. I am in broad agreement with the old left's analysis and condemnation of capitalist societies, and with the new left's rejection of authoritarian socialism. But what I lack to be a true believer is an optimistic faith in the goodness of man. The moral superiority of the oppressed over the oppressor is a by-product of their powerlessness, and revolution is little more than the circulation of tyrannies. The best that can be hoped for is a slight improvement if the previous regime was more than averagely corrupt, exploitative, and despotic; but, statistically, change is probably as often for the worse as for the better. Furthermore, we know too little about society to anticipate with much reliability the consequences of our actions. It is easy enough to change things, but to change them according to our wishes is quite a different matter. Naturally, such a conclusion is not conducive to an activist stance.

Acknowledgments

Twenty years have now elapsed since I took the fateful step in deciding to be a sociologist and entering the Department of Social Relations at Harvard as a graduate student. My next six years were spent accumulating a staggering intellectual debt, both in Harvard and in Paris, in the awe-inspiring company of such outstanding mentors as Clyde Kluckhohn and Claude Lévi-Strauss in anthropology, Gordon Allport in psychology, George Homans, Pitirim Sorokin, Talcott Parsons, Barrington Moore, Samuel Stouffer, Raymond Aron, Georges Balandier, and Roger Bastide in sociology, Frederick Mosteller and Louis Guttman in statistics, and Herbert Marcuse in philosophy. Later, my field work in Africa and in Latin America put me in contact with the Mexican anthropologist, Gonzalo Aguirre Beltrán, and with a number of sociologists and anthropologists in the British tradition, especially Leo and Hilda Kuper, Max Gluckman, and Michael G. Smith. With such stimulation, I could not help but become reasonably literate. However, the heterogeneity of my gurus insured that I became no one's disciple, as this book, I think, shows. Various portions of this work have received the benefit of a critical reading by my friends and colleagues Robert Burgess, Gary Hamilton, Cullen Hayashida, Michael Hechter, Edward Gross, Pamela Kennedy, Lionel Lewis, George Primov, and Pepper Schwartz.

A harried clerical staff consisting of Mary Whiting, Beulah Reddaway, Ina Howell, and Laura Bergeson cheerfully transformed my unsightly scribblings into a neat typescript with a devotion well beyond the call of duty. My wife Irmgard deserves credit for putting up with my disagreeable self during the process of gestation. My greatest tribute to her patience and devotion is that the thought of having to trade places with her makes me shudder. I should also put in a good word for that great sociology editor, William Gum, who not only had the good taste of publishing three of my previous books, but who possesses an unerring knack for attracting to his lists of authors a vastly disproportionate share of sociologists who are intellectually alive.

For the defiant use of the word "man" in the title of the book to designate both sexes of *Homo sapiens,* I gratefully acknowledge the irritation provided by some of my feminist friends. Their proselytism in trying to expurgate the word from the English language is unfortunately based on linguistic ignorance. "Man" means, in the first instance, a member of the species *Homo sapiens* or of closely related fossil species, such as *Homo neanderthalensis.* When one wishes to specify gender, the word "man" is preceded by the morpheme "wo" for the female sex, and by what linguists call a "zero morpheme" in the male case. Besides, has it not occurred to feminists that "person" is also a sexist substitute for "man," since "son" likewise suggests the male gender? So we should really say "perchild," but then "perchild" has obvious connotations which make the term intolerably "agist." Since *Homo sapiens* is also a clear misnomer, I shall stick to "man" as a generic term for our brainy but, alas, none-too-wise species.

Seattle, April 1974   P. L. v. d. B.

MAN IN SOCIETY
A BIOSOCIAL VIEW

1

Introduction:
Why Sociology
Is Not a Science

Most authors of textbooks define sociology as the "science of society" or the "study of the social behavior of man." They concede that other disciplines, such as anthropology, political science, and economics, overlap in subject matter with sociology, but the authors are usually quite defensive about sociology being a real science and, indeed, the queen of social sciences, through the greater generality of its scope. Such a conception of the field is replete with self-indulgence. Sociologists, resentful of their low position on the academic totem pole, have generally tried to show that they are as scientific as the physical scientists and that the reason that they are not as successful in predicting events lies not in their stupidity but in the complexity of the subject.

If by the word "science" we mean a logically coherent body of generalizations concerning causal relationships between observable, measurable, and predictable phenomena, sociology is not a science. Only by extending the meaning of the word to include observations, descriptions, hunches, opinions, tautologies, statistical tendencies, concepts, and taxonomies, does sociology qualify. Sociology *is* more scientific than alchemy, water witching, or palmistry; however, put to the test of prediction, sociologists seem to do no better than politicians, psychiatrists, stockbrokers, priests, parole officers, or journalists, and considerably worse than economists. It might be supposed that, at least in their ability to run their own affairs, sociologists would have an edge over their fellow mortals, but any acquaintance with the American Sociological Association quickly dispels that notion. For several decades that group called itself the American Sociological Society and, apart from the fact that the acronym was unflattering, the old name was, in terms of sociology's own jargon, a clear misnomer. Similarly, sociologists would have a difficult time showing that they do a better job running their department in a university than do chemists or mechanical engineers.

How do sociologists get away with claiming an expertise they do not possess? Why is their bluff not called? The latter question is easy to answer: scarcely anybody does any better. Like the rainmaker, all the sociologist has to do is convince enough people that his sustenance is a relatively small price to pay for the virtual certainty that he cannot do any harm, and the hope that he might do some good; and like other priests and professionals, the sociologist creates that favorable climate by Sanscritizing his trade; that is, by making it esoteric to laymen. The two main weapons in the sociologist's arsenal of obscurity are jargon and statistics. Any intelligent layman needs only a few hours of effort to crack the first barrier and a couple of months for the second.

Let us now examine why sociology is not now what it claims to be nor probably ever will be. Many answers have been suggested. The two least convincing ones are also the most common: (1) we are a young science, and (2) we are dealing with an extraordinarily complex subject matter.

It is true that the label sociology is only about a century old (Auguste Comte, the founding father, is given the credit for it), but intelligent people had been doing sociology for thousands of years, in hundreds of societies. Any anthropologist going to the remotest culture is likely to find among a few hundred (or thousand) people an exceptionally intelligent, detached, alienated individual who, though illiterate, is no less a social scientist for being called an "informant." A few people have always critically questioned the nature of their social order. Sociology is new only by self-misdefinition. It would be analogous to date the origin of medicine by the establishment of university medical schools in the nineteenth century. Much as the Western medicine man invidiously calls his colleagues of other times and places "witchdoctors," the Western sociologist dismisses his intellectual superiors from previous epochs as "social philosophers," "historians," "essayists," or some such mildly opprobrious label.

The second excuse is as bad as the first. Of course, human affairs are extremely complex, but so is everything. What is simple about a molecule, a cell, a chromosome, a solar system? Such simplicity as classical physics presented in the nineteenth century was created by the theory itself and not by the reality. From the seventeenth to the late nineteenth century, physicists constructed a simple, elegant theory around a very limited body of facts, and were thus able to account remarkably well for certain gross phenomena. Today, physicists know better than to call their subject matter simple; only sociologists, whose conception and knowledge of physics are often at the level of high-school experiments with cat skins and resin balls, assert that their subject matter is inherently more complex. In fact, many sociologists' notion of what their science of society ought to be remains curiously fixated on the model of Newtonian physics.

Other reasons for the unscientific character of sociology are far more convincing, and have been suggested for a century or more, mostly by German philosophers of science, but dismissed by most sociologists, especially in the United States. The oldest and most fundamental issue is that of free will. Although it is obvious that individual human behavior is conditioned by innumerable biological and social constraints, man does retain a sufficient measure of autonomy and free will, which makes his behavior often difficult to predict. Different brands of sociology have tried to deny or to trivialize human freedom. For example, social behaviorists have been fairly successful in accounting for certain simple forms of learning and response in terms of a simple hedonistic model of "operant conditioning." The master plan for learning, they tell us, is that "subjects" (human or animal) respond predictably to rewards and punishment ("positive and negative reinforcement"), and since human behavior is nearly all learned, we can predict it quite well by manipulating "schedules of reinforcement," and without any reference to free will.

Freedom and Prediction

The most common sociological approach used to evade the problem of freedom is to restrict the field to the prediction of aggregate behavior. This tradition goes back to Emile Durkheim's famous study of suicide, published in 1897. To ask whether, when, how, and why an individual commits suicide, Durkheim said, is not a sociological question. The sociologist is interested in explaining fluctuations in the suicide rate. Why do more men kill themselves than women, more whites than blacks, more Swedes than Zulus, more Protestants than Catholics —and so on. The person who pulls the trigger may think that he has a choice, but, even if that is true, it is sociologically irrelevant because, in a large enough population, his choice will not make a difference. The sociologist can "explain" aggregate behavior (suicide, crime, birth, stock market, and so on) by invoking causes that are totally unrelated to the conscious motivations of individuals.

Aggregate behavior is extremely important for certain purposes, and sociology is at its best in answering questions having to do with the determination of statistical trends. Often the prediction of trends is far more crucial than the understanding of individual actions. For example, in educational planning, we need not be concerned about whether John and Mary will decide to have a baby next year, but we would be fools not to look at trends in birthrates. But aggregate data can also be worthless to explain other extremely important events. A sociologist of prerevolutionary France might have argued that the statistical probability that a commoner baby born in Corsica in the 1760s would become Emperor of France was less than one in a billion. The same sociologist showing me that, say, before the Revolution 65 percent of all French army officers were aristocrats compared to only 3 percent afterwards, has given me a significant fact. The social-class composition of the French army is an important sociological fact, but so is Napoleon.

In their inability to account any better than newspaper columnists for events such as the outbreak of World War I, the Bolshevik Revolution, the decay of the Ottoman Empire, the creation of the state of Israel, the Nazi concentration camps, the breakup of Pakistan, the Nigerian Civil War, the overthrow and reinstatement of Peron in Argentina, the attack on Pearl Harbor, and the downfall of European colonialism, sociologists "pass the buck" to historians. Since sociology is a generalizing science, say many sociologists, unique events are not its concern. That is hardly a satisfactory escape since in some respects, all events are unique. It is well within the province of sociology to understand what causes wars, revolutions, and ethnic conflicts in general, and, thus, specific instances thereof in particular. By and large, the more significant the question is, the less capable sociology is of giving an answer. And that inability has a great deal to do with the partially indeterminate, or *self-determined,* character of human behavior.

Objectivity and Ideology

Another important factor that limits the scientific character of sociology is the closeness of its subject matter to the observer. The sociologist studies fellow-humans, frequently in his own society. This has two major consequences which, though not exclusive to the social sciences, are much more pronounced there than in the physical and even biological sciences. First, the very process of studying social behavior affects it, because the sociologist's own behavior is part of the reality he observes. Sometimes, in experimentation, the behavioral modification brought about by the sociologist is intentional, but, more often, it is not. There are many complex manifestations of this phenomenon. The self-fulfilling prophesy is one: that is, one's prediction of, say, race riots or a business recession may help to bring these conditions about. Happily, most people do not take sociologists seriously enough for that problem to be grave but, in some fields, such as public policy in race relations or in colonial affairs, sociologists and anthropologists have appreciably contributed to the official definition of the situation.

Second, the closeness of the observer to the subject matter raises the problem of objectivity. This problem is not unique to the social sciences: the astronomer has a greater stake in his own solar system than in those a few million light years away; or the zoologist can identify better with his household dog than with his tapeworm. Nonetheless, the problem is greatly magnified in the social sciences, and doubly so in sociology where a person frequently deals with his own society or a closely-related one. The closer the observer is to the observed, the more difficult it becomes for the former not to let his biases affect his perception of reality. When the two belong to the same society, speak the same language, and thus share, knowingly or unknowingly, much the same kinds of values and assumptions on the nature of social reality, the resulting social science is apt to be, to an unstated and unascertainable degree, a sociological self-portrait by the author. However, unlike in avowed self-portraiture, sociologists generally claim some measure of detached interest in an outside subject, thereby producing an inextricable amalgam of facts and biases.

A large literature is devoted to problems of objectivity in social science, with a wide range of disagreement on its degree of feasibility. My position is that it is an empty statement to maintain that science is objective when scientists patently are not. The writings of sociologists are so obviously permeated with ideology, value judgements, and moralism that any pretense to objectivity is the hallmark of either dishonesty or naivete. Paradoxically, those who claim objectivity are often the farthest from achieving it, and those who disclaim objectivity, frequently come closer to it. The paradox is easily resolved: the sociologist who is sophisticatedly aware of his biases and their effect on his perception of the world is likely to be more objective than the one who is so confident of his objectivity that he is not conscious of his inadequacies.

Perhaps one illustration of how closely sociology has been linked with ideology and policy-making is in the field of "race relations" in the United States. Until the 1920s, racist and social-Darwinist ideas were prevalent in the social sciences (Frazier 1947). It was widely believed that the "whites" represented the highest form of human evolution, and "blacks" the lowest, and theories of racial superiority and inferiority were widely resorted to to "explain" slavery, the depressed position of American blacks, and other aspects of racial oppression in the United States. Then, in the 1930s, the intellectual climate changed, and so did the social science vision of race relations. Cultural relativism was preached by the anthropologists, especially by the students of Franz Boas, (Benedict, 1934). Each culture was equally valuable in its own terms, and could only be evaluated in its own terms. Man's behavior was almost infinitely malleable, and the product of his social environment, not his heredity. Thus, inequalities were to be interpreted in terms of social circumstances, not by innate differences.

In the field of race relations in the United States, this liberal credo was transformed into meliorative, integrationist ideology and social policy. Racism was a social disease to be eradicated by promoting racial integration and abolishing all forms of racial discrimination (Myrdal, 1944; Allport, 1958). The famous 1954 Supreme Court desegregation of schools decision, which quoted liberal social science literature extensively, represents the policy application of that social science ideology. Although, a few sociologists, (for example, O.C. Cox, 1948), took a more radical view, and interpreted race relations in terms of a broader analysis of class exploitation in a capitalist system, the dissidents vegetated in academic Siberia, stigmatized as Marxists.

With the sudden (and largely unpredicted) resurgence of "black nationalism" in the late 1960s, the social science weathercock made another abrupt turn. Blacks who had been, a few years before, loudly proclaimed to be just like whites, except that they had been discriminated against, were suddenly described by a flock of social scientists as having a unique and distinct culture, experience, soul, language ("black English"), and so on. On the left, academic radicals began speaking of the Third World and internal colonialism (Blauner, 1972); on the right, theories of racial differences in intelligence were resurrected (Jensen, 1969). At the policy level, the universities in general, and the sociologists in particular, implemented a system of ethnic studies programs,ethnic cultural centers, ethnic quotas, and the like, eagerly responding to minority (and women's) groups' demands for self-segregation. Information about a person's "race," which academic liberals had spent a quarter century eliminating from application forms, reappeared everywhere, and the American Sociological Association started electing its officers on racial and sex tickets and appointing a "Minority Affairs Specialist."

Examples of the intrusion of ideology into social science abound. The phenomenon is most blatant in fields like social stratification, race relations, and criminology, and less so in demography or ecology. Nevertheless, it is ubiquitous in the social sciences. Thus, the better part of wisdom is not to deny that social science is in fact always permeated by ideology, or piously to proclaim that it should be "value-free," but to become as self-consciously and sophisticatedly aware of the ideological positions of others and of oneself.

Ethnocentrism and Ignorance

Another common source of the failure of sociology to achieve its self-proclaimed scientific canons is the sheer ignorance of sociologists. If generalization is a key aim of science, its achievement presupposes that one be conversant with the whole range of phenomena about which one wishes to generalize and theorize. Here sociology, as conventionally defined, is handicapped by its ethnocentrism in comparison to its allied discipline—anthropology. I believe that the distinction between these two fields has always been inane; it is traceable to the racism prevalent in late nineteenth-century Europe and America, the period when the two disciplines became self-consciously distinct. An invidious distinction was made between "primitive" and "civilized" peoples, which became, *de facto,* a racial distinction. Sociology became the science of the Western, white, master race: anthropology became the study of colored colonials.

Apart from its invidiousness, the distinction between the two fields was an enormous liability to the development of sociology. By limiting itself almost exclusively to industrialized Western societies, sociology restricted its field to a narrow band in the spectrum of human behavior. The power and wealth of Western industrial societies gave sociologists the illusion that they were studying the "real" world, and that the rest of humanity was little more than archaic curiosities to be casually mentioned for the amusement of undergraduates, but not to be taken seriously. The joke was on the sociologists, however. Much like the so-called primitives whose ethnocentrism they found so amusing, sociologists confined themselves to studying The People, leaving the exotic savages beyond the pale to the anthropologists. Consequently, what they thought to be a science of society became little more than a descriptive ethnography of their own society—often not a very good one at that. A science of society can hardly be based on a single case, however politically and economically important. Much of the superiority of some of the early sociologists, like Durkheim, over most of the contemporary ones is because they did not accept the distinction between sociology and anthropology. Today, anthropologists are intimately familiar with at least two societies—their own and one more. Eighty percent or more of sociologists cannot make a similar claim.

This distinction between the scope of experience of the average anthropologist and the average sociologist is significant. The sociologist who has only experienced his own culture is, almost of necessity, more naive about his society than is the anthropologist who knows in depth at least one or two more. A comparison with language is appropriate here. The monolingual person is likely to be a naive speaker of his language, in the sense that he will take the entire syntaxic structure of his language for granted, and will let that unperceived linguistic structure shape his vision of the universe without his being aware of it, and without his being able to conceive alternative ways of looking at the world (Whorf, 1956; Sapir, 1921). The main intellectual asset of multilingualism is that it helps one realize the relativity of syntaxic structure, and, thus, makes one a more analytically sophisticated and conscious speaker of one's own language. To take a crude example, the naive speaker of French will assume that the moon has intrinsically feminine qualities and that the sun is inherently masculine. The naive speaker of German will assume the reverse. The Franco-German bilingual, on the other hand, cannot help but become aware of the relativity of noun genders.

What is true of language is true of culture in general. One cannot be intelligently and analytically aware of one's own culture without being intimately conversant with a different culture. An academic exposure to other cultures is better than nothing, but books are no substitute for an extended personal experience, such as the anthropologist typically gains "in the field." The more unrelated the foreign culture is to one's own, the more valuable the learning experience. Thus, the American undergraduate is likely to learn much more by spending his or her junior year in Papua or Chad than in London or Paris. To return to our simple linguistic example of noun genders, the French speaker who learns Spanish would still not question the intrinsic femininity of the moon and masculinity of the sun. Indeed, these two romance languages are so closely related that perhaps 90 percent of noun genders are the same. The "moment of truth" would come much sooner had he learned German, a tongue more distantly related to French, where any similarity of gender is little more than coincidental.

Sociological ignorance has manifested itself not only in space, but also in time. Much as sociologists have left the so-called savages to anthropologists, they have left the past to historians. To most sociologists history began, at best, with the Industrial Revolution. Spatial philistinism led to ethnocentrism; temporal philistinism led to self-imposed limitations in the development of a theory of social change.

It should be axiomatic to sociology that the present grows out of the past, so much so that there is no such thing as "the present." It is impossible to study an evanescent instant without reference to the sequence of events that preceded it. In the last analysis, a "society" is nothing more than humans interacting, and interaction is, of necessity, a sequence of events. The distinction between "social statics" and "social dynamics," borrowed from physics by some of the early sociologists (Spencer, 1874), is one of the great intellectual liabilities of sociology. To be sure, it makes some heuristic sense to describe social structures at a given moment in time, just as it makes sense to take snapshots of the members of one's family. Both make sense, if only from the viewpoint of economy of resources: a government cannot afford to keep a day-by-day census of its population, nor can a father take 24-hours-a-day home movies of his loved ones. However, a single snapshot or a single census tells relatively little. We want a series of snapshots or censuses; with them we can trace change. The more snapshots we have, the better we can reconstruct the gaps in between: the longer the time period they cover, the better we can trace developmental sequences. Even when we take snapshots, censuses, or other static recordings, we do so as a cheap and convenient way of recording change. Thus, the disciplinary distinction between sociology and history is completely artificial and constitutes a liability for both fields. The historian cannot but be a sociologist, and the sociologist must be a historian. Unfortunately, both disciplines find it chic to sneer at each other, to the detriment of both.

This book is a conscious attempt to overcome both the temporal and the spatial provincialism that has characterized so much of sociology. Unless we are successful in transcending the limitations of our experience in a single society and in the relatively short time-span of our individual existence, we cannot be intelligent analysts of the events we witness. Consider the 1970 U.S. Census. By any standards, it constitutes a costly and massive collection of data. Yet, by itself, what does it tell us? It tells us exactly what it says, and no more: on a certain day, so many males and females of such and such an age, lived in such and such a place, and so on. Only by comparing the 1970 U.S. Census with the previous ones, or with censuses taken in other societies, do these raw data acquire meaning. Only then can we begin to see changes in the structure of American society and glimpses of what kind of a society the United States is, compared to other societies.

Almost all sociologists would agree wholeheartedly with all of the above: it is elementary and axiomatic. Wherein, then, lies my criticism of the field? Simply in the fact that sociologists, individually and collectively, spend an astonishingly small proportion of their professional activities learning about the real world. For the most part, they are nearly as ignorant about it as laymen because they do not *live* their sociology. Instead of systematically observing the processes of interaction around them, as do ethologists, or immersing themselves in primary historical sources, as do historians; instead of living for extended periods in foreign cultures, as do anthropologists; they endlessly play with statistical techniques and computer gadgetry, spin jargon-laden pseudotheories, and rehash each others' recondite cogitations in an empirical near-vacuum. Much of the truly hard data that is collected is gathered by demographers in the U.S. Census Bureau rather than by academic sociologists, and much of what passes for data in sociology is indeed the softest imaginable, namely attitudinal survey data. After half a century or more of supposedly empirical research, such basic factual issues as the nature of community power structure, for example, are still hotly debated in the profession.

I cannot claim to be a student of American society, but after a few months' stay in the half-dozen communities I studied in detail (in South Africa, Nigeria, Mexico, Guatemala, and Peru), I felt that I had a fairly clear idea of what the community power structure was and, what is more, so did in every instance a few intelligent laymen who were participants in that power structure. These communities could not be said to be in any sense "simpler" than many American communities, so the difficulty does not lie in the complexity of the

subject matter. The difficulty, rather, is to be found in the unwilling-
ness or inability of most American sociologists to study ongoing social
processes around them. How many American sociologists, for example, can claim to know what the power structure of their own university is? Since that power structure vitally affects their day-to-day
interests, one might expect that a healthy combination of scientific
curiosity and self-interest would have spawned a deluge of sound
sociological studies of university power structures. Yet, the
sociologists who study their own profession and the academic world
tend for the most part to study such narcissistic trivia as the prestige
ranking of sociology departments and the "productivity indices" of
their colleagues (so many points for a textbook, so many for an edited
collection, so many for an article).

The Nature of Human Nature

Finally, a root cause of sociological ignorance is our reluctance to take
human biology seriously, a theme to which we will return. It has been
a matter of sociological dogma for over half a century that *Homo
sapiens*, as a "culture-bearing" animal endowed with speech and
higher intelligence, was radically different from other species. Nearly
all of his behavior was learned rather than genetically inherited. His
body was nothing more than a carnal vector for his culture, a set of
capabilities (such as a larger brain, opposable thumbs, erect stature,
and vocal cords) rather than a biological code of behavior, as is the
case of social insects, such as bees and ants.

The rapidly accumulating results of animal ethologists, especially
of those who study primates (monkeys and apes), invalidate this
conception of the uniqueness of *Homo sapiens*. Other primates have
been found to possess at least the rudiments of culture (in the sense of
socially transmitted learned behavior) and, conversely, there is accumulating evidence that several fundamental aspects of human behavior are biologically predisposed (though not rigidly determined).
That is, there is such a thing as human nature which sets broad

biological parameters to our behavior. Our behavior is, of course, highly modifiable through learning (as is that of other mammals), but we are not infinitely plastic. Clearly, if sociologists are concerned with human behavior, they must know what the biological limits and predispositions of that behavior are. This, in turn, is only possible by comparing human and nonhuman behavior. Sociologists, in short, should look at behavior across species, as well as across cultures, instead of continuing to state dogmatically that human behavior is so different from that of any other animal that it does not bear comparison.

At this stage, the reader may well ask why he should read any further. The fare I shall endeavor to offer him will be a conscious corrective to what I see as the crippling shortcomings of sociology. Conventional sociology has long suffered from intellectual constipation. Its fixation on consensus, norms, sanctions, values, equilibrium, legitimacy, roles, statuses, and sundry concepts that pepper the standard textbook has given us a frozen and formalistic view of society. Its "law-and-order" perspective on social relations, for all its elaboration and indigestibility, is no less clearly a social philosophy of liberal industrial capitalism than, say, Confucianism was the social philosophy of a mandarin class in an agrarian society, or the Bhagavad Gita the philosophy of a priestly group in a caste society, or Lenin's elitism the philosophy of a party bureaucracy in a worker's paradise.

"Radical sociology," with its roots in socialism, anarchism, syndicalism, populism, and other antipower and antihierarchical social philosophies, has long provided an alternative model of society focused on the conflicts brought about by differential relations of power and of production. The socialist Old Left, to the extent that it became politically successful, became frozen into a fairly unimaginative orthodoxy in support of a new form of tyranny. The New Left was an attempt at administering an intellectual laxative to socialist constipation, but so many of its brighter proponents have felt so guilty about being more intelligent than the "people" that they have made a virtue of irrationality and inchoateness, both organizationally and ideologically. Old and New Left share the crippling limitation of an optimistic view of human nature for which there is, alas, very little empirical evidence.

The need for a sociological bowel movement is greater than ever. This book is not—perish the thought—another attempted grand theory of society. It is little more than an attempt at concocting a more powerful laxative. The best laxative against theory is, of course, facts; thus a more powerful laxative calls for drawing in facts from a wider empirical spectrum than sociology has typically done. This means, in the first instance, taking the past and non-Western societies as seriously as we do our own time and place. Sociologists have long paid lip service to the "cross-cultural approach," but they continue to treat "comparative sociology" and "historical sociology" as separate specialties when these terms should be nothing but redundancies, which indicates their continued provincialism. In the second instance, we must reexamine the basic questions raised by human biology, and that means looking at other species, especially at our fellow primates.

Specifically, this book does not attempt to survey the various approaches to the field of sociology or to summarize its "findings." Any attempt to do so would lengthen this work by two or three hundred pages without any commensurate gain in content, and besides, there are scores of texts in existence that do little else. I shall use a minimum of jargon, except in areas such as kinship, where terms have precise meanings and have no counterparts in everyday language. Much sociological jargon, however, is of too little value to be worth plowing laboriously through a chapter on "Sociological Concepts." I try to stay clear of theory in any formal, deductive sense. To strive for theoretical closure at a stage when we still have so much to learn about the real world would be comparable to that of the proverbial blind men describing the elephant. Rather, we shall look for uniformities in human behavior, in an attempt to arrive at empirical generalizations, however tentative.

My purpose is to raise fundamental questions about the nature of human behavior and the bases of social order. This can be done only by exposing oneself to a much wider range of data than sociologists have typically done. The cost of trying to embrace the whole spectrum of human behavior is that one must suppress the urge to subside it all under a neat general theory. Definitive answers will have to wait, perhaps forever. Many sociologists will see the last phrase as a counsel of despair. I do not, if only because I find questions far more interesting than answers; thus, I do not share my colleagues' impatience with an indeterminate world. In fact, I shudder at the thought that human affairs could become highly predictable, and rejoice at the probability that they never will be.

All sociology, as I have suggested, is imbedded in ideology, and this book is no exception. Like most of my colleagues, I do not like much of what I see of human behavior. Having lived in many different societies, I have felt alienated from all of them, though for different reasons. There are, however, two ways in which I have tried to differ from most of my colleagues' practice of sociology. First, instead of hiding biases, as many sociologists do, under a thick crust of ostensibly bland jargon, I try to bring mine into the open. When a value judgement appears in these pages, it is not a slip of the pen, but a deliberate attempt to inform my readers of where I stand, so that they will be provoked into examining more critically what I am saying. Second, I try not to let wishful thinking and unwarranted optimism color my perception of events. If there is one thing in common between most sociologists of the right, the middle, and the left, it is their optimism.

What we do not like will not go away by our pretending that it is not there. We should strive for a realistic conception of human nature, realistic in the sense that it is consistent with actual observable behavior, not with what we hope our behavior might be. We must, in short, develop an ability to take an unflinching look at what we do not like, however painful or distasteful that might be. Seeing, for example, murder, violence, snobbery, deceit, treachery, and the egotistic pursuit of self-interest occur with unflagging regularity throughout human history, we should stop considering these traits as pathological aberrations, and start entertaining the hypothesis that we are dealing with eminently normal human behavior. To be sure, man is also capable of love and altruism, but we must carefully probe under what conditions these sentiments express themselves, instead of assuming that they represent our true nature, uncorrupted by society. We must retire Rousseau's dream of the Noble Savage. Rousseau had never met any "savages": he just hoped that they were better people than the Frenchmen and the Swiss that he did know, but, alas, he was wrong. Chimpanzees, it seems, come much closer to the peaceful utopia than any human society.

Perhaps the most glaring omission in my treatment of human behavior is that of psychological concepts. This omission reflects my bias against having recourse to mentalistic constructs that cannot be observed in actual behavior. Several brands of social psychology, notably psychoanalysis, symbolic interactionism, and the currently fashionable "ethnomethodology" rely heavily on a conceptual apparatus that presupposes questionable inferences from people's behavior, rather than being directly derived from readily observable behavior. Behaviorism is perhaps the social psychology closest to my own position, insofar as it makes a limited number of simple assumptions about human behavior, and that these assumptions hold up remarkably well to observation and experimentation. Behaviorism assumes that humans will seek what they find pleasurable and profitable, and will avoid what is painful and injurious. Although this does not tell us anything that we have not known for thousands of years, and, thus, is not intellectually exciting, it works remarkably better than any other set of assumptions in manipulating and predicting human behavior, and the behavior of other species as well. The applicability of behaviorism across species is powerful evidence of its validity. Other brands of social psychology are premised on the incomparable uniqueness of our species, and are even remarkably culture-bound within our species. It is difficult enough to conjure a Zulu or an Eskimo with an Oedipus complex, but just try a rhesus monkey or a pigeon.

This book, then, while accepting the basic premises of behaviorism does not seek to elaborate on them. Frankly, I find behaviorism a bore whose elaboration I would rather leave to others. Rather, with minimum reference to the hedonistic model of behaviorism, I shall try to define, first the biological predispositions (or *Anlagen* as German ethologists say to avoid the troublesome term "instinct") that make our behavior peculiarly human and different from that of other species, and, second, the modes of social organization within which we act. The fundamental premise of this book is that human behavior, though similar in some basic respects to that of other animals, is also uniquely human in other respects. Indeed, every species is in some sense behaviorally unique. Since humans are social animals, biologically capable of complex symbolic communication, it makes no sense to separate nature and nurture, our biology and our culture, in attempting to understand our behavior. Human behavior is, by definition, the product of the interaction between our species-wide *Anlagen* and our culture–specific social arrangements.

Most sociologists have so studiously avoided any serious consideration of the biological determinants of human behavior that this book is bound to disturb, irritate, or scandalize. I claim little originality for the point of view presented here. It represents the mainstream of contemporary ethology and primatology, and the biosocial perspective is becoming increasingly incorporated into anthropology. Sociologists, as usual, lag behind intellectually, fearful of having to reorient their thinking along unaccustomed channels. Their main alibi for not taking human biology seriously is that to do so would again raise the spectre of the racist heresy. In fact, as this book will show, a serious examination of the biological parameters of human behavior constitutes the best antidote to racism: it clearly demonstrates the unity of the human species and the remarkable uniformity of basic forms of human behavior throughout the species. In any case, fear of ideological consequences should hardly stop an intellectual from raising questions. If nothing else, I hope to show that it has not stopped me.

In Part I, we will look at the human animal, at his habitat, and at his ways of coping with it in terms of both technology and the most universal and basic forms of social organization, namely kinship and marriage. Then we will examine different types of society, focusing on the most central aspects of social organization—the network of differential relations of power and production and its resultant group inequalities. In Part III, we will look at what man does to keep his mind busy. Finally, we will raise the question of how much ability man has acquired to control his destiny, with or without the help of sociologists.

ADDITIONAL READING

More conventional approaches to introductory sociology can be found in Broom and Selznick (1963) and in Lundberg *et al.* (1963). The latter book takes the position that sociology can be a science in the same sense as the natural sciences. The sociology text that most closely resembles this one, at least in its comparative emphasis, is Lenski (1970), but Lenski stresses technology more and biology less than the present account. Good sources on comparative sociology are Andreski (1964) and Marsh (1967). Gouldner (1970) takes a critical stance to sociology similar in many ways to my own. Insofar as the subject matter of this book also covers what is conventionally defined as anthropology, the student should also consult some textbooks in that discipline, especially the classic Kroeber (1948) and the more recent Bohannan (1963), both of superior quality.

Minimum literacy in sociology also presupposes at least nodding acquaintance with the great classics of social thought, such as Plato's *Republic*, Machiavelli's *The Prince*, Adam Smith's *The Wealth of Nations*, Malthus' *An Essay on the Principle of Population*, John Stuart Mill's *On Liberty*, Rousseau's *The Social Contract*, a selection of the writings of Marx and Engels, especially *The Communist Manifesto, The Eighteenth Brumaire of Louis Bonaparte,* and *The Civil War in France,* and Alexis de Tocqueville's *Democracy in America*. Durkheim's classic introduction to Sociology, *The Rules of Sociological Method* (1938), may still be read with profit.

The best descriptions of complex Western societies can be found much more easily and enjoyably in the great social novelists of Europe and America than in accounts by professional sociologists. For Russia, Gogol's *Dead Souls*, Tolstoy's *Anna Karenina* and *War and Peace*, Dostoevski's *Crime and Punishment*, and the novels of Turgenev stand out. Balzac, Maupassant, and Zola have best captured the reality of nineteenth century French society. In particular, Zola's novels, although not great literature, are certainly great ethnography of a complex society. For Britain, Dickens is unsurpassed, but Jane Austen, Defoe, and contemporary novelists (and playwrights) like Graham Greene, G.B. Shaw, and C.P. Snow have produced perceptive accounts of their society. In the United States, the works of Hawthorne, Steinbeck, Marquand, Sinclair Lewis, and Richard Wright are among the best. Good social novels about non-Western and colonial societies are less numerous, but Ciro Alegria's *Broad and Alien is the World,* Chinua Achebe's *Things Fall Apart,* Alan Paton's *Cry the Beloved Country,* and E.M. Forster's *A Passage to India,* which deal respectively with Andean Peru, Southern Nigeria, South Africa, and India, stand out. A good anthology of literature with a sociological slant is Coser's *Sociology Through Literature* (1963).

PART
I

Gonads, Guts, and Grub

2

The Human Animal

Since the 1930s, the social sciences have been dominated by a doctrine of extreme social determinism. *Homo sapiens,* we were told, was a uniquely culture-bearing animal whose behavior was almost entirely learned and socially transmitted, and thus almost infinitely plastic. Human biology was held to be significant only in the obvious sense that it gave us certain capabilities (binocular vision, opposable thumbs, bipedal locomotion, intelligence) and imposed certain needs (food, shelter, sex, infant protection). Practically everything of social significance, sociologists and anthropologists assured us, was a cultural creation of man.

This extreme social determinism was a reaction against simplistic theories of unilinear evolution, social Darwinism, and racism which had been popular in the late nineteenth and early twentieth century. At that time, for example, it was widely believed in Europe and the United States that different "races" of man represented different stages of biological evolution, with whites at the apex and blacks at the bottom of the human pyramid. When these racist theories were later invalidated and shown to be convenient rationalizations for slavery and colonial exploitation, social scientists tried to atone for their intellectual sins by dogmatically rejecting any notion that biological heritage helps to account for behavior.

The new social determinist orthodoxy was that man was unique in having developed a learned culture transmitted through language. Since culture was learned from other humans, and since human behavior was almost entirely patterned by culture, it followed that man was unthinkable without society. To be sure, man *is* a social animal, and culturally transmitted learning plays an extremely important role in his development. However, it is becoming increasingly clear that the sharp distinctions between nature and nurture, and between man and other animals, drawn by the past two generations of social scientists, are untenable. Learning occupies a large place in animal behavior, and at least some of the primates have shown some rudiments of culture. Some biologists dispute man's supreme position on the scale of intelligence and believe that some cetaceans, like porpoises, may be close rivals.

If there is no radical discontinuity between man and other mammals in the ability to modify behavior through learning, why should there be a discontinuity in the role of what used to be called "instinct"? Why should biology suddenly cease to influence behavior in *Homo sapiens* when it clearly does so in other species? In other words, if other animals exhibit the kind of intelligence that we once thought uniquely human, why should humans not be born with a set of genetically transmitted behavioral predispositions (*Anlagen*), such as we once believed were limited to subhumans? A look at our primate relatives, especially the great apes and the Old World monkeys, helps us regain consciousness of the importance of our biological heritage.

The failure of sociologists seriously to consider the biological bases of human behavior and the complex interplay of organism and environment makes this chapter especially controversial and tentative. Clearly, the old formulation of nature versus nurture is untenable. We must discard this false opposition, and think in terms of two sides of the same behavioral coin. The ideas suggested in this chapter are derived principally from ethology, primatology, and human paleontology (Alexander, 1971; Kummer, 1971; Tiger and Fox, 1969, 1971; Morris, 1967b, 1969; Bigelow, 1969; Lorenz, 1966; Collias, 1944; Scott, 1958; Washburn and Hamburg, 1968; Washburn and De Vore, 1961; and Wynne-Edwards, 1965). The fossil record of early hominids is still quite fragmentary, and even if it were more complete, the intellectual leap from bone splinters to behavior would, of necessity, remain quite wide. As for ethology and behavioral primatology, the systematic observation of primate behavior in the wild is barely two decades old. The evidence that primate ethology has yielded is extraordinarily fascinating, but the field is evolving rapidly and we are still a long way from definitive answers.

Much of what is to follow in this chapter is to be read as a set of inferential and inductive hunches (or "hypotheses" as many of my colleagues might prefer to say, when they seek to cloak their brainstorms in the mantle of scientific terminology). These ideas are still tentative and need to be further examined and tested. The one thing, however, that sociologists can no longer afford to do if they claim an interest in understanding human behavior, is to dismiss or to ignore the fundamental problems raised here. I am prepared to be found wrong in some of my hunches, but I feel reasonably confident that I will prove wrong for the right reasons—a far more exciting prospect than being right for the wrong reasons.

The comparative study of animal and especially mammal behavior has taught us the following:

1. The behavioral repertory of every species is determined in part by a set of biological predispositions that are, at least to some extent, specific to the species in question.
2. Animal behavior is modifiable through learning in response to environmental conditions, and the degree to which behavior is modifiable is a function of the organism's complexity and its intelligence.
3. Many forms of behavior (known as "imprinting" or "critical period" behavior) are the product of a necessary interplay between biological predispositions and environment, which points to the artificiality of opposing these two sets of behavioral determinants.
4. The above propositions hold for both human and nonhuman behavior, most certainly for mammalian behavior, and the "uniqueness" of human behavior has been misunderstood. In-

deed, human behavior is unique in the sense that the behavioral repertory of every species is unique in some respect, but human behavior is not radically discontinuous from that of other species.

The implication of these propositions is that we should conceptualize human behavior much as we do that of other mammals; namely, as the product of a *complex interplay of biogenetical and environmental factors*. That is, the human body is not simply a bundle of drives (hunger, sex, and others) and a set of capabilities (opposable thumbs, a large convoluted brain, vocal cords, upright stature). For all the plasticity and diversity of behavior on which we pride ourselves, our behavioral repertoire, though probably greater than that of any other animal known to us, is far from infinite. There *is* such a thing as human nature, just as there is a chimp nature, or an elephant nature.

The Problem of Survival

Perhaps the most fundamental question about *Homo sapiens* is how we survived to tell the tale. This question, too, can only be answered in relation to other animal species. Most species represent extremely specialized adaptations to a certain environment; they occupy a well-circumscribed ecological niche, living with other species in a relationship of competition, symbiosis, or parasitism. What kind of an animal were we as early hominids? How did we compare with the other primates? How did we compete with other species? How did we survive?

Basically, early hominids were large, terrestrial, bipedal primates, turned omnivore. The gorilla and orangutan surpass us in size, and the chimpanzees approximate us, but all other primates are much smaller. Only about one-tenth of the 189 living primate species show a predominant degree of terrestrial adaptation, mostly the macaque and baboon species; and to a considerable degree, the gorillas and chimpanzees. Some primates occasionally walk on their hind legs, but man is unique in his exclusive bipedalism (except for a brief phase of quadrupedal locomotion in infancy). Man has long, strong hind limbs adapted to endurance, but he is rather slow compared to large carnivores (felines and canines) and the large herbivorous mammals on which carnivores feed. Most primates are predominantly vegetarian, though several terrestrial species have been observed to eat insects, crustaceans, lizards, and even occasionally small mammals. Hominids, however, became much more reliant on meat as a major and regular part of their diet than did other primates.[1] Man is thus the most omnivorous of primates. In fact, we are so little picky about our food that we even eat members of our own species, a rare feat among mammals.

In common with other primates, we have good binocular vision enabling us to see things at great distances, and a poor sense of smell compared to the carnivores and herbivores (respectively the main predators and preys of the open tropical plains that were the early habitat of hominids). In comparison with other terrestrial primates, we are relatively devoid of protective natural weapons like the long canine teeth of male baboons. Other primates have partly opposable thumbs, but ours are much bigger and handier. Our hands are more dexterous than those of other primates, but our feet, specialized exclusively for locomotion, are much less movable. Bipedalism makes us the ungainliest of primates in trees, the main source of protection for even the more terrestrial species, such as baboons, chimpanzees, and macaques, who spend the night in the security of trees. On the other hand, we can swim much better than other primates.

All in all, we were a rather implausible plain-dwelling hunter, devoid of natural defense against predators, practically unable to flee large cats or canines through either escape in the trees or bursts of speed on the ground, and too slow and lacking a good scent to hunt down large prey. How did we avoid being food to the lions long before the Romans developed the practice as a spectator sport?

[1] However, with the population explosion made possible through the invention of agriculture, man in the last few millenia is reverting more and more to reluctant vegetarianism, since animal husbandry is a costly and inefficient way of raising food.

The textbook answer to that question is that, and let it be said without false modesty, we are very smart. Other primates are also rather clever, especially the large apes, but we hold an appreciable edge over all of them. Other primates are also capable of learning through experience and even of transmitting learned behavior through observation and imitation. Swimming and food washing, for example, have been observed to spread "culturally" through a troupe of Japanese macaques. Tool-using and even tool-making can no longer be considered a human monopoly. Chimpanzees pick up and throw sticks to scare away predators; they strip twigs of leaves to use as poles with which to extract termites from hills, and they chew on leaves to make water-absorbing sponges (van Lawick-Goodall, 1971). Culture, defined as socially transmitted learned behavior, is not a human monopoly, but the fact remains that we are spectacularly better at it than even our closest relatives, the chimpanzees.

Whether language is a human monopoly is a matter of definition. If by language we mean a social communication system between members of the same species (by means of gestures, vocalizations, facial expressions, and so on), then, clearly, many animals have it, including animals as remote from us as the social insects (bees, ants, termites). If we restrict the meaning of language to articulate speech, then we are unique. Other primates, and indeed other mammals and birds, make meaningful noises, and some species such as parrots can emulate human sounds in a meaningless fashion, but only humans speak, in the sense of using our vocal cords to emit a code of meaningful, arbitrary, learned symbols. All attempts to train chimpanzees to talk have failed, but chimps have been trained to use nonverbal arbitrary symbols in such a way as to make simple sentences. Thus, if we define language as a system of learned arbitrary symbols, whether verbal or not, then language is not an absolute human monopoly, though nearly so.

Too much has been made of the eminently *cultural* nature of language. To be sure, there is an immense variety of human languages, and all of them have to be learned from scratch to be intelligibly usable. Conversely, even the most extreme cultural determinists concede that the vocal and cerebral equipment necessary for speech are biological. The problem, however, is far more complex. First, it is obvious that not all human communication is verbal (or written), and certain forms of nonverbal communication (such as expressions of fear, mirth, harmless intent through smiling, and sexual attraction through eye contact) are too uniform throughout our species not to postulate a biological basis to them. These forms of nonverbal communication can be regarded as not different in principle from those existing among subhuman primates. Two members of totally unrelated cultures who do not speak a word of each other's language are as capable of communicating sexually as any two monkeys. The only requirement is that the mating partners be of the same species. If they are not, communication breaks down. Thus, we can safely assume that each species, man included, has a biological code of sexual behavior.

Sex, the cultural determinist will concede, is obviously a basic biological drive. But sex, at least among primates, is not purely a biological drive. Experiments isolating rhesus monkeys from contact with members of their species have shown that such isolation in infancy incapacitates monkeys to interact normally with other monkeys (Harlow and Harlow, 1965). Males are even incapable of properly mounting a female and of achieving copulation. Among humans, too, we know that complex environmental conditions can block such basic biological urges as copulation and produce impotence.

Nature and Nurture

It seems then, that at least for the gregarious primate species, both human and nonhuman, much behavior can only be understood as the product of an *interplay* between biological predispositions and social learning. To attempt to separate the two, or to pretend that one does not exist, is plainly untenable. This is why this book is subtitled: *A Biosocial View*.

If the ostensibly biological phenomena of mating behavior are so susceptible to social environmental conditions, could not the reverse be true of ostensibly cultural phenomena like speech? The answer, I think, is affirmative. Even forms of behavior that we think of as entirely learned, operate within biological parameters. Language is a good case in point. First, some linguists believe that, underlying the seemingly endless diversity of human languages, all languages share some syntaxic regularities (Chomsky, 1968). In addition, the ways in which language is learned are amazingly similar across cultures. In all societies, infants begin to learn to speak at roughly the same age (between one and two years of age), in a relatively short time span, and at roughly the same speed. This suggests a phenomenon akin to what bird ethologists have called "imprinting"; that is, irreversible learning at a critical period of an organism's maturation, as a result of a combination of biological predispositions (*Anlagen*) and environmental conditions (Lenneberg, 1967).

Gender identification of the human infant, as either male or female, also seems to occur in all societies at the same time as the infant learns speech. In all societies mentally normal individuals achieve gender identification by age two or so, and, once achieved, it can be reversed only with great difficulty and at the risk of serious adjustment problems. The universality of gender as a key component of self-identity contradicts the belief of those who claim that the learning of sex roles is purely a social phenomenon. If that were the case, we might expect that in some societies the biological accident of gender would be of no social importance. As far as we know, no such societies have ever existed.

A large convoluted brain, then, allowed us to develop complex speech, tools, and weapons, and thereby to overcome some of the shortcomings of our unprepossessing physiques as killer apes. But that is not the whole answer of why we survived. In fact, we had to start surviving as killer apes long before we evolved an impressive arsenal (efficient throwing weapons, such as spears and bow and arrows), and probably long before we developed complex speech as well. We did so by *organizing,* much as did the other primates that live on the ground in the open plains. Like all terrestrial primates, hominids needed the safety of numbers to survive.

The smallest hunting-and-gathering societies are organized at least at the level of the family and the band. The latter typically numbers a minimum of 25 to 30 individuals, much the same order of magnitude as many monkey societies. A few ascetics or eccentrics seek solitude in adulthood, but no human infant can grow up in isolation from adults, and the gregariousness of man is a nearly universal trait. We even have cases of cannibalistic groups, such as the Tupinamba of Brazil, where war prisoners sometimes did not seek to escape their captors even though they knowingly faced the prospect of being clubbed to death and eaten after a few months of fattening.[2]

Humans are so gregarious, in fact, that they are simply unthinkable as isolated individuals. Quite apart from surviving predators, human infants are totally helpless to feed themselves for over a year, and certainly incapable of fending for themselves for several years. Without close and constant contact with other members of the species in childhood, humans are incapable of developing normal human behavior, even if their physical needs are provided for. This has been shown by the severe mental retardation and disorders exhibited by unloved institutionalized infants. Even in adulthood, the greatest punishment that can be inflicted is solitary confinement, as any policeman knows. Gregariousness is so much part of primate nature that even seemingly biological functions like mating seem contingent on it, as suggested by the Harlow (1965) monkey experiments. Male monkeys raised in isolation were unable to copulate. In this, we are not

---

[2] A sixteenth century Portuguese writes of a prisoner, about to be clubbed to death and eaten, who turned down a chance to escape because "his relatives would not consider him brave, and all of them would avoid him" (Magalhães de Gandavo, 1922). Other sources refer to Tupinamba prisoners who did escape, but generally with the wife given to them by the captor group. The usual practice among the Tupinamba groups was to give the prisoner a desirable young maiden from the captor's group. The prisoner's wife was to pamper and fatten her husband, of whose flesh she would later partake, after ritual killing. Any child born to her and fathered by the prisoner would in turn be eaten, sometimes several years after birth. The Tupinamba are now extinct, not, as might be supposed, because they ate each other into extinction, but because the encroaching Portuguese wiped them out through a combination of warfare and the European strains of smallpox and influenza to which indigenous groups had no immunity.

fundamentally different from many other primate species. Our sociability is rooted, not only in our culture, but also in our biology. Indeed, it is absurd to try to separate these two aspects of our behavior, because our culture so obviously grows out of our biology. We are gregarious both by nature and by culture. There is simply no other way of being human.

Dominance and Aggression

We must now ask what kind of a society hominids developed. Again, this question can best be answered by comparison and contrast with other primate societies. Perhaps the most salient aspect of human social organization is how much it is based on a *dominance order*. Human societies are the most complexly hierarchical in existence, a theme to which we shall devote an entire chapter later. In this, we are like some other primates and unlike others. Most of the lower primates, like lemurs, and some of the higher ones, like gibbons and chimpanzees, show very little dominance behavior. However, the predominantly terrestrial primates like baboons and macaques form, like ourselves, strongly hierarchical societies with sharp status differences between various age and sex groups, and even among adult males, and among adult females.

Those monkey societies are hierarchically organized for defense against predators. As the band forages in open country, an activity that forces a certain amount of dispersion, the subordinate males act as sentinels on the periphery, the females and the young are in the middle, and the oligarchy of dominant males stays on the alert at or near the center prepared to jump into the fray, to cover the retreat, and to bear the brunt of the fighting if the need arises. Male dominance in monkey societies, incidentally, is strongly correlated with *sexual dimorphism,* that is, the anatomical differences between males and females other than those linked with the reproductive organs. In the highly male-dominated species, the male weighs twice as much as the female, and has much more developed canine teeth. In the relatively sex-egalitarian primate species, males and females are of nearly equal weight and size.

It is also important to note that in these dominance-ordered primate societies, dominance behavior continues unabated even under conditions where there is no threat from predators, as, for example, in zoos. Under close confinement, male dominance sometimes becomes even more pronounced than in the wild, taking the form, for example, of an enhanced concern for monopolizing females in heat, and constant "displacement" behavior (that is, forcing a subordinate to yield ground). This clearly shows that this dominance, while demonstrably a defensive adaptation to predation, nevertheless persists even when environmental conditions no longer make it useful. Dominance, in short, has become inborn.

The universality of dominance in human societies, under an extremely wide range of environmental conditions, indicates that human dominance is probably also built into our "biogrammar" as Tiger and Fox (1971) called our codes of biologically predisposed behavior. In fact, human hierarchy and dominance are far more complex and elaborate than in even the most hierarchical nonhuman societies. Man not only faced the problem of defense against predators. By becoming a hunter, he turned into a predator himself.

Much has been said about the "killer-ape" theory of human behavior, popularized by Ardrey (1961, 1966), but generally rejected by most anthropologists and other social scientists for a wide variety of reasons and motives, both intellectual and ideological. In simple terms, the theory explains the high level of aggressiveness in *Homo sapiens* through his evolution during millions of years as a predator. The main flaw in the theory is that it confuses predation and aggression, and attempts to explain the latter in terms of the former. I find it useful to distinguish clearly between predation and aggression. Predation is the killing of animals of other species for food. Aggression, as I shall define it, is the display of violence or the threat thereof, toward members of one's own species, usually in competition for scarce resources.

There is little, if any, relationship between predation and aggression. Many predatory species, like leopards, are quite unaggressive, while many highly aggressive species, like baboons, engage in little predation. Aggression is the product of competition, but prey and predator hardly ever compete with each other. Predation is generally lethal, aggression seldom so. Humans have blurred the distinction between the two because they are both highly predatory and highly aggressive, and because their aggression is so often lethal. In fact, man is one of the rare mammalian species that is cannibalistic, and thereby achieves the trick of being both prey and predator to himself. But, killing a fellow human in anger, or shooting grouse for fun or trapping beaver for profit, are two different forms of behavior, and the former cannot be explained in terms of the latter. We shall return to the problem of aggression presently.

Let our sociological imagination roam the plains of Pleistocene Africa with our hominid ancestors. What does our knowledge of primate paleontology and ethology allow us plausibly to infer on conditions of hominid survival and social organization? (Washburn and De Vore, 1961).

Early hominids confronted the double problem of "bringing home the bacon" and of avoiding becoming someone else's bacon. They also had to defend themselves against other hominid bands. Actually, to call early hominids "killer apes" is too flattering a term, for they were probably at least as much scavengers as killers. Without efficient throwing weapons and lacking speed, it was much easier to steal carcasses from some of the larger cats, such as cheetahs, than it was to make a kill. Whether as hunters or as scavengers, it took several hominids banding together to be successful. Futhermore, these hominids had to be male. Female baboons, even pregnant and lactating ones, can easily keep pace with a slow-moving foraging band, and, what is more, they have no alternative but to come along if they are to feed themselves. For a hunting primate, the problem is entirely different, however. Pregnant and lactating females (and most adult females would be in one or both of these conditions most of the time with a nine-month gestation and two-year lactation period for every child), and infants would be of no use at all on the hunt. Indeed, they would be a hindrance. With the killing of large game, the meat could be taken home to the females and children, and women could be relieved from part of the onus of feeding themselves.

Gender Roles and Mating

Thus, hominids evolved a mode of social organization with a sharp sexual division of labor: the adult men hunted and scavenged for meat, fought in war, and ruled politically; the adult women and the children stayed closer to home, gathered vegetable foods, prepared food for consumption, and engaged in handicraft production. This basic pattern of sexual division of labor has since remained fundamentally unchanged (Gough, 1971; Washburn and De Vore, 1961). In a sample of 175 contemporary societies drawn by G.P. Murdock, hunting is *confined* to men in 97 percent of the cases, and is *chiefly* a male pursuit in the remaining 3 percent.

Mating patterns also seem to have a partly biogenic origin. A number of early anthropologists postulated sexual promiscuity and "group marriage" in earlier stages of hominid evolution, but evidence to that effect is completely lacking. Many primate species, including some closely related to man, such as the chimpanzee, are promiscuous, but others are not. For example, the gibbon lives in stable, "monogamous," nuclear families with no mating between siblings or between parents and offspring. The Hamadryas baboon has stable, "polygynous" family units which, in turn, group together to form foraging bands. *Homo sapiens,* like other primates, seems to exhibit a basic mating pattern that is relatively uniform within the species. There is a definite tendency to pair-mating rather than promiscuity.

Humans are not as rigidly pair-mated as are some birds who mate for life. It is also true that Man uses his brain to play sexual (as well as other) games, and that stable pair formation is often preceded by considerable experimentation and trials. Once established, a pair can be broken, but not without considerable trauma. Also, to say that humans tend to pair-mating is not to say that they are by nature monogamous. Indeed, the widespread existence of polygyny (one man married to several women) indicates that man is not naturally monogamous. Several stable, sexually bonded pairs may, and often do, share one common member, almost invariably a male. (Polyandry, the marriage of a woman to several men, is extremely rare.)

Attempts to establish a promiscuous pattern of sexual relations are made repeatedly, but the interesting fact is that they seem to be very unsatisfying. Even prostitutes, who are promiscuous for gain, experience the need for pimps, in defiance of any economic self-interest. Very few of them find promiscuity satisfying. Noneconomically motivated forms of promiscuity (Don Juanism, mate-swapping, orgies, and similar parlor games) do not seem to be any more successful. There seems to be a deeply human need for lasting relationships as opposed to fleeting acts of copulation. If anyone would doubt it, let him or her observe how quickly groups of unbonded young adults thrown in close physical proximity (e.g., on board ships) form pairs, instead of promiscuously mounting each other, as, for example, chimpanzees would do. It may be that love is nothing more than overstating the differences between one human and another, but the point is that we tend to be picky about our sexual partners, and that, when we find a good one, we tend to stick together for considerable periods of time.

There is an important difference between *Homo sapiens* and the other primates and mammals. In most mammal species, adult males are ready to mate almost any time (barring disturbing conditions of stress, danger, and so on), while females are receptive only when in heat (oestrus). This is also the case in nonhuman primates. While this combination does not absolutely prevent stable pair-bonding (the Hamadryas baboon, for example, has stable "polygynous" groups of a male and several females), it certainly puts a strong strain on it. Human females, on the other hand, are relatively anoestrous, and, thus, are relatively receptive at all times, or, their relative receptivity tends to be more psychologically than physiologically determined. Actually, there is evidence of at least residual oestrus in human females as shown through temperature rises around the time of ovulation, but compared, for example, to the female chimpanzee in heat, whose genitalia swell to grapefruit size, the ovulating human female is very discreet about her menstrual cycle. Let us speculate a bit further on the consequences of oestrus for our evolution.

The cultural expression of this universal human tendency to pair-mating is marriage, a topic to which we shall turn in detail in Chapter Four. The universality of marriage is easily explained in terms of the biology of human mating. But why pair-bonding (or love, if you prefer) in the first place? We have seen that the shift from foraging to hunting in hominids made the male into a provider of food for females and children. Let us assume, for a moment, a sexually promiscuous species with oestrous females. Out of a group of 30 to 50 individuals, perhaps 6 to 12 would be nubile females, out of whom 1 or 2 would be in heat at any given time. What incentive would "the boys" on the hunt have to bring the food home to unreceptive females and their brats, instead of gorging themselves on the spot of the kill and saving the bother of carrying the carcass into the bargain? They might bring a few scraps to the females in heat, but why bother about the others?

With each male being stably bonded to one or more females who are sexually receptive at all times, each male now has an incentive to feed his females. As we shall have occasion to discuss presently, man (meaning now both sexes, but especially so the male of the species) is a rather nasty, aggressive, egoistic animal, with outstanding exceptions that all make very good sense in terms of the survival of the species. There are two powerful human bonds that bring out the "good" side of human nature. First, there is the bond between mother and child, which is not a human monopoly. That bond is powerful in practically all mammals, but especially so in primates where infant dependency is so drawn out and so complete. (On the other hand, it is totally absent in most fish and reptiles whose parental responsibilities end after laying the eggs.) The second is the mating bond that we have just discussed. It, too, is not uniquely human, but it is absent in most higher primates (except the gibbon and the Hamadryas baboon). The closely related chimpanzees and gorillas, for example, who have extremely strong and long-lasting mother-child bonds, totally lack pair-mating. With females completely able to fend for themselves, "love" becomes a dispensable luxury.

There is a third human bond that has been discussed intensively by Tiger (1969), namely, the bond between adult males. For early hominids, solitary hunting or even scavenging was not a realistic possibility, even with the help of that extraordinarily useful fellow scavenger, *Canis familiaris,* with whom hominids established a symbiotic relationship a long time ago. If it took several men to hunt successfully, what then prevented these particular men from bashing each other over the head as they showed an easy propensity to do with males from other bands? No doubt, the realization that they needed each other to survive, but also, probably, the swapping of women through the simple little device known as the "incest taboo." If each male is "programmed" not to form pair-bonds with his daughters or sisters, then these females become available to form bonds with other males, and thus indirectly to create bonds between males.

Incest

The anthropological literature on incest taboos and exogamous marriage is enormous, and most anthropologists adopt a cultural interpretation of these phenomena. To Lévi-Strauss (1969), for example, it was through the incest taboo that man made the crucial jump from nature to culture. Through exchanging women, men created social manmade bonds between each other, both at the individual and at the group level. There are at least two lines of evidence that cast doubt on the sociocultural interpretation of the incest taboo within the nuclear family. First, the incest taboo within the nuclear family is nearly universal in the human species, and the institutionalized exceptions are very special indeed. (For example, the Inca and Egyptian kings married their sisters to preserve the purity of their mythical divine descent.) There are, to be sure, a number of instances of actual incestuous relationships (most commonly between fathers and daughters), but seldom with happy endings, and practically never condoned. The occasional occurrence of incest within the nuclear family is no argument against a biological predisposition against it. Homosexual relationships also exist, yet we are certainly biologically programmed the other way. If not, we would not be facing a catastrophic population explosion.

The usual argument in favor of the sociocultural interpretation of the incest taboo within the nuclear family, is that without it, sexual competition within the family would make life intolerable (Parsons and Bales, 1955). Granting that neither the mother nor the father would much care for the other to interfere with their pair-bond with their common offspring, that theory does not explain the near-universality of brother–sister incest taboos. Why should not as yet unbonded brothers and sisters bond with each other? Surely, brothers might find themselves in competition for the same sister. But siblings are notorious rivals for all kinds of things without making family life anything more than a little noisy and boisterous at times. Besides, there are all kinds of families with only one boy and one girl who become nubile at the same time. Why should they not be allowed to establish a nice warm relationship that would consolidate ties of blood? After all, in hundreds of societies, first cousins (who are only one step removed from being siblings) are expected to do just that (Lévi-Strauss, 1969). Yet, within the nuclear family, there is a powerful blocking of incest.

My argument here is that if an item of behavior is universal or nearly so in a species, there is a very good reason to suspect that it is *at least in part* biologically predisposed. The second bit of evidence for biological predisposition of the incest taboo in the nuclear family is that it seems *not* to be unique to *Homo sapiens*. One of the higher primates which has a clear nuclear family pattern of social organization also apparently has an "incest taboo." Gibbons (or at least the best known of the seven closely related species of gibbons, *Hilobates lar*) live in territorial groups of two to four individuals; an adult couple, plus one or two offspring of different ages. When any offspring reaches sexual maturity it is expelled from the parental territory, presumably to pair-mate with an outcast from another nuclear family and to establish a new territory. Birth spacing and slow maturation prevent brother–sister mating (van den Berghe, 1973).

We shall return in Chapter Four to the fascinating subject of kinship and marriage, but at this stage, I wanted to suggest at least the strong possibility that fundamental aspects of our social organization, such as hierarchy, family, and marriage are biologically predisposed. Biology does not explain everything, but it is foolish to pretend that it does not explain anything.

Territoriality

Another key aspect of human behavior to which social scientists have paid scant attention is *territoriality*. The concept is a rather loose and elastic one, covering a wide range of behavior in thousands of species. Here we shall define territoriality as the defense of fixed space against intrusions by members of the same species. Numerous species exhibit that behavior, from fish and reptiles to birds and mammals, but some species are much more territorial than others, and *Homo sapiens* clearly is at the high end of the spectrum, even by comparison with the higher primates. The gibbon is highly territorial, and so are some lower primates, but most monkeys and apes are much less so. Man, on the other hand, defends a great many territorial boundaries at many different levels, and, unlike practically all other animals who threaten but seldom harm intruders, man needs very little provocation to kill trespassers. At the highest level, territoriality takes the form of precisely drawn international boundaries, which even extend to bodies of water which cannot be permanently occupied. The elaborate rituals that take place at frontier posts, the impounding of fishing vessels, the waves of nationalistic indignation provided by the most trivial border incidents are, of course, cultural and fairly recent in their *specific form,* but they all fall into too general and universal a pattern to enable one to discount that man is by nature a territorial animal.

Human territoriality is not limited to the national level, but it is repeated at practically every level of social organization, down to the family. Provinces and municipalities have jurisdictional disputes with each other that often can be settled only through the intervention of a higher authority. Hunters have precise rules as to where game may be killed and pursued. Agriculturalists have for thousands of years fought each other over the precise boundaries of their fields.

In practically every society, the dwelling space of family groups (house, tent, courtyard, fenced enclosure) cannot be casually penetrated by strangers without incurring retaliation. It is not only to Englishmen that their home is a castle. Admission into the familial dwelling space is almost invariably subject to a ritual of recognition, statement of purpose, submission, surrender of offensive weapons, offering of propitiating gifts, all subject in the last analysis to the consent of a member of the household. Infractions elicit violent anger to the point of killing. The shooting of a prowler in one's home, for example, is one of the most sanctioned forms of homicide in Western societies. Even forcible entry without the owner's consent is frequently ritualized, as exemplified by the search warrant in Anglo-Saxon law. The ritual of penetration into someone else's territory is remarkably similar from culture to culture, sufficiently so that complete strangers can survive travel in foreign parts by observing that fundamental etiquette of showing good will and harmless intent. There are, of course, infinite gradations and variations in the symbolic or actual "no trespassing" signs that we erect around our social space, but the universality of this behavior begs for more than a cultural explanation. (Even hippy communes post "no trespassing" signs!)

The territorial behavior of man is so deeply ingrained that it manifests itself even when spatial occupation is quite temporary. Groups are quick to establish territorial claims to tables in restaurants, to portions of playgrounds in schools, or to railway compartments. Even within the household, specific seats, beds, places at the dining table, or entire rooms (e.g., father's study, mother's boudoir) become inviolable to other members of the immediate family. Much of human behavior becomes incomprehensible without reference to the concept of territoriality. This is clearly evident, for instance, in conflicts between juvenile gangs in urban areas. Aggressive behavior is elicited for violations of territory, even when occupation of "turf" confers no material advantages. Spacial claims frequently are an end in themselves.

Aggression, Hierarchy, and Territoriality: The Biosociology of Order and Conflict

Let us now return to the problem of aggression, one of the most fundamental problems we face, both intellectually and practically. The unpleasant fact is that our species is the most sweepingly destructive on the planet. Our brains have made us ruthlessly exploitative of, and predatory on, a wide range of other species, but we are also the only species that constantly threatens to destroy itself. That we should be predatory is easy enough to explain: as our capacity to exploit our environment grew, we made the most of it, even at the cost of the ultimate destruction of our natural resource base. Many species have specialized themselves into extinction, so why should not we? By our brains we survived; by our brains we might well perish.

Yet, the "killer-ape" theory does not explain human *aggression*. We could very well make mincemeat of other animals, and yet be gentle and civilized among ourselves. Other predators are, but clearly not *Homo sapiens*. If the old Roman adage, *homo homini lupus* ("man is a wolf to his fellow man"), were true, we should be far better off: wolves practically never kill each other.

Many species are aggressive to their own kind, but almost never to the point of death. Animals fight when they compete for scarce resources, such as food or access to females in heat, but once it is clear who is the stronger, the fighting stops, in the overwhelming majority of cases, short of serious injury. Not so with man, who is not only very aggressive compared to many other species, but whose rate of *fatal* aggression is quite difficult to match in the animal world. Many fish

devour their young when confined in an aquarium, but this is misguided predation, not aggression. Fish do not know their young,
because they have no parental responsibilities. In open waters, the
chances of their meeting their young would be quite limited. Sharks,
chickens, and other animals have been observed to finish off wounded
members of their species. But no mammal, besides man, routinely
kills his fellows at the slightest provocation, or even for the slightest
chance of gain.

The fact of human aggressiveness evokes passionate emotions
among scholars (who find in intellectual controversy one way of
venting their aggressiveness). The basic line of battle is between those
who believe that aggression is inborn, and those who believe it is
learned. Once more, it is wrong to state the question in "either-or"
terms. Clearly, the incidence and forms of human aggression must be
partly accounted for in cultural terms. If one seeks to explain specifically why blacks are lynched by whites in the southern United States,
why the Nazis sent millions of Jews to gas chambers, why the Romans
delighted in seeing Christians torn to shreds by lions, or why the
Tupinamba eat their war prisoners after fattening them, one clearly has
to resort to cultural and historical explanations. However, there is no
question that we are biologically predisposed to be aggressive. The
theory that man is by nature gentle and is made nasty through a vicious
social system is wrong. If anything, the reverse is true: through life in
society we sometimes learn to suppress the most damaging aspects of
our aggressiveness. Although we are socially encouraged to kill in
cold blood during wartimes, social order also imposes some restraints
on our homicidal propensities.

What is the evidence that we are aggressive by nature? The most
unambiguous evidence is the sex-linked nature of aggression. Males
are much more aggressive than women. Yes, say the cultural determinists, but that is only because they are taught to be. True, in many
cultures males are indeed taught to be aggressive, but this is mere
reinforcement of their inborn predispositions. If males were not
biologically more predisposed toward aggression, would it not be an
extraordinary coincidence that they turn out to be that way not only in

all human societies, but in the vast majority of primate and other mammalian species as well. Furthermore, the level of aggression can be manipulated through hormonal treatment. For example, we can make females more aggressive by injecting them with hormones, such as testosterone, that are naturally present in higher levels in males. Conversely, animal breeders have long known that castration is a sure way to make male animals more docile and placid.

At the very least, then, the *potential* for aggression is inborn, and it is considerably higher in males than in females. However, the specific circumstances that bring out aggression or that suppress or deflect it are in good part cultural. Experiments have shown that frustration is one of the conditions that calls forth aggression, even the displacement of aggression against objects quite alien to the source of the frustration. Scapegoated minority groups, for instance, have often been the victims of aggression resulting from the frustration of the majority as a result of war, economic catastrophes, and the like (Allport, 1958).

As usual, let us try to answer the question of human aggression by looking at other animals as well. What makes animals fight? The answer, in general terms, is resource competition, which is exacerbated by population pressure. The higher the pressure of a species' population on the resources of its habitat, the more aggression we might expect to see, but it is clear that the threshold of aggression varies greatly from species to species. Some species are highly aggressive, others much less so. There are, however, two ways of regulating competition for resources and, thereby, aggression. One is hierarchy and the other is territoriality.

Hierarchy establishes, among other things, a rank order of access to, and a scale of distribution of, resources. These resources might be material (such as shelter or food) or social (right to displace, to be groomed, to copulate). If a hierarchy is firmly established, little contest need take place concerning the sharing of resources. The contest has already taken place and has been settled—at least for the time being.

Another way of regulating aggression is territoriality, which is a method of establishing monopoly rights to the resources of a portion of a species' habitat, for a defined group within that species. These groups are often quite small; a mated pair or a mother and offspring. So long as the territorial boundaries are known and respected, no aggression needs to take place: to each his own.

Even among the so-called lower animals, however, these two solutions to aggression are far from perfect. It is in the nature of privilege and monopoly that they are not suffered gladly by those they exclude. Territories are often contested, as, for example, when the population expands, and new individuals have to carve out new territories out of a fixed amount of space. If territories are attacked, it follows that they must be defended. This brings forth aggression. Thus, territoriality has the paradoxical effect of regulating competition for resources by cutting up space into small monopolies, and thereby reducing aggression; but also, of generating aggression through the challenge and defense of territorial rights.

The same is true of hierarchy. In a social order in which everyone "knows his place," there should, in theory, be no fighting over dominance. However, knowing one's place seldom means accepting it. Hierarchies, therefore, are constantly challenged and defended. Hierarchies are typically both established and overthrown through violent aggression.

Perhaps the best way of stating the relationship between aggression, hierarchy, and territoriality is to say that, while the latter two prevent the *continuous* outbreak of aggression, they certainly do not prevent periodic challenges to the *status quo*.

Looking at primate species, one notes an inverse correlation between territoriality and hierarchy. Primates, such as lemurs and gibbons, who are highly territorial, show little dominance behavior, not even between males and females. Conversely, highly hierarchical species, such as baboons and macaques, are not territorial. Among primates, man stands out as being both highly hierarchical and highly territorial. No wonder, then, that he should also be so aggressive: within the group, he fights over dominance; between groups, he fights over territory. As an example, consider the aggressive behavior within and between street gangs in the United States. Fights between gangs are typically over "turf," and status within the gang is established through individual confrontations.

This high level of both hierarchy and territoriality in humans implies a high level of resource competition, and indeed this is the case. Population pressures are not unique to man. Most species tend to reproduce beyond what is best for them. But war seems a uniquely human alternative to famine and disease in reducing population pressure. Human aggression, then, is not only a consequence of population pressure; it is also a means of reducing it.

There is another way in which human competition for resources is fundamentally different from that of other animals. For "lower" animals, resources are mainly for the satisfaction of basic needs like food and sex. These needs are easily satiated. Beyond a certain point, the prospect of further copulation or food ingestion is no longer attractive. Human needs, on the other hand, are mostly social and artifactual, and thus intrinsically unsatiable. There is no way of ever satisfying the desire for material possessions, money, prestige, attention, glory, power, and the other needs that human intelligence has created for the species. Thus, the competition for resources can only become more and more fierce, calling for more and more aggression, territoriality, and hierarchy. Indeed, human evolution has generally shown that the more surplus wealth human ingenuity created, the more unequal, the more concerned with territoriality, and the more aggressive man became, although, in contemporary industrial societies, wealth is somewhat less unequally distributed than in many agrarian societies of the Third World. Even if the level of aggressivity did not increase, the lethally destructive power of human aggressivity increased exponentially with human technology.

It is true that the frequency of certain forms of violence seem to be decreasing over certain periods of time: lynchings in the United States and public hangings in Britain, for example, are far less popular than they once were. This is hardly a ground for optimism, however, because in every epoch human creativity discovers new forms of barbarism. Some years ago, the optimist might have thought that the horrors of the religious wars of seventeenth-century Europe were an obsolete form of bestiality, but a glance at Northern Ireland, or at communal strife on the Indian subcontinent in the 1940s should quickly disabuse him.

Similarly, nationalism, which was until recently seen as a nineteenth-century European malady, has again flared up and unleashed violent conflicts throughout the world from Nigeria and the Congo, to Bangladesh and Belgium. Racism, which showed signs of receding, is enjoying a revival in the United States. Crimes of violence seem to be increasing in industrial countries, the apparent superiority of nonindustrial countries being possibly attributable more to poor statistics than to greater morality. The world's most industrialized country, the United States, also leads in homicide rates. The Second World War was far more murderous than the First, itself a previous record. Never in human history has a country been as ravaged by three decades of war as Vietnam with its defoliated forests, displaced population, and crater-dotted landscape. The United Nations is no less of a farce than its predecessor, the League of Nations. Amounts and proportions of national budgets devoted to armaments keep escalating. The country that calls itself the world guardian of democracy has constructed the greatest permanent war machine ever, with the fatherland of the proletariat not far behind.

The French Revolution began, modestly enough, by decapitating a few thousand people in the name of freedom, equality, and brotherhood; the Bolshevik Revolution showed a preference for the firing squad that improved on the scale of massacres. By the 1930s and 1940s, the Nazi and Stalinist death camps numbered their inmates in millions, markedly refining the technology of gassing and cremation.

Even the world of entertainment has hardly become less sanguinary over time. The bullring of Madrid is a lineal descendant of Rome's Colosseum. Where live spectacles get too expensive, we produce satisfyingly realistic massacres on celluloid, in the form of endless shoot-outs at O.K. Corral, displays of Samurai swordsmanship, or some reenactment of the bloodiest pages of our history.

The intent of this chapter has not been to vilify man, but rather to take an unflinching look at ourselves as a biological species. For far too long a time, sociologists have left the question of human nature to "social philosophy" (a term of mild opprobrium in the sociological lexicon). Many have even held dogmatically that there was no such thing. Cultural diversity was such, they argued, that, to all significant intents and purposes, man was manmade. It would be foolish to deny the great plasticity of man and his enormous capacity to learn and to transmit his learning culturally. The diversity of cultures and their potency in shaping human behavior are obvious.

Equally obvious are the biological constraints on human behavior. Even the most extreme cultural determinists have to admit that the physiology of age and sex impose limits on the performance of social roles, but they regard these problems as trivial and alien to sociology. Let us take the question of war and peace, which hardly any sociologist would regard as trivial. All societies impose constraints on the expression of violence, yet nearly all fail in suppressing it, even when there is nearly unanimous agreement that violence is senseless. Practically everybody agrees that war today does not pay and has become an extremely dangerous and destructive game. Yet presumably sane and mature leaders continue to plunge their countries into holocausts for reasons as trivial as which flag is to flutter over a stretch of sandy wasteland in the Sinai, or what political complexion the government of a fourth-class power is to have on the other side of the globe (Vietnam), or even the outcome of a soccer game (1969 Salvador-Honduras conflict).

Within societies, lethal violence can be repressed only insofar as the state is successful in so monopolizing the means of violence as to make the threat of its use a convincing deterrent. Even then, success is far from complete. Not until World War I was dueling effectively stamped out in Europe, for example, despite the fact that it had long been illegal in most countries. Only after the war swept aside the last remnants of the aristocracy among whom dueling had been a pastime to relieve the tedium of parasitic indolence, did that particular form of violence become obsolete. Or, to mention another form of endemic violence in a highly "advanced" society, hardly a day goes by in any large American city without a cops-and-robbers shoot-out.

The seemingly ineradicable character of intraspecific aggression in *Homo sapiens,* whether between groups or between individuals, suggests that we are dealing here with a fundamental feature of human nature. That it has outlived its evolutionary usefulness is, alas, no guarantee that it will promptly vanish. The cultural level of explanation accounts for the specific forms that violence takes in a given society, but scarcely for its causes and incidence.

Konrad Lorenz, after a lifetime of study of animal behavior, concluded that the missing link between the apes and *Homo sapiens* is man. The central point of this chapter is that an understanding of human behavior requires us to place man equally squarely in nature and culture.

ADDITIONAL READING

The notion that the social behavior of man should be compared to that of other species owes much to the work of ethologists, and more especially of primatologists. Among the best accounts of primate behavior are Kummer (1971), Morris (1967a), and De Vore (1965). The problem of aggression is dealt with cross-specifically by Lorenz (1966) and Scott (1958). Among the most articulate proponents of the "zoological perspective" on human behavior are the primatologist Morris (1967b, 1969), and anthropologists Tiger and Fox (1969, 1971). I have dealt with age and gender as biologically based aspects of social differentiation in *Age and Sex in Human Societies* (1973). Other sources that develop arguments on the role of aggression, territoriality and hierarchy similar or parallel to the views presented here are Alexander (1971), Bigelow (1969), Collias (1944), Scott (1958), Washburn and Hamburg (1968), and Wynne-Edwards (1965). Many social scientists have advanced non-biological theories of aggression, such as the psychoanalytic "frustration-aggression" theory (Dollard *et al.,* 1939), or learning theory (Bandura, 1973). A culturally determinist position is represented by Montagu (1957).

3

Habitat, Tools, and Weapons

Man is by nature a tropical animal. Nearly all primates live in the tropics or subtropics, and the few that do not, like the macaques of Northern Honshu in Japan, spend half of the year miserably shivering in the cold. Human technology, however, made possible survival in nearly all habitats on earth, from semideserts to subarctic tundras, and from sea level to altitudes of 15,000 feet in the Bolivian Andes. Among mammals, man is one of the most ubiquitous; only the dog and some of the rodents successfully compete with man, and then largely as either domestic animals or parasites of man.

Technology, Adaptation, and Evolution

There is no human group, no matter how isolated, that does not possess, as a minimum, a technology of fire, shelter, and tool-and-weapon-making. Some humans go naked or nearly naked, not out of ignorance, but because they live in a climate where clothing is not essential to survival. Even these groups, however, know how to make fire and build shelters. Indeed, the association between ''primitiveness'' and nudity is an ethnocentric one, as many of those groups engage in agriculture and animal husbandry. Archeological evidence suggests that while fire-making may not be over 50,000 to 100,000 years old, man captured, used, and fed natural fire long before learning how to produce it; shelter and tool- and weapon-making were developed at the dawn of hominid evolution, several million years ago; and other primates, especially the chimpanzees, seem to be on the threshold of that technology. Fire-making is a human monopoly as far as we know, but wild chimpanzees build nests in the trees to sleep in safety from predators, make crude tools, and use sticks and other objects as defensive weapons.

Even this rudimentary technology rapidly enabled early hominids to spread over much of the land area of the planet, and thus achieve a geographical distribution incomparably greater than that of any other primate. Interestingly, the spread of *Homo sapiens* had as a concomitant the disappearance or severe restriction of man's most closely related species including the still barely surviving great apes and the extinct lines of hominid evolution such as *Homo neanderthalensis*. The early technological breakthrough of the paleolithic hunting culture allowed man to escape the narrow confines of the specific ecological niche to which the other primates are confined, and thus gave man an enormous adaptive advantage over all of them. We may also ask why only the evolutionary line that led to *Homo sapiens* survived while other closely related hominid lines became extinct. Our best guess is that these various hominid species competed directly with each other for food, and that the one species with an intellectual edge, and hence a better technology for killing man, near-man, and beast had enough of an edge to push his competition into extinction.

The most significant fact about man's ecological adaptation is that so much of it is *cultural* rather than biological. Biological adaptation is not altogether absent, however. There is some evidence that humans adapt genetically to climate and geographical milieu. Skin pigmentation may be a climatic adaptation, and so might be the incidence of certain genes such as the one for sickle-cell anemia which, in its heterozygous form, gives some resistance to malaria. In addition to genetic transmission of adaptive traits, much physiological adaptation is acquired in early childhood. Such is the case of adaptation to high altitude among Andean Indians, which takes the form of enlarged lungs, shorter stature, subcutaneous fat, and capillary development. These adaptations are acquired principally during the first two years of life. Compared to other primates, and indeed to most other mammals, man is biologically unspecialized. His digestive system, for example, can accommodate to practically any kind of vegetable or animal food, which is one of his most obvious biological assets.

Other primates also learn to adapt to environmental changes, but in a much more rudimentary and undramatic way than does man. It is highly unlikely that even the chimpanzee—the most humanlike of primates—could successfully adapt to subarctic environment, even after a few thousand years of "cultural" evolution. He would probably need several million years of *biological* evolution. With man there is a dramatic quantum jump: thanks to technology, he immensely accelerates his capacity for ecological adaptation, and hence enormously enhances his capacity to survive practically anywhere on the landed surface of the earth, and, indeed, more recently, on and under water, in the air, and even in outer space.

Man's capacity to adapt to and make use of his environment has been so dramatically successful that humanity is suddenly recognizing that its very success brings it on the threshold of catastrophe. Much like parasites whose proliferation eventually kills both their host and themselves, man now threatens not only other species, but his own as well. While it took man at least two or three million years of cultural evolution to achieve the capability for extinguishing life on our planet, it would now only take a few hours of madness by a few key people in the two superpowers to realize that potentiality. Starting around the seventeenth century, our capacity for self-destruction has increased exponentially. We are now squarely in the era of mega-tons and mega-deaths.

Our cultural beginnings were much less spectacular. We may end up in a bang, but we started with a barely audible pop. In fact, after the ancestors of *Homo sapiens* became moderately successful paleolithic hunters, scavengers, and gatherers, nothing dramatic happened technologically for the next two or three million years, except for the invention of fire-*making* (as distinguished from fire-using), and of long-range weapons that could be accurately thrown, like spears and arrows. Some paleontologists, as Leakey, believe that speech evolved only slowly and gradually in early humans perhaps as recently as a quarter of a million years ago. Technologically, however, no drastic change happened until the so-called Neolithic Revolution some 10,000 years ago. The only domesticated animal was the dog who, as a carnivorous scavenger, was a natural companion of man. The dog's bark was man's first (and cheapest) "advance warning" system, and its keen sense of smell greatly increased man's efficiency as a hunter. Unlike the more parasitic relationship existing between man and his more recently domesticated animals, the man–dog relationship is truly symbiotic; that is, mutually beneficial.

The Neolithic Revolution

Although paleolithic technology included the use of a wide range of mineral, vegetable, and animal products, such as wood, grass, stone, clay, bones, horns, and hides, it had several limitations. Food had to be continuously searched for, and its supply was often irregular and unreliable. No sources of energy other than raw human muscle power were tapped, and thus *control* over the environment was virtually nil. The need to be continuously on the move and the absence of modes of transportation other than human portage restricted the accumulation of goods to the bare essentials of weapons, a few simple tools, and clothing. Under such conditions, population density remained low, probably well under one inhabitant per square mile in most environments.

Then, some 5000 to 10,000 years ago in various parts of the Old World, and a little later in the Western Hemisphere, a dramatic breakthrough took place, sometimes referred to as the Neolithic Revolution. This set of interrelated technological changes was probably independently invented, or at the very least semiindependently developed, in about half a dozen different parts of the world, in most cases along great river valleys, where the combination of alluvial soils and irrigation water facilitated food-growing. This moment of history is perhaps the greatest leap forward which humanity ever took. Hitherto, man had been a predator making up for his bodily limitations through the use of artificial weapons. In competition with other species, he had achieved some success in terms of adaptability to a wide range of habitats, but man was still very much part of nature rather than a master over it. The great quantum jump was one from *adaptation to,* to *control over* the natural environment.

The most essential control to establish was over the food supply. What is referred to as the domestication of plants and animals is, in the first instance, a set of techniques enabling man to keep his food reliably on hand. Not only was the reliability of the food supply greatly increased, but also its quantity. Growing corn or tending flocks are more productive ways of securing food than chasing after elusive game or picking wild berries.

In turn, this revolution of food-growing and food-raising enabled man to greatly increase his numbers, and thus his competitive edge over other species. The first human population explosion began a few thousand years ago when it became possible for the same environment to support human populations 10 or more times greater than before. In the rich river valleys, irrigated agriculture made for extremely dense populations and for the rise of powerful empires. In less privileged environments, but where rainfall was still adequate, slash-and-burn agriculture (which still prevails in most of the tropics) supported medium-density populations. Marginal dry lands were gradually taken over by nomadic or seminomadic pastoralists. Even where grazing is scanty, herds of cattle, sheep, and goats can feed many more people than wild game.

The Neolithic Revolution was so named because this development of agriculture and livestock breeding coincided roughly in various parts of the world with polished (as opposed to chipped) stone technology. Too much stress, however, has been put on that aspect of technology. Stones are permanent, and thus convenient pebbles in the archeologist's reconstruction of human evolution, but the food-raising technology was far more significant. It opened the era where man and his domesticated plants and animals began to displace, destroy, or exploit to extinction numerous other species, especially large mammals. Along with food production, techniques of food conservation and storage further increased the reliability of the supply. This period also marked the beginnings of the use of nonhuman sources of energy, especially of wind, water, and large animals. Particularly developed in Asia and around the rim of the Mediterranean, these techniques greatly magnified the productivity of human labor as well as man's control over his environment. The use of the horse as a mount in the Old World was at once a great leap forward in man's speed on land (unsurpassed until the nineteenth century), and in his destructive capacity in warfare.

Agrarian Societies and Pastoralism

Some 4000 to 5000 years ago, the use of the wheel, of metals, and of writing began to spread to various parts of the Old World, and Western historians have used these criteria, along with stone architecture, to differentiate the "great civilizations" from the not-so-great ones. That the stress on these achievements is probably excessive is shown by the fact that most sub-Saharan African civilizations have lacked the wheel and (until contact with Islam) writing, and only a few have extensively built in stone; yet their technology of iron and other metals was more advanced than that of cultures that possessed the three other features. Similarly, the New World civilizations of Meso-America and the Andes knew the principle of the circle and the wheel, but made virtually no practical use of it, in part, probably because so much of their terrain was mountainous.

Of the pre-Colombian civilizations, only the Maya had a true system of writing, and although their metal technology was advanced, it was remarkably impractical, being largely limited to the use of copper, gold, and silver in jewelry and decoration. Weapons and tools were largely made of stone, such as the sharp and brittle obsidian. The American civilizations also lacked large domesticated animals, except, in the Andes, the llama and alpaca. The latter is too small and frail to carry any weights, and even the larger llama has a maximum carrying capacity of some 20 kilograms, far too little to serve as a mount. Largely limited to human portage, without appreciable utilitarian use of metal tools, for the most part without writing systems, and with a fairly simple agricultural technology, the pre-Colombian cultures attained high levels of political organization and achieved brilliant feats of megalithic architecture and sculpture. Inca stone work, for example, with its enormous fitted blocks weighing up to tens of tons, such as in the citadel of Sacsahuaman overlooking Cuzco, staggers the imagination, considering the simple technology with which it was achieved. Conversely, the often more technically advanced tropical Africans who were master blacksmiths, with the exception of the Zimbabwe civilization and to a limited extent some West African cultures, remained relatively uninterested in carving or utilizing stone.

A common misconception in the way of looking at human social evolution is to regard agriculture as more ''advanced'' than pastoralism. Defining as pastoral those societies that derive most of their food from domesticated herbivores, pastoralism is almost necessarily associated with nomadism or semi-nomadism. It is true that a sedentary mode of life is typically possible only with agriculture (and, exceptionally, in certain fishing economies, such as the salmon fishermen of the Northwest Coast of North America), and that sedentary life in turn allows greater population densities, accumulation of surplus production, and more complex forms of political and social organization. However, agriculture and livestock breeding are, from an evolutionary perspective, nearly synchronic developments. Indeed, nearly all of the agricultural societies have raised domestic animals for food, if not cattle, then smaller livestock, such as poultry, swine, goats, and sheep; or, in the New World, turkeys, guinea pigs, llamas, and alpacas. Many of the cultures that are thought of as pastoralist, because they attach great social and economic importance to cattle, do have a mixed economy of livestock breeding and agriculture. Such, for example, are many peoples of Eastern Africa, from the Southern Sudan to South Africa, to whom cattle is a socially all-important form of wealth, a medium of "bridewealth" payment, and even a link to ritual activities. If anything, it seems probable that man domesticated most animals (except the dog) somewhat after cultivating plants. Herbivores probably were first attracted to human settlements by crops and thus gradually tamed.

The pure pastoralists are relatively few, and most of them live more or less symbiotically with agriculturalists (as indeed do by now practically all of the few surviving hunters and gatherers, such as the Pygmies, Bushmen, and native Australians). The purely pastoral way of life is thus not a more primitive prelude to sedentary agriculture, but rather a successful adaptation to marginal lands, often arid or semiarid ones, or, in the Andes, to high altitudes, where agriculture is extremely difficult. The Bedouins of Arabia, the Tuaregs of the Sahara, the Fulani of the Sudan, the high-altitude Andean herders, and other pastoralists have numerous trade and other contacts with agriculturalists. Nomads may graze their cattle over areas occupied by peasants whose land they thus fertilize. Cattle herders also frequently come to urban centers to sell livestock and buy a wide range of goods, such as salt and weapons. Sometimes, they become specialized in long-distance trade by using their camels as beasts of burden across deserts. In any case, they seldom if ever live in isolation from other societies. They merely fill an ecological niche more specialized and limiting than that occupied by agriculturalists. The limitations on their social organization are imposed by the marginal environment rather than by the technology.

Nomads have been notoriously successful in warfare against sedentary, urbanized civilizations, despite being often greatly outnumbered. A number of nomadic pastoralists, such as the Mongols in much of Asia and Hamitic groups in Eastern Africa, have conquered settled groups, and have become sedentary themselves after becoming a ruling class over agriculturalists. Most of the time, however, contacts between pastoralists and agriculturalist have been peacefully symbiotic; while, among nomads competing with each other for scarce pasture, warfare has typically been endemic.

Another misconception in our view of human evolution is to see it in too schematized a way, as a continuous, unilinear growth from the simple to the complex. As a gross summary statement of the general trend, such a view is tenable. But it does not follow, for example, that *contemporary* hunting and gathering societies represent living fossils, or arrested forms frozen dead in their evolutionary tracks. There is evidence that, as a result of conquest and displacement to more marginal habitats, some societies have in fact *de*volved to a technologically simpler mode of subsistence than they once possessed. Such, for example, seem to be the Lacandon of the Southeastern Mexican forest, linear descendants of the Maya who represent the most literate and artistically brilliant civilization of pre-Colombian America.

Many of the contemporary "primitives" live in marginal ecological niches, which they originally did not occupy by choice, but into which they were probably pushed by more powerful societies. The precariousness and austerity of material existence exhibited by these people are frequently attributed to the alleged primitiveness of their technology, when, in fact, they are much more validly ascribable to environmental limitations. The Eskimos provide a good illustration. The Arctic wasteland is scarcely a Garden of Eden for a tropical primate like man. Survival in that wasteland, however precarious, is the product of a long line of inventive adaptation, which represents one of the greatest technological achievements by any preindustrial society. The problems of transportation (solved by one of the most effective uses of the dog developed by any culture, and by the most ingenious use of animal hides for boat construction) and of the conservation and generation of heat in an environment where fuel is scarce are staggering.

Thus, it is ethnocentric to apply the criteria of technological "advancement" of non-Arctic societies to the Eskimos, and to wonder why the Eskimos did not build pyramids, invent steamships and snowmobiles, or develop flush toilets. The Eskimo miracle is sheer survival in the Arctic, a feat that "advanced" industrial societies could emulate only in the twentieth century, and then at fantastic expense and by imitating the ''primitive'' Eskimos. Eskimo technology is as far a cry from that of paleolithic tropical hunters as that of many seemingly more complex and impressive agricultural societies.

Ecology

Human ecology, the relationship between man and his environment, is qualitatively different from that of other animals in that it is only marginally biological and predominantly cultural. This is not to say that man does not continue to evolve biologically as well. In fact, there is no evidence that his biological evolution is any slower than that of many other animals. The big difference is that technology enables man to adapt to a wide range of conditions in his physical environment with a speed that is incomparably faster than biological evolution.[1] Not only is social evolution much faster than biological evolution, but the cumulative character of technology has accelerated exponentially the rate of change. So incredibly rapid has the pace become in the last century that man is now caught up in an adaptive race *with himself*. Technology changes sufficiently within the life span of an individual so as to create serious problems of social adaptation to the technological adaptation to the physical environment. No longer concerned about the biological obsolescence of his species, man now faces the problem of social obsolescence of the individual.

Another staggering consequence of the technological explosion is that ecological problems have suddenly escalated to the point where our glaring successes in the mastery of our planet raise the spectre of

[1]A reminder is necessary here. To say that biological evolution is slow on the scale of human history, and, hence, does not go far in explaining how we have adapted to our environment in the last few thousand years, is not to argue that our biological heritage as primates is irrelevant to an understanding of our contemporary social behavior. Indeed, in the previous chapter, I have argued for the relevance of human biology to our social behavior. Furthermore, biological evolution need not be as slow as it has been in the past. Indeed, our controlled breeding of domestic animals shows that we can profoundly alter the anatomy of a species in the space of a score of generations or so. The range in size, for example, between a Chihuahua dog and an Irish wolfhound is well over one to a hundred. Horses range from the two-foot midgets raised in Argentina to the Belgian workhorses weighing close to a ton.

our extinction. Our technology of environmental control and exploitation has become so efficient and destructive that, unless we quickly develop a technology of control over the technology of destruction and the biology of reproduction, our future is bleak indeed.

So far, we have tried to take an unflinching look at what kind of an animal we are, and at how we have coped with our environment to insure our survival as a species. We have examined, if only cursorily, the biological and material foundations of human behavior. These topics, however basic they obviously are to an understanding of human behavior, have long been peripheral to the concerns of sociologists. Anthropologists have done much better in this respect, but the social sciences in general have only recently rediscovered the immense relevance of both human biology and of human ecology to our social behavior.

Let us briefly recapitulate the central arguments. In the previous chapter, I stressed that, for all his idiosyncracies, man is nonetheless an animal; specifically, a mammal and a primate. This is true not only in the obvious and trivial sense of our biological functions, capabilities, limitations, and needs, but also in the determination of our social behavior. Most sociologists have assumed that there was a sharp discontinuity between what determined animal and human behavior, and they spread the credo of autodeterminism in human social behavior. Yet, equally bothered by the implications of individual free will and the limitations this position implied on the development of sociology as a predictive science, the dominant sociological credo was one of *collective* autodetermination. Man was shaped by Society; that is, by the transcendental force that mysteriously emanated from the interaction between people. Sociology became in effect a quasi religion with Society as its God, Auguste Comte as its prophet, consensus and solidarity as its morality, and, of course, sociologists as its priests.

We suggested that important and recurrent features of human behavior, especially aggressivity, dominance, gregariousness, pairmating, nuclear family incest taboos, and territoriality, are far too ubiquitous in the species to be explained purely or even predominantly in terms of learning. Next, we turned to the equally glaring fact that man is indeed a very special kind of animal through his greater intellectual capacity to modify his behavior through learning—and to transmit learning socially. The discontinuity with other primates is not as great as once was thought, but it is significant enough to make social evolution distinct from biological evolution, and human ecology different from that of other animals. Man is practically alone in mediating his interaction with his nonhuman environment through a socially learned technology. The first great human achievement was the essentially adaptative technology of paleolithic hunters; the second one was the ever-accelerating technology of control that started a few thousand years ago with the domestication of plants and animals.

Thus, many of the predicaments of *Homo sapiens* came because, on the one hand, he is an animal who adapted biologically to a specialized environment, and on the other hand, he is a highly intelligent animal who was able to transform his environment and his society at a rate far exceeding his biological adaptation. In many ways, then, man's intelligence has made him a biological misfit so enamored with his cultural creations that he refuses to look at his biological heritage, and, therefore dismally fails to control it. This theme is eloquently developed by Desmond Morris (1971) who suggests that urban life made possible by agricultural technology has in fact created an artificial environment for man, similar to what zoos are for animals. Man has domesticated *himself* along with plants and other animals, and the result all too often has been a miserable, caged, trapped parody of the paleolithic hunter and gatherer which he still is biologically. A few thousand years of cultural history cannot undo millions of years of biological prehistory. History has, of course, profoundly transformed human destiny, but it has not wiped the biological slate clean. Human behavior must always be understood as the interplay of biology and culture, with both continuities and discontinuities between them.

Having sketched here how man related to his nonhuman environment, we can now turn to the more traditional concerns of sociology and social anthropology—the social relations of man.

ADDITIONAL READING

The subject matter of this chapter usually receives little attention from sociologists, with a few notable exceptions, such as Lenski (1966, 1970) and Ogburn (1950). Anthropologists have stressed the material basis of society to a much greater extent. Among the classics are Morgan's *Ancient Society* (1877), which greatly influenced the work of Engels (1942). More recent anthropology texts that give the subject its proper place are Kroeber (1948) and Herskovits (1950). Morris (1971) analyzes the biological implications of urban growth and industrial technology.

4

Kith and Kin

All human societies are organized on at least four bases: age, gender, descent, and marriage. Although all societies possess at least these four principles of social differentiation, many resort to other bases of organization as well. The family is the universal human group in which all four principles are found, and, in that sense, the family is the most fundamental and probably the most intractably irreducible form of social organization. Even in its most reduced "nuclear" form, the family contains two adults of opposite sexes married to each other and their offspring. In most societies, family groups are far larger and more complex than that, but in all societies families normally include adults and children of both sexes and of at least two different generations, linked together by ties of marriage and descent.

The Family: Age and Sex Dominance

The universality of the family as the basic mode of social organization raises the important question of its biological basis. Indeed, anything universal to the human species can be presumed to have at least partly biological foundations. This is not to say that the structure of the family is not importantly shaped by culture, but, more than any other major complex of social institutions, the family is our main mediating link between nature and nurture.

In Chapter Two, we explored these biological foundations. *Homo sapiens* is characterized by relatively stable pair-bonding between adult males and females (a pattern facilitated by the anoestrous character of human females who are sexually receptive at practically all times), by extremely strong mother–child ties (due to prolonged lactation and utter infant dependency), and by an incest taboo between parents and children and between siblings, which, we have tentatively suggested, might be in part biologically predisposed and linked with the establishment of bonds between adult males. These biogenic foundations establish the minimum conditions for the existence of the simplest and most universal form of human family, the nuclear family, composed of a married couple and their common unmarried offspring. Now we shall explore how these biological foundations were elaborated on culturally, giving rise to far more complex arrangements.

Two distinct theoretical perspectives on the family have pervaded the sociological literature. The dominant approach has been that of functionalism, making the family the cornerstone of the social order. The family, functionalists have argued, is the minimum and indispensable form of social organization necessary for the proper socialization and protection of children. The regulation of sex in marriage and the incest taboo in the family prevent destructive conflict, make for stable relationships, and provide for emotional and sexual gratification as well as for reproduction. Exogamous marriage (marriage outside the family, clan, etc.) establishes ties between families and, thus, a wider and more secure basis of social solidarity. This functionalist approach has, by and large, dominated American sociology textbooks, and became the standard fare of "Marriage and the Family" courses (Parsons and Bales, 1955).

An equally old but much less influential tradition has made the family the villain of the sociological farce. Associated with Marx and with Engels (1942), this approach has looked at the family as the ultimate source of inequality in the transmission of property and other forms of privilege. Not only does the family perpetuate inequalities of class through the inheritance of property and the transmission of educational advantages, but it is internally tyrannical and conflict ridden. The family, in short, is a microtyranny dominated by male adults, and the most universal model of human inequality. Clearly, both views have some validity: the family does make for inequality and conflict, but, utopian attempts to eliminate it have met with quite limited success. The apparent conflict between the two perspectives is easily resolved if one accepts the view that inequality, aggressiveness, and conflict are indeed very human, as suggested in Chapter Two. Perhaps we should take a sober look at the biological bases of inequality within the family; namely, age and gender differences, instead of theorizing about the functions of the family, or moralizing about its nastiness.

Looked at as a system of interrelations, the family is strikingly hierarchical: adults dominate children, and males dominate females. This is the case in all human societies, although the degree of female subordination varies from extreme to moderate. Age and sex differences account for much of the hierarchical structure of the family, and do so consistently in all cultures. Even if one chooses to focus primarily on the *social* dimensions of *descent* and *marriage*—the two basic relationships within the family even in its simplest nuclear form—the conclusion is inescapable that these two sets of ties are closely linked to age and sex differences respectively. Descent is the socially recognized filiation that exists between members of different generations; marriage is the socially sanctioned pair-mating. The family is a group of people tied together by descent or marriage, which means that its members belong to different generations or to opposite sexes. Age frequently enters into the ties between siblings, since their birth order establishes a natural hierarchy.

The biological basis of the age and sex hierarchy within the family is equally obvious: sheer brute strength is by far the best single predictor of who is dominant over whom. The main element in male dominance is sexual dimorphism in size, and thus in strength. (Dimorphism comes from Greek *dimorphos,* having two forms.) Some mammals are much more dimorphic in size than others. Even among primates, some, like the gibbons, are minimally dimorphic, while others, like baboons, have males that weigh twice as much as females. The more sexually dimorphic a species is, the more it tends to be male-dominated. On that scale *Homo sapiens* is a *moderately* dimorphic species. Human females weigh approximately four-fifths as much as males, giving the latter a decisive, but not an overwhelming, edge. Some females are stronger than some males, but it is interesting to note that deviations reducing sexual dimorphism are often socially disapproved of: big women and small men are stigmatized.

That male dominance is largely a product of differences in strength is confirmed by the structure of age dominance within the family. Adult females dominate children of both sexes, and older girls are dominant over younger boys. In fact, as age differences in strength are much larger than sex differences, adult domination over children is far more extensive than adult male dominance over adult females. In the last analysis, the authority structure within the family is based on the use or at least the threat of force. By the time most infants are one or two years old, they know that they will not be effective in a contest with an adult, an extremely frustrating discovery which is perhaps related to the tantrum behavior characteristic of that age. On the other hand, much of the rebelliousness associated with adolescence may well grow out of the child's realization that the balance of physical strength is rapidly shifting to his advantage.

Age dominance is maintained not solely by force, but also by the knowledge that grows out of experience. Not only are adults dominant over children, but middle-aged adults are dominant over younger adults. However, seldom are the oldest in actual political control: most often the power resides in persons in mature middle age. This indicates that, when physical senility sets in, power declines, the peak period of dominance clustering around the intersection between a declining curve of physical strength and an ascending curve of knowledge and experience.

Nuclear and Extended Families: Who Lives Where?

The simplest form of the human family is the *nuclear* one. It is virtually universal in the species, and attempts to eliminate it have met with quite limited success on a societywide basis. However, as an exclusive form of family organization, the nuclear family is exceptional. That is, in the overwhelming majority of societies, nuclear families aggregate in larger and more complex kin groups known as *extended* families. Common in contemporary Western societies, the monogamous nuclear family as a preferred and predominant kin grouping is, in fact, a rather rare and exotic arrangement. The far more common extended family includes relatives other than a married couple and their unmarried children, and this typically means relatives belonging to at least three different generations. The principle that determines the composition of the household of kinsmen who live in physical propinquity to one another is known as the *rule of residence* (Murdock, 1949). This rule determines who goes where with marriage. In Western societies, the normal expectation is that the newlyweds both hive off from their respective families and establish a new, separate household where they will raise their offspring. This rule is known as *neolocal residence,* and produces nuclear families, since it precludes the possibility of three generations or married siblings living together.

All other rules of residence give rise to extended families. The most frequent arrangement is the one where the bride leaves her family upon marriage and joins the household of her husband and his relatives. This is known as *virilocal* (or *patrilocal*) residence, and obviously results in a much larger family group incorporating at least three and often four generations of blood-related males and their spouses. A much less common rule, known as *uxorilocal* (or *matrilocal*) residence, is the one where it is the wife who stays put and the husband who comes in to live with his in-laws.[1] This also results in an extended family composed of three or four generations of related females and their in-marrying husbands.

---

[1] My reason for preferring the terms "virilocal" and "uxorilocal" to the seemingly less exotic "patrilocal" and "matrilocal" is not, as might be thought, to irritate my readers. "Patrilocal" and "matrilocal" refer to father and mother, and are thus complete misnomers. The issue is whether it is the bride who goes to live with her husband and his parents, or the groom who moves in with his wife and her relatives. In both cases, one of the spouses lives with both a mother and a father. The difference is which spouse lives with in-laws, and which spouse lives with relatives. This obviously has nothing to do with papa or mama, as the terms "patrilocal" and "matrilocal" very misleadingly imply.

There are some other complicated and rare forms of extended families but the virilocal form accounts for some four-fifths of all extended family systems and the uxorilocal for nearly all the rest. Within these three basic types of family residence (neolocal, virilocal, and uxorilocal), there are however, a number of more complex combinations or alternatives. In few societies do all family groupings actually conform to the dominant or normative type. In nearly all societies, there are some family groups that contain kinsmen or in-laws that "normally" should not be there. Let us take the American case as an illustration. American family living groups are among the smallest in the world because of a combination of neolocal residence and low fertility. Yet we know that not all families conform to the norm of father, mother, and two or three children that we see on billboard posters ("The family that prays together stays together"). For one thing, many families do not stay together, and thus include children by previous marriages, or are composed of a female head of household and her offspring by a succession of lovers. Many families also include a widowed grandparent, an unmarried sibling of either wife or husband, or some other relative. For reasons of economy, a number of young couples temporarily live with the parents of either spouse before establishing separate residence. All these "exceptions" to the stereotypical middle-class, suburban, nuclear family add up to a good many extended households, but neolocality is the preferred pattern, at least in the middle class.

In some societies, more than a single rule of residence may be practiced. For example, a variant of the extended family is the *stem* family. The stem family is a reduced extended family of the virilocal type, in which only one of the sons (often the oldest, sometimes the youngest) is expected to stay with his parents after marriage. The other sons are expected to establish neolocal residence. This system is usually found in peasant societies where land is scarce, and where an attempt is made not to fragment land holdings beyond minimum viability. The one son who stays on the farm inherits it, and his brothers are expected to go and settle in town or to emigrate. Such a system existed in Japan and some rural parts of Europe. Those societies can thus be said to institutionalize both virilocality and neolocality.

Another system of multiple residence rule is the fairly common arrangement of temporary uxorilocal residence followed by permanent virilocality. For a period of months or a couple of years, the groom lives with his in-laws and performs certain services for them as part of the marriage contract, and then the young couple go and live permanently with the groom's family.

The significance of the rule of residence lies not only in the size of the family group, but also in the types of relative that live together. In virilocal families, the men in the family group are related by blood to each other, and the married women are linked to the men by marriage, but frequently unrelated to each other by blood. In the uxorilocal situation, the opposite is true: the women are linked by blood, and the married men are the often unrelated spouses of these women.

The advantages of extended over nuclear families in all but the most mobile industrial societies are obvious. A larger family group has a built-in margin of flexibility in the allocation of tasks and distribution of resources. For example, to have the onus of child care spread from the child's mother to half-a-dozen adult or adolescent females in the household obviously frees the women for other tasks. For example, in many African societies, women do a good deal of the agricultural labor, and much of the infant care is left to the mother's older daughters, to co-wives, or to sisters-in-law. For the men, the extended family provides a ready basis for the organization of tasks which require cooperation: the extended family is a readymade work or hunting party.

Similarly, the extended family provides for the wider and hence more equal distribution of resources: it constitutes a simple but efficient system of economic risk-spreading and social security. It is little wonder then, that only in Western industrialized societies where the search for jobs entails great spatial mobility, and where job specialization and turnover make it difficult for several relatives to find employment in the same location, is the nuclear type of family dominant. Even in those societies, the convenience and economy of having at least some other relatives around is not lost on many people. A grandmother may be a convenient babysitter; or a young husband finishing college may find that the guest room in his in-laws' house is a cheap abode until he and his wife can afford a place of their own.

Moreover, industrial systems can adjust to a prevailing family system just as easily as the family system can adjust to industrial modes of production. The assumption often made by Western sociologists that it is the family system that must yield to the "functional imperatives" of industrialization is plainly untenable. Japan is a good example of a highly industrial society where the industrial structure has made the necessary adjustments to be compatible with the traditional stem family. To be sure, there probably are more nuclear families in Japan today than a century ago, and more in the cities than in the rural areas, but the stem family with three generations living together is still a viable and desired alternative. The stem family continues to be common in the rural areas, and subsists even in larger cities as a less common alternative. In any case, the sense of obligation to, and membership in, larger patrilineages remains very much alive (Dore, 1955, 1967).

The traditional pattern of rural Japan before the industrial era was one of primogeniture. The eldest son inherited the land and stayed with his parents, while the younger sons were expected to emigrate, often to urban areas. Younger sons either established new families of their own, or sometimes they became adopted sons-in-law in families that did not have sons. The eldest son, his parents, his wife, and his children established the traditional Japanese three-generation stem family. When industrialization came, the existing extended family structure proved compatible with it. The traditional family system permitted, indeed encouraged, extensive urban migration. Furthermore, the industrial system itself developed along lines very different from the Western pattern of great labor mobility. Much of the industry was made up of small-scale family firms where the extended family was more an asset than a liability. Even large-scale industry developed a quasi-familistic model of industrial employment. The Japanese system of company paternalism with a stable permanent labor force covered from birth to death by the protective blanket of company welfare may seem archaic and irrational to ethnocentric Westerners, but it has not prevented Japan from successfully competing with Western industrial societies. With such labor stability, and frequent employment of several members of the same family in the same firm, the extended three-generation stem family is perfectly compatible with industrialization. This example shows, once more, how wary we should be of generalizing from our own experience in Western societies.

Descent: Who Are the Ancestors?

Another important principle of kinship organization is the *rule of descent*. It may appear obvious to Westerners that in all societies people have two parents, four grandparents, eight great-grandparents, and so on. This biological fact (which is recognized in the vast majority of societies, but not in *all* of them) is more often than not of minimal social import. The overwhelming majority of the world's societies ascribe much more social significance to a single line of descent to the detriment of all others. These societies are said to have *unilineal* descent.

Societies such as ours, that attribute equal or nearly equal significance to all lines of descent, are misleadingly called *bilateral*. (*Omnilineal* would be a better term, since *bilateral* implies that there are two sides to a family. This, in turn, leads to confusion with *double descent*, as we shall see later, but unfortunately "omnilineal" is not in common use.) Although Westerners inherit their surnames in the father's line, they otherwise pay approximately equal attention to all their ancestors, or, in the American case, they pay precious little attention to any of them beyond their grandparents. (Many Americans do not know the first names of all four of their grandparents, nor the maiden names of their grandmothers.) Bilateral descent societies are relatively rare for a simple reason: bilateral descent makes it impossible to divide a society into clearly distinct, mutually exclusive kin groups beyond the nuclear family. Indeed, only full brothers and sisters have identical ancestors. If one chooses to recognize all lines of descent, it means that, beyond the nuclear family, there can be no corporate kin group, membership in which is common and exclusive to any specific kinsmen. First cousins, for example, share only half of their sociologically significant ancestors. Thus, they cannot establish a wider descent group that would include all their sociologically relevant ancestors and only those. That is why Western societies, with their bilateral descent, do not have clans or lineages.

The alternative of giving salience to a single line of descent has the automatic consequence of creating solidary kin groups that may include thousands of people, and which are quite unambiguous and mutually exclusive. These unilineal descent groups are called *lineages* and *clans*. The distinction between these two terms is that in lineages the common ancestor can actually be traced genealogically, but in clans he or she lies too far back in the past for actual filiation to be traced. Indeed, the clan ancestor may well be a mythical figure. Typically, a lineage is a subdivision of a clan, though not all unilineal descent societies have clans. The lineage itself can be segmented and subsegmented at each generation. The number of generations of ancestors through whom a lineage or segment of a lineage has to trace descent before it gets to the one common to all its members is said to be the *depth* of the lineage. Those societies that attribute great importance to lineage depth, and that are made up of complex pyramids of major lineages of, say, eight or ten generations' depth, subdivided into ever-smaller segments and subsegments of decreasing depth, are called *segmentary lineage societies,* and are quite common in Africa (Evans-Pritchard, 1940, Radcliffe-Brown and Forde, 1950).

Another common form of social structure to which a rule of unilineal descent can give rise is a *moiety* system. This type of social organization is common in aboriginal American and Australian societies, and consists of dividing the entire society into only two clans (Lévi-Strauss, 1969). The term "moiety" (derived from the French *moitié* for "half") designates a clan when a society only comprises two. The significance of this arrangement is that the two moieties of the society are typically linked through complex exchange relationships that almost invariably involve intermarriage (Lévi-Strauss, 1969). Men of moiety A get wives by exchanging their daughters and sisters against women from moiety B. The daughters and sisters of A men, in turn, become wives of B men. Men in the two moieties are obligated to marry only each others' women.

There are two basic ways of tracing descent in a single line: one can opt for the male line of father, father's father, and so on; or for the female line of mother, mother's mother, and so on. The first alternative is called *patrilineal* and gives rise to *patrilineages* and *patriclans,* and the second rule of descent is *matrilineal* and generates *matrilineages* and *matriclans.* There are at least twice to three times as many patrilineal societies as matrilineal ones, and although a number of societies have been documented to have evolved from a matrilineal to a patrilineal system, none have been observed to evolve in the opposite way (Murdock, 1949).

A lot of nonsense has been printed about matrilineal societies. Some early anthropologists assumed that matrilineal descent was a remnant of "matriarchy," supposedly the original condition of mankind. In fact, not a scrap of evidence has been adduced that any society has ever been collectively dominated by women. (A few have been ruled by a female head of state. But to argue that Great Britain and India are matriarchies because of Queen Elizabeth and Indira Gandhi is obviously ridiculous.) Men are dominant in both patrilineal and matrilineal societies, and this makes the latter not simply mirror images of the former. The relative infrequency of matrilineal societies, and their tendency to turn patrilineal are probably due to the fact that the lines of male authority are a bit more awkward to maintain in a matrilineal system, as we shall see presently.

The transmission of authority within kin groups follows closely the rule of descent. In patrilineal (or indeed bilateral) societies, authority over children is vested in the father, the father's father, or the father's brother. In matrilineal societies, jural (the ultimate legal) authority over children lies with the mother's brother or the mother's mother's brother; that is, with the male members of the mother's matrilineage to which the children also belong. The father exerts no jural authority over his children who do not belong to his matrilineage, but has authority over his sister's children who do. (When there is no actual mother's brother, a "classificatory" mother's brother is substituted, such as a mother's mother's sister's son.)

The difficulty in matrilineal societies comes from the fact that sisters and brothers normally do not live together after marriage, but husbands and wives do. That means that the father lives in daily contact with his children, and often tries to lay some jural claim over them, while the mother's brother who has the legal authority is typically some distance away. This is true whether the rule of residence is virilocal or uxorilocal. The mother's brother may live nearby in the same village (and he typically does), but not in the same household as his sister's children. Thus, matrilineal societies often have endemic conflicts of authority over children between fathers and mother's brothers. The latter has the law on his side, but the father is in closer physical contact with his children.

There is a neat, though infrequent, solution to this problem of matrilineal societies, known as *avunculocal* residence. After infancy, the boy moves away to live with his mother's brother, whose daughter he subsequently marries. Avunculocal residence is, in essence, a special case of uxorilocal residence in which a husband, by going to live with his wife, also manages to reside with his mother's brother by becoming the latter's son-in-law.

A few societies, known as *double descent* societies, are both patrilineal and matrilineal. Double descent is not the same as bilateral descent. Double descent societies recognize only two lines of descent; namely, the father's male line and the mother's female line, to the exclusion of the father's mother, mother's father, and father's father's mother, and so on. Bilateral societies recognize two parents, four grand-parents, eight great-grand-parents, and so on. (This is why it would be less confusing to call bilateral societies *omnilineal*.) When patrilineages and matrilineages exist side by side, they obviously are not mutually exclusive, each person being a member of one of each. Instead, the two kinds of lineages typically have different functions, such as the inheritance of various types of property, or a distinction between ritual, political, and economic functions.

Rule of descent and rule of residence are correlated to each other, but not perfectly. Uxorilocal and avunculocal residences are the norm only in matrilineal societies, but a good many matrilineal societies are virilocal. The great majority of patrilineal societies are virilocal, as are some bilateral societies. Neolocal residence tends to go together with bilateral societies (Murdock, 1949).

As we have already seen, the rule of descent is closely associated with succession to authority in the kin groups. In patrilineal systems it is passed on from father to son, and typically from older brother to younger brother, if authority extends to collateral relatives. In matrilineal societies authority is transmitted from mother's brother to sister's son. In both cases, authority is held by men, but in patrilineal systems the transfer operates *directly* between patrilineally related males, while in matrilineal societies, authority is passed on *indirectly* between males who are linked through a female relative.

Inheritance of property is also associated with the rule of descent, but not as closely as is the transmission of authority. Most often, the bulk of the property stays within the lineages (apart from the marriage transactions) if such exist and is bilaterally inherited in bilateral systems. There are, however, many complicating factors, such as different types of property being differently passed on, or males and females inheriting property differently. In many patrilineal systems, for instance, children may inherit some property from their mothers, and in numerous matrilineal societies children can inherit both from their father and their maternal uncle.

Marriage: Who May or Must Marry Whom?

We must turn now to another essential structural feature of kin group organization—*marriage*. The social institution of marriage gives moral and jural sanction to the biological propensity toward pair-bonding in the human species. It is not coincidental that all human societies institutionalize some form of marriage; that is, a relatively stable contractual agreement solemnized by ritual (and often the transfer of property), and establishing well-defined sexual, parental, economic, and jural rights between an individual man and woman and their offspring. Despite evolutionary speculation about the existence of promiscuity and "group marriage" at earlier stages of hominid development, there is no evidence of either in any contemporary or historical society (except, sporadically and unstably, as utopian experimentation). In rare cases, marriage is permitted between persons of the same sex, but the overwhelming majority of marriages in all societies are between members of opposite sexes. Marriage, then, as a social institution follows closely biological pair-mating, although it does not completely coincide with it in any society. Once more, we are dealing with a complex interplay of biological predispositions and social institutions. Much sexual intercourse takes place outside of marriage, but in most societies most stably mated pairs are in fact married. With few exceptions, women marry younger than men, but not earlier than the onset of puberty. (In a few societies, marriages are contracted in infancy, but not sexually consummated before the onset of sexual maturity.) In nearly all cases, husband and wife are expected to cohabit, but, in some societies, adulterous sexual relations are permitted under certain conditions to either or both partners. (For example, a Masai man may have intercourse with the wife of any age-mate of his when he is visiting him.)

A few terms need to be defined at this point. Marriage can be either *monogamous* or *polygamous*. Polygamy, in turn, can be of two sub-types: *polygyny* (one man married simultaneously to more than a single woman), or *polyandry* (one woman simultaneously married to more than one husband). A rule of marriage is said to be *prescriptive* if it is obligatory and *preferential* if there is some option. *Endogamy* rules define the group or groups *within* which marriage is prescribed or preferred. *Exogamy* rules refer to the group or groups *outside* of which one should marry.

Westerners are handicapped in understanding most systems of marriage because their own system is so unusual in several ways. First, prescriptive monogamy is the exception rather than the rule. Over three-fourths of all societies have preferential polygamy, and nearly all of those are polygynous; polyandry is even more exceptional than prescriptive monogamy. Second, modern Western societies are highly unusual in making marriage primarily a matter of individual choice between the prospective spouses. In most societies, marriage is considered far too important a matter to be left to the whims of individuals, and marriage is primarily (but not exclusively) a contractual agreement whereby women are exchanged, either directly or indirectly, between kin groups. Third, Western societies have relatively flexible rules of preferential endogamy and few rules of prescriptive exogamy, except for the nuclear family. Westerners are thus unusually free to choose as a prospective spouse almost any member of the opposite sex. There are exceptions, of course, such as rules of "racial" endogamy in South Africa or the United States, but it is generally a matter of relative indifference which of several million women a male Westerner chooses as a spouse. The actual choices are, of course, far from random, being determined by propinquity, education, income, religion, ethnicity, and other factors, but the rules of preferential endogamy tend to be loosely defined.

Finally, Western societies stress the sexual component of marriage far more than most others. In nearly all societies, eroticism is a component of marriage, but one has to read Western marriage manuals to find the marital bed on the center stage of the relationship. In most societies, procreation is stressed far more than sex. In addition, social, political, and economic considerations typically loom large in most non-Western marriage systems. This is not to say that other societies do not consider sex important, but they tend to dissociate it far more from marriage than do Westerners. Romantic love, for example, is a theme in Hindu literature, but its overlap with marriage is purely coincidental. Suicide rather than marriage is the Hindu solution to an impossible love, and the Hindu caste system makes most spontaneous loves impossible, an inexhaustible source of tear-jerking plots for the Bombay film studios.

In contrast to the highly individualistic and permissive Western marriage systems, most societies make marriage a collective concern hemmed in by restrictive rules of both exogamy and endogamy. In biological terms, this means that all societies allow pair-mating to take place, and go to some length in sanctioning and stabilizing it, but almost everywhere pair-mating is hemmed in by social rules. It should be stressed here that all societies have rules of both endogamy and exogamy applying to different groupings, and that, while rules of exogamy tend to be prescriptive, rules of endogamy are frequently preferential. Exogamy rules generally apply to kin groups, at a minimum the nuclear family, and commonly the lineage, moiety, and clan in unilineal descent societies. In contrast, endogamy rules typically apply to non-kin groups, such as castes, classes, and ethnic, racial, or occupational groups.

A good illustration of a highly restrictive system of marriage standing in sharp contrast to relative permissive Western systems is that of traditional Hinduism. A Hindu must, on pain of outcasting (which in a caste society is tantamount to total ostracism), marry within his caste and subcaste group, of which there are several thousand in India. That is, the caste is strictly endogamous. In addition to the thousands of caste and subcaste groups, there are language groups differing widely in customs, and while these language groups are not prescriptively endogamous they certainly are preferentially so. It is theoretically possible for, say, a Gujarati-speaking Brahmin to marry a Tamil-speaking Brahmin, but wide differences in language and culture make this unlikely. In practice, then, a person is restricted both by caste and ethnic endogamy, in addition to religious endogamy, which underlies the entire system.

The problem, however, only begins there because the rules of exogamy are as restrictive as those of endogamy. In the Northern Hindu groups, there is a strict rule of lineage exogamy prohibiting marriage with anyone related up to seven generations back in the father's lineage and five generations back in the mother's lineage.

Southern Hindu groups, on the other hand, have preferential cross-cousin marriage (i.e., a male must preferably marry his mother's brother's daughter). Frequently, there is no suitable spouse anywhere within the local town or rural district, and spouses have to be sought hundreds of miles away. Not surprisingly, Indian newspapers carry columns of matrimonial want ads specifying religion, language, caste, and subcaste, as well as age, physical appearance, occupation, income, and other characteristics of the prospective partners. To a traditional Hindu, "boy-meets girl" is an exotic custom known through Western films.

It is important not to confuse incest and exogamy. There is some overlap between the two concepts, but they are far from synonymous. First, incest applies to sexual relations and exogamy applies to marriage, and, as we all know, sex and marriage are not the same. Second, the nearly universal incest taboo between parents and children and between siblings makes the nuclear family an exogamous group. Beyond the nuclear family, however, incest and exogamy part company. In fact, in hundreds of societies, a strict rule of lineage or class exogamy that prohibits marriage with extremely distant relatives in one line of descent is combined with preferential cross-cousin marriage, which makes marriage between mother's brother's daughter and father's sister's son, or between father's sister's daughter and mother's brother's son the most desirable. ("Parallel cousins" are the children of one's mother's sister or father's brother and, under unilineal descent, one of these two groups of parallel cousins, of necessity, belong to the same lineage and clan as oneself. "Cross-cousins," being the children of one's mother's brother or father's sister, can never belong to the same descent group as oneself if there is lineage exogamy.)

Marriage as an Exchange

In the vast majority of unilineal descent societies, marriage is primarily an exchange between men of nonmarriageable kinswomen against marriageable women from other kin groups. This typically takes the form of lineage exogamy, so that two or more lineages are linked through a multiplicity of marriage ties. The simplest model for such a system of exchange is a society divided into two exogamous moieties with a rule of preferential cross-cousin marriage, since cross-cousins will automatically belong to opposite moieties.[2] Marriage by exchange can involve any member of exogamous lineages, with or without preferential cross-cousin marriage.

In a more complex but widespread variant of exchange marriage, the exchange is "generalized" (Lévi-Strauss, 1969). Instead of group A giving women to group B, which in turn gives its women to group A, there are now several exogamous groups who may both seek and give women in and to any of the others. A dowry, or "bridewealth," is

[2]The skeptical or puzzled reader might want a demonstration of this statement. If I live in a patrilineal society with lineage exogamy, then the children of my father's sister belong to the lineage of her husband. Her husband has to belong to a different lineage from my own and my father's sister's, otherwise my father's sister, who belongs to my lineage, could not have married him. The children of my mother's brother belong to the lineage of my mother and of my mother's brother. But my mother, in order to marry my father, had to belong to a different lineage from my father's, and thus from my own. A mirror image situation prevails in a matrilineal society. There, the children of my father's sister belong to my father's and my father's sister's lineage, and I belong to my mother's lineage. My father and my mother had to belong to different lineages in order to marry, therefore, I cannot belong to the same lineage as the children of my father's sister. The children of my mother's brother, on the other hand, belong to the lineage of his wife. My mother's brother belongs to my lineage, and he had to marry a woman who did not. Therefore his children and I must belong to different lineages.

This seemingly complicated, but actually simple combination of lineage exogamy with cross-cousin marriage resolves the apparent paradox that vast numbers of even distantly related kinsmen may not under any circumstances intermarry, while certain types of first or second cousins *must* intermarry.

In turn, this raises again the question of incest. In Chapter Two, we have suggested that the nuclear family incest taboo may have become built into our biological *Anlagen*. Yet, the terms "incest" and "incest taboo" have also been loosely applied to such rules as lineage and clan exogamy, which are clearly sociocultural in character. This loose usage has then been used to "demonstrate" the cultural nature of incest taboos. The biogenic argument for the incest taboo applies only to the nuclear family, and, indeed, it is only in the nuclear family that one universally finds an incest taboo. Clan and lineage exogamy rules, far from being extensions of the incest taboo and attempts to avoid intermarriages between close relatives, are commonly associated with rules that prescribe or strongly favor the intermarriage of first cousins. Exogamy and incest, then, are two clearly distinct phenomena. The first is clearly cultural, and the second is possibly in part biogenic.

received by the donor group and paid by the recipient group, thereby obviating the need for the recipient group to give the donor group a nubile woman in return. The donor group may well use the dowry to get a nubile woman for one of its male members, but the prospective spouse may freely be sought in any other group in the system, not simply in the last recipient group. One of the functions of the dowry in such systems, then, is to free the contracting parties to a marriage from the constraints of direct reciprocation in kind. I may not have a nubile unmarried daughter to give to my son's father-in-law in return for my son's bride, and, if I did, my son's father-in-law may not have a marriageable son, or his son might not care for my daughter. Therefore, the dowry for my son's bride cancels my obligation to my son's father-in-law, and allows him to use that dowry to get his son a bride (or himself a second wife) anywhere he pleases within the limits of the prevailing rules of exogamy and endogamy.

Again, the Western tradition is unusual in having the dowry paid, if at all, from the bride's family to the groom's. In most societies, the dowry (often misleadingly called "brideprice" or "bridewealth") goes from the groom's kinsmen to the bride's. It often involves a substantial amount of wealth, frequently livestock, but sometimes rare and valuable artifacts such as metal objects. Ethnocentric Westerners have often misinterpreted these marital exchange systems as commercial transactions in which women are bought and sold like chattel, but it is a gross distortion to give these facts an economic interpretation. The dowry, besides making possible the "generalized exchange" system just described, is at the core of a complex network of social ties between descent groups. In many stateless societies (i.e., societies lacking the centralization of executive power in the hands of a ruling class), marriage exchanges constitute the principal basis of social solidarity beyond the lineages and clans.

The dowry not only establishes ties of mutual obligation and solidarity between descent groups, thereby making possible the creation of larger societies, but it also constitutes a legal warranty of the legitimacy of the marriage, and, in patrilineal systems, of the claim of the husband's patrilineage over the offspring of the in-marrying woman. Often the dowry might be better termed "childprice" than "brideprice," because the claims of the lineage over the women's offspring are far more important than the sexual claims of the husband over his wife. Commonly, if the marriage should prove barren, a divorce takes place and all or most of the "brideprice" is returned.

In class-stratified societies, marriage is typically restricted by status group. The general tendency is for classes to be preferentially endogamous. When two persons of the same class status marry, the union is said to be *isogamous,* in contradistinction to *hypergamy* (where the woman marries a man of higher status than herself) and *hypogamy* (where a woman marries "down"). It is interesting to note that, insofar as exceptions are made to class endogamy, they are almost invariably in the direction of hypergamy. There are two plausible and complementary explanations for the relative prevalence of hypergamy and the rarity of hypogamy. One is that husbands feel their male dominance threatened by a wife of higher class status, and, hence, seek to avoid such situations. (In sociological jargon, hypogamy creates strain due to the "status inconsistency" between gender and class status.) Another explanation (not incompatible with the first one) is that nearly all highly stratified societies have patrilineal or bilateral descent, and confer class status on the children through the father rather than the mother. Thus, by marrying "up," a woman "promotes" both herself and her children without appreciably lowering the status of her husband, while by marrying "down," she and her children would be losers without a compensating gain for the husband (van den Berghe, 1960).

Marriage selection in stratified societies frequently is regulated by complex and multiple rules. There typically are several dimensions to social stratification, and one dimension of status may be "traded off" against another in marriage, as when the daughter of the impoverished aristocrat marries the son of the rich bourgeois, or when the middle-class black man marries a working-class white woman in a racially stratified society. Generally, status group endogamy is preferential, but it can also be prescriptive as in the Hindu caste system, or in the

South African or, until recently, in the United States racial caste system. (South Africa and many states in the United States passed a number of laws prohibiting interracial marriages. Such laws are still in full effect in South Africa, and have only recently been declared unconstitutional in the United States.)

Monogamy and Polygamy

Yet another important feature of marriage is whether it is monogamous or polygamous. Westerners often assume that monogamy is the rule, and that polygamy is a problematic and, on the whole, rather unworkable exception. How prevalent polygamy (and especially polygyny) is, is a moot question, because the answer differs depending on the criterion chosen.

The situation is as follows: in roughly three-fourths of all societies, polygyny is a permitted and often preferred form of marriage, but the prescriptively monogamous Western societies have been so large and powerful that monogamy has been spreading to some non-Western societies under Western influence or domination. This does not prove the superiority of monogamy over polygyny, but rather that of the machine gun over the bow and arrow. Of the major continental masses, polygyny seems to hold its own well only in Africa, but most of the large Asian societies were preferentially polygynous until recent times.

It is also true that the approximately equal sex ratio insures that, even in polygynous societies, most men are *de facto* monogamists at any given time. Thus, the difference between a "monogamous" and a "polygamous" society hinges on whether an alternative to monogamy is permitted. Paradoxically, the great majority of people all over the world are monogamously married, but, in the great majority of societies for nearly all of human history, polygyny has been permitted and indeed preferred.

The ethnographic curiosity is not polygyny, a highly viable and thriving arrangement even in urbanized societies, but polyandry, which is exceedingly rare and found under circumstances that suggest that, wherever it is found, it is merely a way of making the best of a bad bargain. The few cases of polyandry tend to be associated either with conditions of precarious survival where attempts at population control have given rise to female infanticide as in some Eskimo groups, or with stratified systems where hypergamy generates a movement of women up the social scale, and thus creates polygyny at the top of the class structure and polyandry at the bottom. Under hypergamy, high-status men may marry women from all strata. If polygamy is permitted along with a preference for hypergamy, it is clear that women will tend to accumulate at the top of the status ladder and be scarce at the bottom. Polyandry in the lower strata, then, does not express a preference for this form of marriage, but the best of a bad bargain for lower status men left bereft of women by polygynous upper status men.[3]

The usual question raised about polygyny is how a substantial amount of it can exist in a society, given an approximately equal sex ratio, and without condemning some males to permanent celibacy. The answer is simple: by maintaining a large difference in age of marriage between males and females. The most common form of polygyny is "cumulative." A young man of, say, 25 years of age marries a first wife who is some 10 years his junior; 10 or 15 years later he will marry a second wife who may be 15 or 20 years his junior; and in late middle age, as his wealth and status increase, he will marry a third wife who is 30 or 40 years younger. When he dies, his widows will remarry, sometimes preferentially a son or younger brother of their deceased husband. Thus, for men, polygyny tends to be a

[3]In all societies that are both polygynous and stratified by rank, there is a strong tendency toward hypergamy. That is, the higher a man's status, the more polygynous he is likely to be. This means that, given an approximately equal sex ratio at the various class levels, many women from lower status groups marry "up," and thus that women are scarce at the bottom of the status hierarchy. Even then, male celibacy is a far more common solution to the problem than polyandry. Prostitution, is, of course, also common in such situations, but polyandry has nothing to do with prostitution, unless one wishes to adopt the extreme feminist position that all forms of marriage are synonymous with prostitution for women.

privilege of status and age. In many societies, most men who survive late middle age will become polygynists, but, at any given time, only 10 to 20 percent of the adult males are polygynists. (A high mortality rate makes such a system workable.) Men can have several wives simultaneously, but women, in fact, have several husbands serially.

There is no conclusive evidence that polygyny depresses the status of women relative to men. Women as a gender have a lower status than men in all societies, but seemingly no more so in polygynous societies than in monogamous ones. The common belief that polygyny degrades women is probably due to the Western stereotype of Arab "harem" polygyny, in which women are thought to be sexual playthings at the mercy of lascivious pashas. In fact, such "harems" were strictly limited to a tiny ruling class and, even then, they were cases of concubinage rather than polygyny, since Islam limits polygyny to four wives. Concubinage and polygyny are quite distinct phenomena, since institutionalized concubinage frequently exists in monogamous societies, such as Latin American countries or slave societies established by European countries. Marriage, by definition, legitimizes the offspring, but concubinage by definition does not.

Polygyny, in most societies where it exists, is small-scale, the younger men being mostly monogamists, and the middle-aged or older men having typically from two to five wives. In most systems of polygyny, the rights, obligations, and seniority of each wife are carefully defined. The first wife often has some authority over the others, and she gains in status what she may lose in sexual attention. Frequently each wife retains a great deal of economic independence, constituting with her children a subfamily with a separate dwelling, cooking place, and domestic economy. Norms of equality of treatment, such as rotation in sleeping with the husband, often prevail as well. Of course, jealousy and conflict exist in polygynous families, but that is also true in monogamous ones.

As we have seen, the family is indeed the cornerstone of the social order. The network of ties of kinship and marriage that it establishes both within kin groups and between them is a fundamental aspect of the social structure of all human societies, and constitutes the principal mode of social organization in many of the simpler, small-scale societies. Kinship and marriage relations are closely linked to biological differences by age and sex, and thus they make for role differentiation and a division of labor based at least on age and gender. Descent ties regulate the transmission of property and authority within kin groups, and marriage ties, through rules of exogamy, establish networks of political and economic relations between kin groups.

The family, as has been belabored in sociology textbooks, is a "multiple-function institution." It protects and socializes children, provides sexual and emotional gratification for adults, and performs a multiplicity of economic functions in the production and consumption of goods and services.

Granting that the family stands for all of the good things that sociologists have told us, it equally obviously is a male-adult dominated microtyranny ridden with age and gender conflicts, and, thus, must also be studied as a network of power relations. The universality of such age and gender conflicts in human societies is quite striking. Conflicts between husband and wife, or parent and child, rivalry between siblings or co-wives, and bitter feuds between close relatives are all extremely common. Stable harmony is the exception. The prevalence of conflict in the family does not make the latter any less important. It merely suggests at least two things: first, that hierarchy is a universal aspect of even the simplest forms of social organization; and, second, that hierarchy is resented and generates conflict. Egalitarian ideology notwithstanding, any two people in any actual interactive situation are scarcely ever equal, and inequality is probably the most fundamental feature of social organization. To this vast problem we shall devote the next section of this book. Here we may simply conclude that the great insight of Marx on the link between inequality and conflict certainly has to be extended from the analysis of class to that of the family.

ADDITIONAL READING

The literature on the family and kinship is immense. That produced by sociologists is generally pedestrian and ethnocentric. Goode (1963), Bell and Vogel (1960), and Coser (1964) are exceptions. The anthropological literature is generally of much higher caliber, but most of it is quite technical. Murdock (1949) and Lévi-Strauss (1969) are classics, and the Bohannan textbook (1963) is excellent on kinship. See also van den Berghe (1973) for the relationship between the family and age and gender differentiation. Radcliffe-Brown and Forde (1950) edited a useful collection of readings on kinship and marriage in African societies, and Evans Pritchard's monograph on the Nuer (1940) is one of the most famous studies of a segmentary lineage system. The Human Relations Area Files, a vast information retrieval system consisting of index cards covering hundreds of societies and available in a number of the main university libraries in the United States, is a good research instrument in the area of kinship and marriage.

PART
II

The Nasty Side of Man

5

Inequality: Forms of Invidiousness

That all men are created equal may have seemed a self-evident truth to the amiable optimists who signed the American Declaration of Independence, but it plainly flies in the face of all evidence. That all men should be treated as if they were equal is a rather exotic and recent idea born in Western culture a little over 200 years ago. Even the proponents of *liberté, égalité, fraternité* for all did not really mean what they said. Washington, Jefferson, Monroe, Madison, and many other American libertarians were slaveowners, and never seriously believed that their human chattel was endowed by its Creator with certain inalienable rights. Africans, somehow, were not quite people. While among today's radicals, it is no longer fashionable to accept racist theories, male followers of Mao, Che, and other saints of the revolutionary pantheon have great difficulty accepting the claims of women's liberationists that women are equal. Women's liberationists themselves are often adult chauvinists, expressing distressingly little concern for the welfare of children or the rights of the unborn.

The Premise of Inequality

In the overwhelming majority of societies for nearly all of human history, inequality has been treated as axiomatic, and human

93

relations have been ordered on the premise that any two people are seldom if ever equal. As we have suggested in Chapter Two, the roots of human inequality are at least in part biological, for we share our drive for status and dominance with many other mammals and birds. However, human inequality goes much beyond the rudimentary forms of dominance behavior found in other species. Egalitarianism may be good rhetoric, but it is bad sociology and rank empirical nonsense. To say, however, that the premise of inequality has been virtually universal is not to say that people have lived happily with inequality. Indeed, the overwhelming evidence is that people low on the totem pole have been both acutely aware of inequality and acutely resentful of it. Frequently enough, their resentment has made them explode into violence, even at the risk of death. Inequality, as was clearly seen by Marx, is one of the most universal and recurrent sources of conflict in human societies. It often takes violence to establish inequality, more violence to maintain it, and more yet to overthrow one particular form of it in order to establish a new one. But, then, violence—as we have seen—is very much part of human nature.

Man is not unique in establishing hierarchies. Chickens and many other birds have "pecking orders," and countless mammalian species establish dominance orders. The terrestrial primates, such as baboons and macaques, whose ecological adaptation and problems of survival have much in common with man's, have highly hierarchical societies dominated by oligarchies of adult males who defend and dominate the females, infants, and peripheral males, and get a near-monopoly of the attentions of the females in oestrus. The urge to dominate, which is much more developed in men than in women, is probably part of our primate heritage. All human societies are stratified at least on the basis of age and sex, as are, indeed, most higher primate societies. Men dominate women, and adults dominate children, a hierarchical order evident in the human family, the smallest and most universal form of human social organization (van den Berghe , 1973).

As we suggested earlier, the dominance order that inequality establishes is a way of establishing a scale of access to, and distribution of, resources (both material and social). Because so many of the resources that man prizes are social and artifactual rather than simply being raw materials for physical survival, human needs are intrinsically insatiable. This being the case, resource competition in the human species is always intense, and this produces a lot of aggressive behavior. Hierarchy, then, is a way of regulating resource competition, and indirectly, aggression. An established dominance order makes continuous fighting over desired resources superfluous. However, there is another side to hierarchy: it not only regulates competition and aggression, it also provokes it. Hierarchies are not suffered gladly.

Human inequality goes far beyond that found in any animal society. The exercise of creativity in inventing bases of individious distinctions is truly boundless and specifically human, a theme beautifully developed by Thorstein Veblen (1899). Generally, the more complex and economically developed a society is, the more multitudinous and arbitrary the bases for inequality. Relatively simple hunting-and-gathering or pastoralist societies, like the Pygmies of the Congo rain-forest or the Masai of East Africa, are stratified mostly by age and sex, and are fairly egalitarian for adult males. Complex agrarian societies are highly stratified. There is perhaps a slight reversal of the trend toward greater inequality in modern industrial societies (Lenski, 1965).

INEQUALITY AND TECHNOLOGICAL DEVELOPMENT

The reason for this close association between the degree of inequality and the degree of technological and economic development is fairly clear. Advances in technology have meant increases in production, and especially in surplus production and in artifactual goods. Surplus production and manmade objects can be indefinitely accumulated, and the "need" for them is insatiable (unlike basic drives like hunger, thirst, and sex, which are quickly satiated). Therefore, the more surplus is created, the more intense resource competition becomes, and the wider the scope for inequality, at least in material possessions and control over human labor and favors (including sexual).

Why, then, does there seem to be a reversal of the trend toward more and more inequality in industrial societies? Industrial societies, whether capitalist or socialist, have experienced some degree of equalization of wealth, but not of power and prestige. Even highly industrial countries like the United States and South Africa have proven completely compatible with the most demeaning and invidious kind of caste system based on skin pigmentation. To be sure, outright legal slavery has been abolished, but differences in power and prestige are as great as ever beneath all the rhetorical cant of democracy and the rituals of equality. The Western politician kisses babies and shakes hands with his constituents, and the Eastern Communist potentate play-works with the peasants, but these rituals are not new to industrial societies. After all, the Pope has been washing his cardinals' feet for a long time, and Marie Antoinette had a play-farm built at Versailles so that she might milk goats just as any other farm maid in her kingdom.

Rituals of equality, affectations of humility, pretentions of benevolent paternity, ostentatious displays of indigence by the wealthy, and similar rituals of debasement are not new to industrial societies. The powerful and the wealthy have long known that displays of vicarious identification with the oppressed take some of the sting out of oppression, and these shabby acts of deception often have the desired effect of pacifying the masses. The elaborate ideologies of equality in industrial societies, capitalist or socialist, serve the same function. The ''Comrade General'' is no less an ''excellency'' than his Tsarist counterpart. Stalin and the Tsars both loved to call themselves the ''little father'' of the millions they tyrannized. Allowing for the slightly different image carefully manufactured by public relations specialists, our ''Mister Presidents'' are not very different. The basic reason why Nixon got into trouble was not that he was any more despotic and devious than his predecessors, but rather that he did not do a creditable job of hiding both his misdeeds and his arrogance.

What has changed in industrial societies, both capitalist and socialist, and to approximately the same extent in both, is the distribution of material resources. Material resources are less unequally distributed in industrial societies than in complex agrarian societies, and it is important to explore why. For the first time in world history, industrial societies have created such a glut of material goods that poverty—in the naked material sense of a dire shortage of basic vital necessities—has been virtually eliminated. The "poor" of the United States are indeed treated as pariahs and are often kept in psychologically degrading conditions, but they are not dying of famine and epidemics, as hundreds of thousands of people a year still do in Asia and Africa. The bottom tenth of the American or Northwest European income distribution are at least ten times as well off in per capita income as the average citizens of at least 30 or 40 African and Asian countries.

As for the very powerful and wealthy in industrial societies (again, both capitalist and socialist) it is now considered bad form to build marble Taj Mahals. Gold-plated Rolls Royces might still do for oil sheiks, but not for a French prime minister, or an American president, or a Soviet general secretary. With the damper on the display of wealth at the top (partly created by the egalitarian ideology, which enjoins the powerful to make a minimally convincing pretense of "common manness"), and a relative glut of expensive mechanical gadgetry all the way down to at least broad sections of the middle class, material goods lose most of their potential for making invidious distinctions, and the society appears more "democratic." What good is a Cadillac if even the ghetto pariah can run one? Industrial societies are so glutted with material artifacts that reverse snobbery is now common: today's snobs run around in Toyotas and Volkswagens, thereby documenting that their status is secure enough not to depend on the vulgar display of wealth.

My point is that the argument for greater and growing equality in industrial societies hinges heavily on a purely material definition of equality. Here it is interesting to note how studiously the elite of both capitalist and socialist countries has defined equality in material terms. Materialism is the cornerstone of socialist and capitalist ruling class ideology because, without it, the entire myth of democracy and egalitarianism collapses. Industrial ruling classes and the social scientists subservient to these ruling classes have proven quite reluctant to analyze inequality in terms of power. Those who do, as for example, Milovan Djilas (1959), are thrown in jail, exiled, or defined as academic eccentrics who may be allowed to indulge in their pastime in the carefully encapsulated environment of the universities, so long as they do not incite their students to riot.[1]

The Bases of Inequality

Besides the almost infinite number of bases for invidious distinctions, human inequality is characterized by the fact that not only individuals, but also groups, are rank-ordered. Hens have a pecking order between individuals but they do not have a class system. Most human societies

---

[1] A number of Western sociologists have advanced the theory of convergence between capitalism and socialism. As capitalism develops, they argue, it incorporates many elements of welfare and social security, and sections of the economy become increasingly state-controlled and regulated. Mature socialism, on the other hand, reverts in part to private enterprise and tends to become more flexible, more pragmatic, and less dictatorial, so goes the theory. These parallel forces of industrialization make the stratification system of capitalist and socialist societies very similar: both are ruled by salaried technicians, civil servants, and managers who operate within very much the same kind of bureaucratic structures. Needless to say, Soviet social scientists and ideologues dogmatically reject the theory. The convergence theory suggests that ideology makes little, if any, difference on the extent of inequality, which makes good Marxian sense, but nevertheless is an inadmissible conclusion as far as the Soviet *apparatchiks* (party bureaucrats) are concerned (Inkeles, 1950; Moore, 1950; Goldthorpe, 1966).

do. It is true that some insect societies, like ants and bees, have a "caste system" of workers, warriors, queens, and so on, which has sometimes been compared to human caste or class hierarchies. There is an enormous difference, however, between the caste order of an ant colony and that of a human one. The queen and worker ants have biologically ordained functions that are not interchangeable: the workers are sterile, and the queen is little more than an egg-laying machine. The human master and slave, on the other hand, are biologically interchangeable on the cotton plantation, and their relative position is purely the creation of social conditions. Paradoxically, it seems to be in the nature of man to create hierarchies which make no natural sense at all, beyond age and gender distinctions. Human invidiousness is a gratuitous end in itself which, in more cases than not, serves no demonstrable function for the survival of the species, though it often serves the individual interests of some.

There are two sorts of inequality that are common to all human societies, based on age and sex. In all societies, adults as a group have more power than children, and men than women. Some societies have been nominally ruled by queens or infant kings, and some individual women dominate individual men. However, nowhere has there ever been a society where children as a group dominated adults, or women men. Queens have shown no more predilection to choose females as ministers, army officers, policemen, or tax collectors than have male monarchs. Infant sovereigns typically ruled through regents. All societies recognize an age below which social and civic responsibility cannot be assumed.

We have already discussed in Chapter Four the biological and social bases for adult male domination within the family. Male domination applies to an even greater extent to societies at large. Individual wives may dominate their husband within the family, or at least share a great deal of authority and responsibility within the family, but the macropolitics of running the society at large are invariably a male monopoly or near-monopoly. The evidence in favor of the existence of "matriarchies" in the dawn of human history is purely mythological.

So far as we know, no human society has ever been matriarchical, or for that matter, child-dominated.

Some of the technologically simpler societies have been stratified almost exclusively by age and sex, not to mention individual differences in prestige, influence and wealth due to personal qualities and abilities in hunting, pottery-making, child-raising, or some such. These societies are *classless* in the sense that they do not have groups of individuals (other than age and sex groups) which, for some reason or other, are collectively assigned a higher or lower position in relation to other groups. These classless societies are also *stateless*. Stateless societies are not anarchical, nor do they lack "social control"; rather, they have no specialized sets of institutions that can be called a government, or individuals who specialize in the wielding of power over their fellows. Such societies have no courts, policemen, judges, tax collectors, bureaucrats, ministers, and so on. Their armies are directed at external aggression, not internal repression.

Karl Marx was among the first social scientists to recognize clearly that the emergence of social classes was directly linked with the development of states and vice versa. Classless, stateless societies are also characterized by a low level of productive technology, in which little or no surplus can be accumulated, and hence appropriated, by the few at the expense of the many. The price of equality, human history seems to teach us, is to live on the margin of want, as do rain-forest Pygmies or semi-desert Bushmen hunters. Even then, democracy applies only to adult men.

Classless Societies

Let us take a brief look at two such classless societies, the Bambuti Pygmies, hunters of the rain forest of the Republic of Zaire (formerly the Congo), and the Masai, pastoralists of the savannah of Southern Kenya and Northern Tanzania.

The Pygmies live from hunting and gathering in the lush rain forest of the Northeastern part of the Congo basin (Turnbull, 1961, 1965).

They lead a seminomadic existence, moving around their hunting grounds in groups of around 50 individuals, divided into several extended families (which may, and often do, shift from one hunting band to another). Though Pygmies number in the tens of thousands scattered in the rain forest of the Congo and Cameroon, there is no social organization beyond the hunting band of two or three scores of individuals.

The variety of forest products gives the Pygmies a reasonably adequate diet, but their material possessions are few. Their housing consists of hastily erected small conical huts made up of a flimsy framework of branches covered with broad leaves. They do no weaving, are sparsely dressed in leaves or animal skins, and have no blacksmiths or other specialized artisans. Every man or woman is supposed to be able to produce the few things he or she uses: ropes, bows, arrows, nets, and so on. Pygmies have no formal government, courts, chiefs, taxes, or any of the institutions that one associates with the state. Decisions to move camp, go hunting, and so on, are taken communally by the adults, with the men playing a dominant, but not exclusive, role. Women do most of the gathering of shrubs, berries, fruits, roots, and the like, and they cook the food, while the men do most of the hunting. However, women help as beaters in the net hunting, and the men also do some gathering. Collected food is quickly and communally consumed, as the Pygmies do not conserve or store food for more than a couple of days. Other than the dog, which is used in hunting, the Pygmies keep no domestic animals, and they do not engage in agriculture.

It is interesting, however, that the Pygmies, whenever they seek a few luxuries like tobacco, beer, salt, iron objects (arrow tips, knives, and machetes), and food crops like bananas and manioc, temporarily surrender part of their independence and freedom by entering into unequal patron–client relationships with villages of more complexly organized Bantu agriculturalists. The Pygmies exchange meat and their labor for these luxury goods: they are regarded by the Bantu as serfs and treated with a kind of amused condescension as semihuman beings or as irresponsible children. The Bantu try unsuccessfully to incorporate the Pygmies into their own social structure, but once gorged on food, salt, beer, and tobacco, the Pygmy band suddenly leaves the semidependence of the Bantu village to regain the roaming freedom of the rain forest.

The Masai are a far bigger and more complex society than the Pygmies. They number some 300,000, and roam with their livestock over several hundred thousand square miles of arid savannah. They are also seminomadic, changing their village sites every few months; but being pastoralists, they have their food always close at hand. Instead of having to hunt it down, they follow their livestock from pasture to pasture. The Masai diet consists mostly of milk and blood (tapped from the jugular vein of their cattle, which they seldom slaughter, because the cattle are too important as an index of wealth and for the payment of "bridewealth"). This is supplemented by the meat of goats and sheep which are slaughtered more frequently. The Masai also use dogs for hunting and donkeys as beasts of burden, but they engage in no agriculture. They trade livestock, meat, and hides with outsiders to buy beads for their elaborate jewelry, metal spears and knives, and the manufactured fabric with which they clothe themselves; but they despise the agriculturalists who rely on vegetable foods.

Until British conquest put an end to their successful war expeditions, they raided their neighbors' cattle and encroached on their territory so that by the late nineteenth century, they had carved a large empire out of the East African savannah. The Masai are a proud, fiercely independent people, with a developed sense of nationhood, yet they, too, are a classless and stateless society. All Masai men are equal, being stratified only by age, and they rule themselves through democratic assemblies in which all initiated men have the right to speak.

The basis of the Masai political and military organization is their *age-grade* system, perhaps the best arrangement ever devised to integrate large numbers of people without imposing the class tyranny of the few over the many (Bernardi, 1955). The age-grade system operates somewhat like an American school system, where, at regular intervals, classes get promoted to the next higher grade. The Masai age-grade system extends throughout the entire society and encompasses most of an individual's lifetime.

Around adolescence, boys are initiated in groups over a period of several years. All the boys initiated within a period of 15 years or so constitute an *age-set;* that is, a solidary group of men who, throughout their lifetime, will have well-defined mutual obligations and rights (including the right to sleep with each other's wives, and the prohibition to marry each other's daughters). Each age-set has a name, and the age-set continues to exist until its last member dies. After initiation, the young men enter the age-grade of warrior; during their 10 to 15 years of military service, they are not allowed to marry, and they live in segregated villages, observing certain food taboos. They always fight side-by-side as a solidary group. When the next initiation cycle is declared open, every age-set is promoted one age-grade. Thus, the warriors are promoted to junior elder, a status that allows them to marry, establish a household, accumulate cattle, and raise children.

The men remain junior elders some 15 years, until the next initiation cycle is opened, and then they are promoted to the grade of senior elders where, for another 15 years, they devote themselves primarily to public affairs. Their most important task as senior elders is to run the initiation and instruction of the youth. Their role as teachers of the youth is quite important, but they are not an executive ruling class in any strict sense. Any age-grade largely runs its own affairs democratically, and Masai society at large is democratically run by the assembly of all initiated males. Senior elders wield disproportionate influence by virtue of their experience and their ritual and pedagogical functions, but they are not "chiefs," if by that one means somebody issuing commands to be obeyed. Finally, after their period of service as senior elders, the men retire from public affairs altogether and become merely respected elder statesmen.

A number of pastoralist societies of East Africa are similar to the Masai in their use of age as the main principle of stratification, and in their absence of social classes and of a state. Although living at a rudimentary level of technology, these societies long proved quite viable, and indeed militarily formidable to their agricultural neighbors. Some three-quarters of a century ago, however, they were conquered by the German and British, and became incorporated in their colonial empires. Today, split between Kenya and Tanzania, the Masai are being ruled by black bureaucrats who succeeded the white ones at "independence," and they are pressured in the name of progress to abandon their pastoralist way of life to make room for land-hungry peasants.

The East African pastoralists represent probably the largest and highest level of integration that can be achieved by a classless, stateless society. The price of social evolution to more complex forms of organization and economic production, it seems, is inequality beyond age and sex. Forms of human inequality have been varied enough to provide hundreds of sociologists with a rewarding specialty. So infinitely imaginative has man been in creating invidious distinctions, that most labels applied by social scientists to various forms of inequality ("class," "caste," "estate," "race," "slavery," or "serfdom") have been ambiguous or misleading. Each of these labels has covered a wide range of phenomena.

Forms of Unfreedom: Slavery, Race, and Caste

Let us look briefly at some of those concepts. Slavery, that loose label used to refer to a wide spectrum of degrees and types of unfreedom, is probably some 6000 to 8000 years old and developed simultaneously with the first agricultural states throughout the world. Throughout history, war captives typically became slaves, though in more "advanced" forms of slavery, humans were also bought, sold, bartered, and exchanged as chattel. Notorious though systems of "chattel slavery'' were (such as the cotton and sugar cane plantations of the Americas, or the salt mines and public works projects of Rome, Egypt, and Mesopotamia), chattel slavery is the more uncommon variety of the phenomenon. More common were institutions usually referred to as ''domestic slavery,'' in which the unfree person lived and worked in the household of his master under conditions often not very different than those of a poor relative. The term ''slave'' refers in the last analysis to a legal status whereby a person is deprived of some of the rights accorded to the commonality of citizens in a given society. Sometimes the position of slaves has been abject and degraded in the extreme. In a few cases, slave-concubines of kings, have wallowed in luxury, and favorite male slaves have become powerful prime ministers. Some West African societies even reserve certain categories of high political offices to a ''slave nobility.'' In most cases, however, slaves have been members of a household, unrelated by blood or marriage to the rest of the household, and obligated to perform unremunerated services.

The modalities of ''unfreedom'' are virtually infinite. Indentured servants are domestic slaves whose labor obligations are of specified duration. ''Pawning,'' an institution widespread in Africa, is an arrangement whereby the services of a child or junior relative are loaned to another person as a sort of collateral for, and interest payment on, a debt. Serfdom is usually distinguished from slavery in that the dominion of the master is not directly over the person, but over the land. The serf in Medieval Europe or in the Spanish American *hacienda* had certain usufructuary rights (the legal right of using the profits of something belonging to another) in the land in return for which he performed labor services to his lord. In practice, since serfs in most cases did not have the practical option of leaving the manor or *hacienda,* the distinction between serfdom and slavery was a mere legal technicality.

However much slavery offends the moral sensitivity of contemporary Westerners, the fact remains that many forms of it were no more degrading or inhuman than some modern brands of inequality. The pacifist who sews mail bags in the federal penitentiary for refusing army induction is the linear descendant of the Roman slave who pulled a galley oar for being a Christian. The lot of the Greek slave in the patrician Roman household who tutored his master's children in the social graces of his culture was little different from that of the French governess in the British aristocratic household. The favorite slave of the Ottoman sultan was in no greater danger of losing his head than the Soviet factory manager under Stalinist terror. The slave on the Old South cotton plantation was materially better off and far more secure than the inmate of the Nazi concentration camp. The distinction between slavery and "freedom" is more often one of legal technicality than of material or social condition. Slavery covers a wide range of forms of inequality, and not necessarily the most blatant ones.

Two other forms of inequality that rank high in the catalog of disapproval of *Homo democraticus modernus* are "caste" and "race." Indeed, in their equal dislike of both, social scientists have often lumped these two rather different forms of inequality in a single category.

In the inventory of human depravity, racism probably holds pride of place. It is none too convincing to claim superiority because of greater wealth, power, morality, or birth, but it is rank stupidity to claim it because of hair texture, skin color, or nose shape. Yet entire social systems of inequality have been erected on such inane premises, and have endured for centuries despite abundant demonstration of the absurdity of racism. The United States and South Africa are perhaps the two best examples of thoroughly racist societies, a fact that has not dampened American pretensions to being the bastion of democracy, or South Africa's claim to being the "free world's" best friend in Africa.

APARTHEID IN SOUTH AFRICA

South Africa, the most insanely stratified industrialized country in the world, is worth a closer look (Adam, 1971; van den Berghe, 1965; Kuper, 1965). Of its total population of some 20 million, some 18 percent are classified as "Whites" or "Europeans"; 10 percent as

"Coloureds" (people of mixed descent); 3 percent as "Asiatics," mostly descendants of East Indian immigrants; and 69 percent as "Bantu" or "Natives." The "Europeans" are divided between a 60 percent majority group of Afrikaans-speaking descendants of Dutch settlers and a 40 percent minority of English speakers. The other three "racial" groups are collectively called the "non-Whites" or "non-Europeans." Each of these groups is subdivided into a number of smaller linguistic and religious groups. The Bantu, or Africans (as they prefer to call themselves) are divided into the Zulu, Xhosa, Sotho, and a number of smaller ethnic groups that were independent nations before they were conquered by the Europeans in the late nineteenth century.

The official government policy for the past quarter century (and the informal practice long before that) has been to achieve maximum feasible segregation between the four racial groups. Known as *apartheid,* that policy is based on the premise that interracial contact breeds conflict—a self-fulfilling prophesy in South Africa—and, hence, that it is best to keep racial groups apart. In fact, the main aim of the government (which to all significant intents and purposes is a white monopoly in South Africa) is not so much to avoid contact between racial groups, but to maintain the white minority regime in power indefinitely. Indeed, there is massive contact between whites and nonwhites, but almost invariably on a master–servant, or employer–employee basis, and whites do not mind that at all. Without black labor, South African industry would grind to a halt, and the whites could not maintain their high standard of living.

Apartheid is thus clearly a policy of white supremacy which, under the guise of pluralism and "separate development," imposes on the nonwhites, and especially on the Africans, a crushing burden of political, social, educational, and economic disabilities. Not only is nearly every public and private facility (schools, churches, hospitals, trains, buses, waiting rooms, cemeteries, hotels, restaurants, cinemas, prisons, toilets, swimming pools, park benches, libraries, zoos, and so on) completely segregated by race, but the segregation is grossly unequal. Facilities for nonwhites are either absent or vastly inferior to those available to whites. African wages are about one-fifth of those of whites, and the law debars nonwhites from most desirable jobs. The schools, from kindergarten to university, are completely segregated for both teachers and pupils, and the state spends roughly 10 times as much on a white child as on a nonwhite one. The South African cabinet, armed forces, parliament, and judiciary are entirely white.

There is a farcical system of "Native chiefs" and "Bantustans," which supposedly represents the Africans, but, in fact, the white government acts completely as a colonial overlord. Africans are forbidden to strike, and numerous laws give the police virtually unlimited powers of search without warrant, imprisonment without trial, banishment, and daily harrassment. Nonwhites pay disproportionately heavy taxes, including some taxes to which whites are not subject, and get only minimal services from the state.

Property rights, especially land ownership, are extremely limited for nonwhites. The whites, with 18 percent of the population, own 87 percent of the land; and nonwhites are prevented by law from buying, renting, or occupying any land in areas which the government decides are "white." Nonwhites do not even have such elementary rights as the freedom to assemble, to travel within the country, or to reside where they wish. To be anywhere at all, an African needs a properly endorsed "reference book" which he has to produce on demand to the police on pain of immediate arrest. Political opposition is tolerated within narrow limits for whites, but completely suppressed for nonwhites.

The whole of South African society is unashamedly racist: any person classified by the government as white by virtue of his physical appearance is automatically entitled to all the privileges of citizenship, no matter how incompetent or uneducated. Any nonwhite, irrespective of wealth, intelligence, education, or any other personal quality, is excluded. The entire system is a vast economic, political, and social ladder, with the Whites on top, the Coloureds and the Asiatics several rungs below, but one or two rungs above the Africans, and the Africans as a vast, disfranchised, exploited *Lumpenproletariat* and a land-hungry subsistence peasantry. Social mobility into the white group is theoretically impossible (though some Coloureds managed to "pass" until the government closed the loopholes by law). Intermarriage and sexual relations between whites and nonwhites are forbidden by law under penalties of up to seven years of prison.

Apartheid, in short, is about as airtight a system of racial domination and exploitation as any human group ever devised. The well-meaning American liberal may wonder that such a monstrous system manages to survive, but, then, racism in the United States was only slightly less monstrous until the recent past. Human history shows us that there is little if any relationship between the moral qualities of a political regime and its longevity. The ghastliest tyrannies can last for centuries; true democracies have proven remarkably few, precarious, and short-lived, except in the simplest societies.

THE HINDU CASTE SYSTEM

The Hindu caste system is another notorious example of an incredibly developed hierarchy of status, of a cancerous growth in the principle of inequality (Srinivas, 1966; Dumont, 1970; Ghurye, 1952; Hutton, 1946). "Casteism" has some elements in common with racism: status is *ascribed* (independent of an individual's merit or personal qualities), membership in groups is assigned by birth and for life, the groups are in a hierarchy, and members of the lower groups suffer under crippling psychological and social disabilities. In many other respects, however, the two are quite different forms of inequality.

Let us look briefly at caste in India. The system originated some 3000 years ago, but, contrary to the opinion of some sociologists, it never remained static. It survived major revolutions and religious reform movements that opposed it, such as Buddhism, Islam, Sikhism, Christianity, and Hindu reformism; and it tended to become increasingly complex and unwieldy over the centuries. The British colonial government, lacking the incentive to fight caste, accommodated readily to it, but the government of independent India since 1947 has made many largely unsuccessful attempts at abolishing the disabilities and inequalities of caste. Caste, in ever-changing manifestations, is probably as much in evidence today as it was 500 or 1000 years ago.

Caste is a European term (from the Spanish or Portuguese *casta*), and is a bad one to use for India. The confusion is all the greater as caste has been used to translate the two very different concepts of *varna* and *jati*. There are four *varnas,* which, in descending hierarchical order, are the *brahmins* (traditionally priests and teachers), the *rajputs* or *kshatriyas* (warriors and rulers), the *vaishya* (merchants), and the *sudra* (peasants and common people). Over the centuries, a fifth group, consisting of people engaged in occupations considered to be defiling (such as scavenging or the killing and processing of animals), developed below the four *varnas,* in a position so lowly as to be regarded as social pariahs. These were known as the *untouchables* (as contact with them defiled any higher caste Hindu), or the "Scheduled Castes" as the British termed them or the *harijans* ("Children of God") in Mahatma Gandhi's gentle euphemism.

In terms of day-to-day life, the *jati* rather than the *varna* is the significant social group. Except for the Brahmins (who technically regard themselves as a single *jati,* but in fact are divided into many sub-*jati*), each of the *varnas* is internally divided into hundreds of *jati* (or "castes" in the restricted sense), and many of these *jati* are in turn divided into sub-*jati*. Altogether, there are many thousands of *jati* and sub-*jati* in India. The *jati* generally has a ruling council, or *panchayat*. The *jati* is a solidary social group from which one may be expelled ("outcasting") for severe offenses, but to which one normally belongs by birth and for life; and is an endogamous group within which one must marry on the penalty of outcasting. Endogamy also often applies to the sub-*jati*.

Nearly all of these *jati* and sub-*jati* regard themselves and each other as being in a hierarchical order, but the immense number of these groups and the great regional variation in the representation, naming, and socioeconomic position of these groups make for considerable lack of consensus on which *jati* fit where in the status ladder. From this complex and confusing situation, there results a keen competition between *jati* to jockey for position and to claim a higher status than they are accorded by others, largely by emulating the customs and dietary restrictions (such as vegetarianism) of the higher *jati*. Although movement of an individual from one *jati* to another is technically impossible, *jati* as groups have been moving up and down the status hierarchy.

There are at least two fundamental reasons for the resilience of the caste system despite legal assaults of the government and the modernizing influences of Western-style education, industrialization, and large-scale urbanization. First, the caste system is legitimized in the religious beliefs of Hinduism (such as *dharma, kharma,* and reincarnation), and it is inextricably interwoven into the myriad of socioreligious practices that dominate the daily life of the Hindu. Rituals of incredible punctilliousness regulate the relations between and within caste groups, determining not only whom one may or may not marry, but also what foods one may or may not eat and with whom, how close one may approach lower caste persons, what purification rites one must undergo for violations of these rules, and so on. Caste, in short, is a central part of Hindu religion, and Hindu religion is a way of life that affects all social relations.

Second, though the caste system as a whole is extraordinarily cumbersome, the *jati* to which one belongs, no matter how lowly its position, is an important solidary group on which one depends heavily for nearly all of one's intimate social relationships, for economic assistance, for political patronage, and so on. In other words, since caste is so all-encompassing, life outside of a caste group is nearly inconceivable. Outcasting is the ultimate penalty, a kind of social death, far worse than membership in a lowly untouchable group. (Outcasts sometimes seek and achieve admission in lowly castes, especially untouchable ones.)

So pervasive is the Hindu caste system that it has even extended itself to the 80-or-so million non-Hindus in the 550-odd million total population of India. The hundreds of "tribal" groups scattered throughout India have become incorporated as lowly "hill castes" in their relations with Hindus. Even the great religions, which have traditionally proclaimed the equality of man, have become affected by the virus of caste in India. Thus, one finds many Muslim, Sikh, Christian, and Jewish minorities in India who have developed quasi-caste systems of their own, based, for example, on the caste or origin of their converts from Hinduism. Inequality and invidiousness, it seems, are highly infectious. Perhaps an additional strength of the Hindu caste system is that, in a society that comprises thousands of hierarchized groups, the pain of subordination is more than compensated for by the relish of being able to look down on at least *some* other groups.

Both race and caste are *ascribed* (as distinguished from *achieved*) forms of invidiousness; that is, the social status in which a person finds himself is unrelated to that person's qualities, efforts, or merits. A Brahmin can be a scoundrel and an Untouchable a saint, but that scarcely affects the fact that the saintly Untouchable ritually pollutes the dissolute Brahmin, should his shadow fall across the Brahmin's path. These overwhelmingly ascriptive systems are also characterized by low rates of *social mobility*. If an individual's status is completely ascribed, it follows that he can do little to change it. However, no society has a completely rigid hierarchy. Even in South Africa, some racial "passing" takes place; and within the racial groups, there is considerable social mobility in class status. In India, there is group social mobility because the relative status of castes changes over time, and there even is individual mobility if one accepts the Hindu theory of reincarnation. An individual will be reborn in a higher or lower caste, or indeed in a subhuman life form, depending on his moral achievements during his previous incarnation.

ETHNICITY

Much more common than either race or caste as a basis for stratification is *ethnicity*. An ethnic group is one that shares a relatively homogeneous culture and a mutually understandable language. If an ethnic group achieves political independence from other ethnic groups, it becomes a nation-state. It is obvious that the vast majority of countries in the world are not nations but rather multiethnic conglomerates that have developed out of a history of conquest. When one ethnic group conquers another, it is, in fact, establishing a colonial empire, whether it is called that or not. For example, the Soviet Union is a Russian empire, Israel a Jewish empire, and the United States an Anglo-Saxon empire. Military conquest establishes one of the most unequal relationships imaginable. To be an Estonian in the Soviet Union, a Navaho in the United States, an Arab in Israel, a Quechua in Peru is to suffer the consequences of imperialism (i.e., of the domination of a foreign ethnic group that conquered others by the force of arms or sometimes by the duplicity of big-power diplomacy, which amounts to the same thing). It is true that some multiethnic countries have attempted to establish conditions of equal or proportional representation for their constituent ethnic groups, but the successful examples have been few. Switzerland stands out as the most successful and enduring multiethnic democracy, but other countries like Belgium, Canada, and Yugoslavia have reached much less satisfactory arrangements because they started out with a historical legacy of economic and social inequality between ethnic groups born out of previous wars and conquests. Where several ethnic groups live side by side in the same state, they generally do so on the basis of ethnic inequality, and this is the main reason for the hundreds of nationalist movements that have developed throughout human history, and which continue to flourish even in modern industrial societies.

Ethnic domination (which is frequently a *minority* domination) ranges from the most ruthless genocide (as with Nazi anti-Semitism) to relatively benign forms of indirect rule, internal autonomy, and near-equality (as between French and English Canadians, where the main sphere of Anglo domination is through the control of the economy). Relatively benign, *laissez-faire* forms of ethnic domination have tended to perpetuate ethnic divisions and conflicts, and to minimize acculturation to the dominant group. Where conquered peoples have been largely left alone to run their own local affairs, and are only moderately taxed and exploited, they have generally preserved their ethnic identity, and therefore also their subordinate status as a group.

Two other types of situation lead to much greater rates of acculturation, and hence of social mobility, between ethnic groups. One is the situation of voluntary emigration, where the migrant ethnic group has obvious advantages in assimilating to the host society. The other is that of extreme exploitation, such as in chattel slavery, or in Spanish American colonialism where the conquered people are literally shattered as a society, and often forced to adopt the language and culture of their masters and conquerors. In some countries of Latin America, for example, ethnic inequalities have largely disappeared through the simple but drastic expedient of wiping out ethnic groups either physically as individuals, or culturally as groups. (Policies of forced acculturation of ethnic minorities into the dominant group have recently been termed *ethnocide*, by analogy with genocide. The two are often sequential, as in the case of United States policy towards Indians. Widespread genocide was followed by various attempts at ethnocide, of which "termination policy" is but the most recent expression.)

Class: Power, Wealth, Prestige

The term "class" is perhaps one of the most confusing in the sociological literature; it has meant different things to different people. To some sociologists, a class is simply an analytical category made up of one or more statistical indices (e.g., the "class" of people with incomes below $10,000). Such arbitrary categories that do not correspond to self-consciously existing groups have sometimes been called *strata*, reserving the use of the term "class" for groups that have some subjective meaning to the people concerned (e.g., the "blue-collar workers"). Here we shall use the term "class" to mean a group that has some subjective meaning to the people concerned in a given society; that is, a group that has at least some measure of *class consciousness*.

Even within that more restricted use of the term, there have been, broadly speaking, three main approaches to class in the sociological literature, each stressing a different set of factors. Some authors, like Karl Marx, have emphasized the *economic factors* of production as most basic; others, like Gaetano Mosca (1939), have stressed *power* as the underlying basis of class; others yet, like Thorstein Veblen (1899), have defined class mostly in terms of *prestige*. Max Weber (1968) is usually credited with attempting to syncretize the three approaches.

Systems of class stratification are too varied for a single theory of class to prove universally valid. There are, however, certain uniformities that allow us to reach some general conclusions. First, there is a close relationship between the development of centralized political institutions and the rise of social classes. Nearly all societies that have social classes (beyond age and sex stratification) also have states, that is, persons who, by virtue of the political office they hold, exercise power over other persons unrelated by blood or marriage, and who are in a position to use violence to insure obedience. Conversely, nearly all societies that have states have social classes, even the socialist countries that pretend otherwise.

Second, social classes seem to be linked with the amount of surplus goods and services produced by a society. Societies with technologically primitive systems of production that live on the margin of sheer subsistence are relatively egalitarian. Generally, the more surplus is produced, the more elaborate the stratification system is. There is perhaps a slight reversal of that trend in the highly productive industrial societies where the standard of living of the ''poor'' has risen dramatically. However, even in these countries where the ''poor'' would be affluent by the standards of the ''Third World,'' class inequalities remain far greater than in societies where everybody is living on the edge of want and starvation. Thus, the relative affluence of a society is not to be confused with equality, even when a substantial part of that affluence is distributed to the lower classes. So far, in human history, general destitution seems to have been the price of democracy. Affluence, even where it is fairly widespread in a society, seems to have more of a stratifying than a leveling effect.

Third, prestige is probably the least important of the three main components of social class. It is true that prestige often attaches to wealth and power, but so do envy and hostility. Many ruling classes have enjoyed little prestige. The approach to social stratification that grants prime importance to prestige assumes more consensus about the legitimacy of inequality than generally exists. In any case, prestige is more an *index* than a causative factor of class differentiation. Furthermore, prestige differences in societies are not limited to class-stratified systems. Indeed, significant differences in prestige between individuals based on personal qualities are universal, and thus are also found in classless societies, whereas appreciable differences in power and wealth are closely linked to class societies.

If it seems well established that power and wealth are the underlying bases of most class systems, which of the two is prior? Does the accumulation of wealth precede the monopolization of power, or, alternatively, does the concentration of power make for the appropriation of surplus production? Empirically, the two so frequently go together that the question may seem like a chicken-and-the-egg one. Nevertheless, it is an important one. Marx's answer was that appropriation of surplus production came first. Material conditions of existence are the underlying basis of any society, and differential relations to the system of production create, by definition, social classes as Marx conceived of them. The class that appropriates ownership of the key factor of production (labor, land, or capital) at a given stage of economic development monopolizes the means of coercion to maintain its class position. The state for Marx is the "executive committee of the ruling class."

Though there are a few historical instances of genuine plutocracies, (e.g., of merchant classes of city-states that became the politically dominant class), it seems that Marx was wrong in most cases. Power, not wealth, is the prior basis of class position in most historical cases.

There are two kinds of evidence for this statement. First, we know of a good many agricultural societies, principally in Africa, that have well-developed states and a complex stratification system, but where economic differences between social classes are not great. Land in these societies is frequently held communally by extended family groups. One's class position is determined largely by the political offices one holds and by the network of patron-client ties. High status entails the obligation to redistribute wealth among one's clients, relatives, wives, and other dependents in the form of hospitality and largesse, rather than to accumulate it. A person's social status is thus measured mostly by the number of his wives and clients over whom he has power, rather than by the accumulation of wealth and items of conspicuous consumption. Even the king's household is different more by size than by quality from those of his subjects. Except for a few regalia that belong to the office rather than to the person of the king, the style of life of the king is much like that of his subjects. The king is often surrounded by elaborate rituals and taboos because his position is sacred, but he does not wallow in luxury.

An example of such a society are the Nupe of Nigeria (Nadel, 1942). They have been a centralized kingdom for hundreds of years and now number approximately half a million people. They are clearly stratified into slaves (formally abolished during the British colonial period); commoners; specialized craft guild members like brassmiths, barbers, weavers, and so on; various classes of noble office holders (some appointed by the king, some hereditary); and three royal lineages alternating in the kingship. Rank differences are clearly evident because certain articles of clothing, such as the blue turban, are restricted to people holding certain offices, but differences in wealth and living standards are not very marked.

Favorite slaves may rise to noble status by being elevated to political office, and slaves are not necessarily poor. Horse ownership is an important status symbol, as is extensive polygyny. A nobleman's walled-in compound might include scores of round dwellings to house his extended family, his wives, his slaves, clients and retainers, whereas the average commoner's compound may include only half a dozen. The architecture of the capital city is quite uniform, except for the Western-style king's palace built after British rule was established. Houses are round with mud floors and walls, and have a conical straw roof. They are single-storied and single-roomed. A group of houses occupied by a virilocal extended family is surrounded by a mud wall. Class differences are not sharply drawn in terms of diet and life style, though distinctions of power and status are clearly marked by rules of etiquette. The main economic equalizer is the extensive network for the redistribution of wealth, which links powerful patrons with their numerous clients. The household of the powerful is both a social security system and a patronage empire.

The second type of evidence in favor of the general priority of power over wealth in the determination of class systems is the widespread existence of the phenomenon of "weak money," or "pariah capitalism." In a great many agrarian societies, the class of well-to-do merchants and moneylenders has been confined to a powerless pariah status and debarred from political power. Often, this class of pariah capitalists has included foreigners or religious minorities kept isolated in commercial ghettoes, such as Jews in Europe, and overseas Chinese and East Indians in various parts of Asia and Africa. But even when the merchant class has been indigenous, it has sometimes been granted very low status as was the case in pre-Meiji Japan. Wealth, then, is no passport to power.

In industrial societies, there generally is a close correspondence between power and wealth, which is almost equally so in capitalist and socialist countries. There may be a slightly greater tendency for the wealthy of capitalist countries to come to power and for the powerful of socialist countries to become wealthy, but otherwise the two differ little in their stratification systems. Socialist practice, it seems, is the best refutation of the Marxian thesis. Socialist countries remain austere and puritanical for only a short time before what Milovan Djilas (1959) called the "New Class" reemerges as a kind of bureaucratic bourgeoisie milking the collective cow for their not-so-collective interests.

Social Mobility

An important feature of systems of social stratification is *social mobility*, or movement up and down the status scale. This complex topic has given birth to an immense sociological literature (Lipset and Bendix, 1959). A widespread belief among Western sociologists until recently was that industrial societies were characterized by high rates of social mobility while "traditional" societies had more "closed" and ascriptive systems of stratification, allowing only limited social mobility. In fact, no simple generalization holds, because there are many different kinds of social mobility and several ways of measuring it.

First, an important distinction must be made between the movement of individuals from one stratum to another, and systemic change in the stratification pyramid. We have seen, for example, that the Hindu caste system, long considered by Western sociologists as the prototype of a static and rigid social order, has undergone much systemic change in terms of the caste groups involved and their relative position, even though individual social mobility as we understand it in the West is theoretically impossible.

Even when individuals move from one class to another, it is important to take systemic change into account, especially what sociologists often call the shape of the social pyramid. In most agrarian societies, some 90 percent of the population has consisted of peasants, about one-tenth consisted of specialized craftsmen and merchants, and a fraction of one percent represented the privileged ruling class. In such a system, the extremely broad basis of the pyramid statistically limits the total amount of possible interclass mobility. The chances that the individual peasant will become anything else are statistically very small. Even in early phases of industrialization, the peasantry and the urban proletariat combined made up three-fourths or more of the total population, leaving room for a growing, but still relatively small, middle class.

In later phases of industrialization, the farming population contracts to one-tenth or less, and the skilled and semiskilled industrial workers to about one-third of the labor force, while the technical, clerical, and other middle-class service occupations expand greatly. Such is the case in advanced industrial countries like Britain, the United States, and Germany today.

Thus, the high rates of social mobility characteristic of rapidly industrializing societies are much more the consequence of the great bulge around the middle of the stratification pyramid which affl ient societies develop, than of any supposed trend toward democratization and equality of opportunity. If the entire labor force is greatly upgraded, there is scarcely any place for individual workers to go except up, particularly if the index of social mobility used by the sociologists is a comparison of father's occupation and son's occupation, the so-called intergenerational mobility. Obviously, a generation's time span is long enough to reflect much systemic upgrading. Considerably lower rates of mobility are obtained if one traces the work history of individuals. Indeed, occupational level is to a large extent determined by the level of formal education attained, and that, in turn, is generally set by the end of the second decade of life.

A less common, but at least as significant, way of looking at social mobility is to inquire about the rate of entry into the ruling class or upper stratum. This is what the Italian sociologist Vilfredo Pareto (1963) did when he developed his theory of "circulation of elites" and pronounced history to be "a graveyard of aristocracies." Pareto postulated that a ruling class had to remain open to the more capable elements from the lower classes to survive at all; otherwise it quickly became incompetent and was overthrown by revolution. There is indeed evidence that closed, hereditary aristocracies become sclerotic, and that many "traditional" societies that had relatively low rates of systemic change had, in fact, a high rate of turnover in the ruling class. The classical example is that of Imperial China, where access to the mandarin class or ruling bureaucracy was through an elaborate examination system. To be sure, the many years of leisure and dedication to learning which preparation for these examinations required gave the gentry an advantage over the ordinary peasant. But, by pooling resources, even poor peasants could finance the studies of their brightest offspring, who thus had a chance to enter the all-powerful bureaucracy and could repay his debts by squeezing taxes out of other peasants in the foreign district to which a mandarin was almost invariably sent. This system of rule lasted for thousands of years, and, except for cycles of growth and decline in the centralized power of the Emperor, Chinese social structure changed relatively slowly until the twentieth century. Yet, a study by Robert Marsh (1963) showed that the rate of social mobility for Chinese mandarins in the nineteenth century was roughly the same as that of American engineers in the same period.[2]

An almost exactly opposite situation existed in eighteenth-century France (Brinton, 1957). The rate of systemic change was quite rapid. There was a considerable quickening of the pace of economic life in the period immediately preceding the Industrial Revolution. The levels of technology, trade, and urbanization increased, and with them the urban bourgeoisie (both the *petite bourgeoisie* of artisans and shopkeepers and the *haute bourgeoisie* of wealthy financiers, bankers, shipowners, and entrepreneurs) grew to unprecedented wealth, numbers, and influence. While the country was changing under them, the hereditary nobility had become increasingly parasitic, frivolous, and incompetent, squandering in Versailles the taxes and compulsory labor squeezed out of their peasants. To a limited extent, the rich bourgeois could purchase army commissions, nobility titles, and other

[2]Many African countries that recently became independent have a stratification system not unlike that of imperial China. Lacking almost completely a native bourgeoisie, these countries are ruled by the state bureaucracy and by army officers who gained their position by passing examinations in a highly competitive school system that has been relatively open, even to poor peasants' children. These black mandarins are the successor elite to the white colonial bureaucracy which they replaced at independence.

royal favors, but, in the end, the relative closure of the ruling class in a dynamic society proved the undoing of the *Ancien Régime*. The genteel debauchery of the Versailles courtiers ended at the guillotine of the Place de la Concorde.

We have seen that there is little relationship between the rate of entry into the ruling class and the rate of change in the society at large. High rates of systemic change can be accompanied by low access to the privileged stratum, usually with revolutionary consequences in the end. (South Africa comes to mind as another example of this seemingly incongruous situation.) Conversely, a society's stratification system may remain relatively unchanged while the personnel at the top is constantly replaced. Such a situation is common enough for the French to have coined a phrase about it: *Plus ça change, plus ça reste la même chose.* ("The more it changes, the more it remains the same.")

It is often assumed that easy access to the top is a measure of how democratic a society is. This, too, is an overgeneralization born out of sociological ignorance. A high rate of entry into, and turnover in, the elite is commonly a symptom of tyranny. Often the crudest forms of personal despotism have been characterized by promotion of low-status persons, such as slaves, eunuchs, henchmen, and other menials, to high political office. The lowly born in high places have several obvious advantages to the tyrant. Lacking any traditional basis for status (such as a powerful family), they are completely dependent on him and devoid of any power in their own right. Their heads can be chopped off without raising any eyebrows, which has the additional advantages of making room at the top and providing scope for the scheming ambitions of the courtiers and sycophants. The privileges of the pariah, slave, foreigner, eunuch, and others of lowly status are likely to be bitterly resented by the high-born whom the tyrant must keep under control. Privileged menials are one of the best counter-weights to an entrenched aristocracy, and thus one of the best instruments of monarchical absolutism. Bodyguards may consist entirely of low-status thugs at the beck and call of the despot. Such were, for example, the infamous *tonton macoute* under the Duvalier dictatorship in Haiti. In its most extreme form, large-scale terror, such as under Stalin, makes for a lot of social mobility. But even more restrained brands of tyranny often give the lowly born a better chance to reach the top than regimes with democratic pretensions. The Cuban or Haitian army sergeant has a better chance of becoming President than does his counterpart in the United States.

ELITISM AND EGALITARIANISM

The sociological study of inequality is permeated with ideological cant. Western sociologists, despite their pretenses at objectivity, have been as ideologically biased as their Communist counterparts. The latter superficially seem more dogmatic, and the explicitness of their dogmatism exposes more clearly the ideological underpinnings of their work than that of their "bourgeois" colleagues, whose conception of objectivity is the careful concealment of their biases. In the end, there is little to choose between them. In both "socialist" and "capitalist" sociology, the most widespread value judgement has been that inequality is bad. A minority tradition in each camp has held the opposite: Lenin's position on the vanguard of the proletariat is not all that different from the theory of the divine right of kings.

The egalitarian tradition in sociology is unfortunately much less convincing than the elitist one. Although elitist theories of the social order are often self-serving, they constitute a fairly good account of reality, whereas egalitarian theories fly in the face of the evidence. In the end, what passes for theory in the field of social stratification amounts to little more than the selective use of evidence to defend an ideological position. Such, for example, has been the famous debate over the "functional theory" of stratification (Davis and Moore, 1945; Tumin, 1953). The sociological "left wing" has argued that stratification is "dysfunctional" while the "right wing" has held that it is "functional," meaning "good" for society. Whether good or bad, inequality undeniably exists in all human societies. The two most universal bases of status differences, age and gender, are obviously rooted in biology, and, as we have suggested before, there is evidence that inequality is, as other basic components of human behavior, the product of a complex interplay of biological predispositions and sociocultural factors. There is, therefore, every reason to expect that, irrespective of ideology, inequality will be with us for the foreseeable future. Other than liking or disliking it, there is not much we can do about it. The eternal tragedy of the revolutionary is that his attempts to abolish inequality have inevitably led to its reestablishment in a slightly different form.

ADDITIONAL READING

Stratification is one of the few areas where the sociological literature has an embarrassment of riches. Probably the best single anthology in the field is Bendix and Lipset (1966), which includes fragments of many of the classics as well as empirical studies. Among the earlier classics, Marx's and Engels' *The Communist Manifesto*, and Mosca (1939), Pareto (1963), Michels (1949), and Veblen (1899) should be part of the minimum intellectual baggage of educated laymen. The works of C.W. Mills (1951, 1959) are important statements about the contemporary United States. Young (1961) is a delightful piece of social science fiction about Britain. Djilas (1959) is a critique of Communist countries by a high-ranking Yugoslav official in disgrace. The reader by Béteille (1969) contains case studies from several important societies, including non-Western ones. My *Racism and Racism* (1967) compares four racially stratified societies, and my *Age and Sex in Human Societies* (1973) analyzes these two universal aspects of inequality. Dumont (1970) and Srinivas (1966) are excellent on the Hindu caste system, and so is Mason (1971) on European colonialism. Tuden and Plotnicov (1970) edited a useful collection on Africa. Lipset and Bendix (1959) give a well-known statement of social mobility in industrial societies. Lenski (1966) presents a broad evolutionary and comparative perspective on the problem of inequality.

6

Politics: Forms of Tyranny

In the broadest sense, politics is the struggle for power. In Chapter Two we suggested that the universality in human societies of a well-established dominance order, based at least on age and gender, called for a partly biological explanation of the phenomenon. All human societies are organized on the basis of power differentials, a fact for which we suggested a threefold evolutionary explanation. As ground-living primates, we needed to organize for defense against predators, much as did the macaques and baboons, who are also dominance-ordered. As predators ourselves, we needed to organize for successful hunting, and this meant a sharp division of labor by age and gender, and coordination of the activities of several males. Finally, and perhaps most importantly, we developed power-ordered (and hierarchical) societies as a way of regulating access to scarce resources. In man, the only animal who has developed social needs that are intrinsically insatiable, the problem of regulating the aggression and conflict generated by competition for scarce resources was especially acute. Territoriality and hierarchy were the dual answer to the problem, but they were not satisfactory solutions, because they were both sources of aggression. That we are so territorially and hierarchically organized helps to explain why we are not continuously at each other's throats, but it also helps to understand why we remain so aggressive and violent.

Every human group is in some sense a political system, irrespective of the ostensible aims of the group. Dominance exists not only in governments and political parties, but also in families, in schools, in symphony orchestras, in monasteries, in chess clubs, and in bird-watching associations. States are merely organizations whose avowed primary purpose is the wielding of power. In that avowed sense of a group of people making it a career to boss over other people, the state is not universal. As we shall see, there are many stateless societies, but none that are not dominance-ordered, at least by age and gender.

The Struggle for Power

If politics is the struggle for power we may then ask: power for what? The basic answer is: control over scarce resources. That problem in turn is twofold. Within the group, if pandemonium is not to be chronic, there must be a system of rules establishing who has access to what, in what order, in what amounts, and under what conditions. Externally, the organization of any group means the exclusion of nonmembers from a share of these resources. The two aspects of the problem, then, are (1) distribution of scarce resources within the group, and (2) monopolization of resources for the group.

If resources were primarily material (that is, for the satisfaction of our basic biological needs), the problem would not be so complex. Indeed, we find that many societies, whose technology is so simple that they have not produced much surplus and that basic material needs still loom large, managed to do quite well politically without creating states. In more technologically complex societies, however, where artifactual and social needs assume more and more importance, the problem of both internal and external order grows in complexity. It is a measure of man's perversity that power, originally a means to an end, so frequently becomes an end in itself. That is, power often is no longer simply an instrument of access to other resources, but becomes a resource in its own right.

In theory, there is no reason why the problem of distribution of resources both within and between groups should not be solved amiably through consensual agreement. Occasionally this happens, especially when resources are not scarce. We do not generally fight over our oxygen supply, for example. Conflicts over water are acute only where there is not enough to go around. Where resources are scarce, however, the consensual solution, though sometimes tried, rarely succeeds. Many human groups cultivate a fiction of consensus. But scratch the myth of consensus and you typically find a power system, even in communities ostensibly dedicated to egalitarianism and the sharing of resources, such as monastic orders.

Similarly, human groups are not only dominance-ordered; they also defend themselves against intrusions from outsiders. Territoriality is a common and universal manifestation of boundary maintenance between competing groups, but not the only one. The restriction of access to membership is another aspect of that behavior. There are innumerable human groups (such as families, castes, and clubs) that exclude outsiders, all the way from complete exclusion except by birth to conditional acceptance, but practically none that accept strangers unconditionally. (In this respect, we are far more tolerant of other species than of our own: we pick up stray dogs far more casually than stray children.)

The study of politics, then, is the study of how power is contested, maintained, and wielded in order to gain access to scarce resources, both material and social, including power itself. A good starting point in our inquiry is the family as one of the simplest and most universal types of human organization.

THE FAMILY AS A POWER SYSTEM

As a micro-tyranny run by adult males, the family contains in elementary form many of the elements of more complex forms of political organization, a fact clearly grasped by Confucian social philosophy, which links obedience to the emperor to filial piety. (That the model is not a bad one is shown by the fact that Confucianism has been the political blueprint for some 2500 years in the world's largest, oldest, and, many would say, most civilized nation.) In many other political systems as well, the linkages between the family and more complex forms of tyranny are explicitly recognized. Before the European fashion changed to egalitarian ideology in the eighteenth century, for example, the theory of benevolent despotism legitimized the position of the king as that of father to his subjects. The religious authority of the priesthood is often rationalized in the same terms.

Paternalism is probably the most widespread model of, and justification for, political rule. The great strength of paternalism is that it appears to reconcile despotism with justice, hence its nearly universal appeal to rulers in search of legitimation. The main elements of paternalist ideology are as follows: the ruler is to his subjects as a father to his children. His authority is justified by the inability of the subjects to rule themselves since they are "grown-up children," and by the ruler's benevolence toward his subjects. If one accepts the double premise of incapacity of the ruled and benevolence of the ruler, it follows that despotism is conducive to the common good.

In most instances paternalism is a legitimizing myth rather than a description of reality. In fact, the two premises seldom hold in practice. Adults are not like children, and rulers can seldom feel toward their subjects as parents do towards their children. That is, the family is, by and large, a *benevolent* tyranny, because it is part of our biological heritage to protect our children, feed them, and attend to their needs. This heritage of infant protection is shared with other mammals. A state, however, is not a biologically based organization, and rulers are not biologically programmed to "love" their subjects. Instead, they are economically motivated to exploit them. The tyranny is most commonly untempered by benevolence. This, however, has not hindered the ideology of paternalism to seek justification for even the ghastliest forms of human degradation and exploitation, such as chattel slavery in the Americas. Our point here is not that the state is like a big family, but rather that the more complex forms of political organization have grown out of the family, that the power relations prevailing in the family have become generalized to bigger polities, and that in the process of generalization the benevolent despotism of the family has tended to become a despotism untempered by benevolence.

The essential similarity between the family and more complex political systems is that, in both, relations of dominance and submission rest in the last analysis on violence or threat of violence. Father can outwhack mother, who in turn can outwhack the children, at least until adolescence when parental authority becomes challenged. Power is not automatically received and unquestioningly accepted. It is in the nature of power to be resented and challenged by those at the receiving end of the stick, and to be retained and defended by those who hold it. Violence or the threat of violence is the ultimate argument in a power contest. The average family is no more exempt of violence and conflict than the average state, though our ideology concerning the family makes us reluctant to accept that fact.

The essential difference, however, between a family and a state is that some type of family organization is necessary to the survival of our species (or at least has been until a few thousand years ago), whereas the state is a recent creation, essentially synchronic with the development of agriculture, when our species ceased to be restricted to the ecological niche for which its biological evolution had adapted it. The *raison d'être* of the state is exploitation of the many by the few.

Order in Stateless Societies

Westerners, as products of a statal tradition several thousand years old, tend to take the existence of a state for granted, and to consider that the alternative is anarchy. Anthropologists know that stateless societies are anything but anarchical. It is possible for human societies numbering in the thousands, or even in the hundreds of thousands, to exist without a state. We have examined in the previous chapter the case of the Masai; there are literally hundreds of such stateless societies that have survived to our day, although most of them had the misfortune of becoming incorporated into colonial empires during the last centuries.

It is, however, a mistake to romanticize and idealize stateless societies. Although they are relatively democratic, at least for adult men, they are also frequently very aggressive. The Masai were traditionally an efficient, permanent war machine with young men spending a decade or more as celibate warriors, capturing cattle and women from their neighbors.

Another cherished myth of American liberals is that democratic societies are peaceful. Few human societies, whether democratic or tyrannical, are peaceful, and the few that are, are the losers of human evolution. Peaceful groups like the Pygmies are the ones that are so weak that their only chance of survival is to avoid conflict with their more powerful, more numerous, and better organized neighbors.

This natural penchant for violence in man raises for all societies what sociologists call the "problem of order." What is there to prevent the war of all against all? Indeed, the minimum definition of a society is a group within which the expression of violence is regulated. Starting again with the family, it is clear that the inhibition of violence, and especially of lethal violence, is the very condition of survival. Men could not wantonly kill women or adults kill children without dire consequences. It is true that some societies practice infanticide or abortion, but they usually do so under ecological conditions that make the pressures of overpopulation evident.

For the some 20 million years when our hominid ancestors were adjusting themselves to their environment by becoming predators and scavengers, the peace group was bigger than the family. The hunting-gathering-and-scavenging band of perhaps 30 to 50 individuals, including six to a dozen male adults, seems to have been the average size of the hominid group for all but the last 8000 to 10,000 years of human history. Cooperation between at least a few adult males was a necessary condition of successful hunting and scavenging. It was perhaps only one hundred thousand years ago that hominids developed moderately adequate *throwing* weapons like spears and bows and arrows. Without them, a lone man with a stone, stick, or bone was a poor match against large felines, man's most direct competitors for animal food. It seems highly probable that until the development of throwing weapons, man was at least as much a scavenger as a hunter; that is, he stole more kills from the big cats than he managed to kill on his own. And it clearly takes more than one man waving a stick to chase away a pride of lions or even a cheetah from a kill. For millions of years, then, multi-family groups numbering several scores of individuals managed to maintain a reasonable degree of internal peace without creating states. Much as they might have liked to bump each other over the head, they had to stick together to survive and to provide food for their females and young.

The large-scale and complex stateless societies that survive to this day are cultural elaborations on this biologically evolved blueprint for human survival. Stateless pastoralist or agricultural societies may include tens or even hundreds of thousands of people. Internal peace is maintained through diffuse social pressures and sanctions which dissuade people from misbehaving under the threat of ridicule, shame, censure, ostracism, and the like; or through mediation mechanisms to resolve conflicts; or through the ritualization of conflicts within well-prescribed channels, such as "feuding." Internal cohesion is often achieved by perpetuating a state of chronic warfare with neighboring societies. Thus, a powerful cement of Masai nationalism was the need to maintain their efficient war machine in order to wage continuous raids against their neighbors. Internal peace and external war are often two sides of the same coin. In the same sense in which a society can be defined as a peace group, relations between societies are frequently characterized by chronic war.

It would be erroneous to assume that there is no authority structure in stateless societies. There is always a well-defined authority structure based on age, sex, kinship, and marriage within the constituent family groups in these societies. Such families are, in most cases, extended and polygynous and typically include scores and even hundreds of persons. Thus, each lineage or clan could be regarded as a micro-state ruled by its older males according to a system of rights and obligations defined by custom. Within the family groupings there is no ambiguity as to who holds power and authority. What differentiates, however, state and stateless societies is that, in the latter, there is no well-defined class of office-holders with clear executive authority over people not related to them by kinship or marriage. What then, beyond these diffuse social pressures already mentioned, holds these family groupings together into a larger society that may incorporate many thousands of people if there is no central authority to order them about?

One of the extremely important sets of ties holding stateless societies together are rules of *exogamy*, which force lineages and clans to enter into matrimonial alliances with each other. In its simplest form, two exogamous moieties exchange women for wives, so that every single family in one moiety has in-laws (and thus relatives) in the other. There is theoretically no limit to the number of lineages and clans that can be linked through ties of marriage. One of the basic reasons why people in stateless societies (and indeed in state societies as well) stick together is that they have invented for themselves a system of exogamous marriage: if they did not stick together men could not get any wives. Rules of exogamy have often been interpreted as extensions of the incest taboo, but, as we have suggested earlier, there is evidence of a biological basis for nuclear-family incest inhibition, whereas exogamy (which does not preclude marriage between first cousins, and, indeed, frequently encourages it) is clearly cultural and extends social bonds beyond those that seem to be built into our *Anlagen*, or biological predispositions.

Beyond rules of exogamy, there are other forces that hold stateless societies together. Ethnicity, that is, the bond of a common culture and language is obvious enough, but it is neither a sufficient nor a necessary condition to constitute a society, for many societies incorporate more than one culture, and many culturally homogenous groups are split into many distinct societies. Nevertheless, most stateless societies are held together through the sharing of important cultural institutions. Among the Masai, we have seen that the age-grade system (and the military organization that is based on it) performs that unifying role. In other cases, great religious festivals have the same function of bringing people together for the performance of rituals seen as essential to the prosperity, health, and well-being of the collectivity. The French sociologists, Durkheim (1915, 1933) and Mauss (1954), for example, put great stress on these religious institutions as reinforcers of what they called "collective consciousness."

These collective institutions and rituals in stateless societies are often run by a "council of elders," typically made up of heads of lineages, and it may well be asked why such a council is not called a state. If, indeed, these elders have executive powers over the society (i.e., if they have the power to give orders and to apply sanctions in case of disobedience), we have the germ of a state. If we find, for instance, that such a council of elders can call on the services of a group of younger men to bring recalcitrants to them in order to be fined or otherwise punished, we have in fact a stratum that would be called a gerontocracy (government by the old). If, however, such a council of elders plays a largely ritual role, going through the motions of presiding over ceremonies prescribed by custom, we can still speak of a stateless society.

In actual practice, the dividing line between a stateless and a state society is not sharply drawn. Indeed, there are hundreds of marginal cases of formerly stateless societies in the process of gradually evolving a centralization of executive power. This process of state formation has been repeated, in several different forms, thousands of times in human history. Why is there this unmistakable evolutionary tendency for hitherto stateless societies to develop that centralization of power and that monopoly of violence in the hands of the few, that we call a state? The answer is that, for all its viability, the stateless society also has a number of limitations that put it at a competitive disadvantage *vis à vis* states.

The basic limitations of the stateless society are in terms of *size* and *organization*. The outer size limit for a stateless society seems to be in the half-million range, as shown by some of the East African pastoralist or mixed pastoralist–agricultural societies, but most stateless societies number from a few hundred to a few thousand people whose activities can be effectively coordinated. By contrast, the largest states have incorporated populations numbering hundreds of millions.

This size limitation is, in turn, closely related to an organizational one. Custom, consensus, social pressures, and ties of marriage are effective means of cohesion up to a certain point, but they are not an efficient way of coordinating the activities of large numbers of people, particularly if these activities involve sustained and complexly interdependent efforts. Organizational limitations of stateless societies are perhaps most obvious in war and in economic production. As we have seen, the Masai and other East African stateless societies had developed efficient war machines, but their type of warfare was sporadic raiding rather than sustained campaigns with protracted wars of conquest, of military occupation, and so on. Furthermore, their military technology was quite rudimentary. It takes little logistics and organization for each man to produce and maintain a spear, a leather shield, and a sword, the weapons of the Masai warrior. But it is beyond the reach of a democratic citizen army without professional officers to keep up a motor pool, to maintain tanks and aeroplanes, or even to keep a machine gun in working order. The industrial machine needed to produce the military hardware presupposes complex forms of social organization.

Agrarian Societies:
The Growth of the State

Technologically, the great leap forward (or backward, depending on one's viewpoint) in the development of the state came with more complex agriculture. Hunting and gathering, livestock raising, and the simpler types of slash-and-burn tropical agriculture are fully compatible with a stateless mode of social organization. More advanced and intensive agricultural techniques, particularly those involving terracing, irrigation, and other large-scale public works requiring the coordinated and sustained work of large numbers of people, are not. The historian Karl Wittfogel (1957) developed the thesis that "oriental despotism" was the product of the need for centralized control in the development and maintenance of irrigation works, and, hence, called these states "hydraulic civilizations." While he seems to have exaggerated the importance of irrigation by itself, there is an obvious link between advanced forms of agriculture and the emergence of large, centralized states. All advanced agrarian societies (and industrial societies) have well-developed states.

A great many of the simpler agrarian societies and, indeed, some pastoralists are also organized in states. Any simple theory of technological determinism is not sufficient to explain the emergence of the state. The evidence indicates that there are several ways in which states emerged. Military conquest, and more specifically, the conquest of people, as distinguished from simple territorial expansion or cattle-raiding, is perhaps the most common one. When a conquering group maintains its dominion over another group, it becomes, by definition, the ruling class of the new larger political entity. Military conquest typically gives rise to multi-ethnic empires, and to ethnic stratification, since the conqueror is often of a different culture than the conquered. Sometimes, a process of cultural assimilation takes place whereby the conquered are absorbed into the conquering group, or, more rarely, where the conquerors adopt the language and culture of the conquered. Even after acculturation has taken place, stratification between the descendants of the conquered and of the conquerors often remains. Nine hundred years after the Norman Conquest, French still remains the prestige language of the English upper classes, even though the Normans assimilated into the Anglo-Saxon culture they conquered.

Conquest greatly fosters the development of a state in a conquering group which may have been stateless before, because there now arises the need to use coercion in order to control and exploit the conquered. Indeed, the conquered can scarcely be expected voluntarily to conform to the will of the conqueror. The bases of social cohesion existing in a stateless society are utterly lacking in a conquest situation. The conquerors must, therefore, apply the threat of organized violence to secure compliance from the conquered; that is, constitute themselves as a ruling class in the newly established conquest state.

The conquerors may already have been organized as a state before they expanded, but whether or not they were, they have to form a state if they are to rule over culturally alien people. Amusingly, a number of African conquest states were legitimized through a myth that the conquerors were freely invited by the conquered to rule them because they were incapable of ruling themselves. Thus, the European colonial myth of the inability of Africans to maintain self-rule had been independently invented by the Africans themselves to justify African colonialism. Nor is this kind of legitimizing myth to disguise the origin of conquest empires in violence unique to Africa. The Incas of the Andes who expanded rapidly through military conquest in the fifteenth century spread the myth that their evident superiority made other peoples welcome incorporation into the Inca Empire, a fiction perpetuated by the sixteenth century mestizo chronicler, Garcilaso de la Vega, and still enshrined in contemporary Peruvian history schoolbooks. Conquest, it would seem, is always in the best interests of the vanquished, unless you happen to be one and know better.

Not every state, however, originated in conquest. Often state formation is an internal process of power centralization within a given society. A council of elders, for example, in an hitherto stateless society may slowly extend its functions from ritual or ceremonial ones to executive ones, and become in effect a ruling gerontocracy. The appearance of a police force, or the use of armed force for purposes of internal control, is a clear symptom that a state exists. So is the existence of courts that have the power to inflict punishment. Conciliation mechanisms to bring about civil reparation exist in many stateless societies, but criminal justice enforced by specialized authorities is characteristic of the state. To the extent, then, that a group of individuals within a society arrogate to themselves the authority to control the activities of people not related to them by blood or marriage, and to back up their authority with the threat of the actuality of violence, a state can be said to exist.

Collective rule by council is a relatively uncommon form of state organization. Monarchy is far more frequent, for it is in the nature of centralization of power to reach its logical conclusion: the ultimate power of one person. A common way in which monarchies have developed is through a curious extension of the principle of seniority. We have seen that, within kin groups, the principle of seniority is almost universally resorted to in order to establish precedence of authority, all the way from the nuclear family to lineages incorporating thousands of people.

A frequent social mutation of that principle is for one branch of a lineage or clan to claim collective seniority over the other branches. It is one thing to have the oldest male in a given descent group assume authority over all members thereof. So long as seniority is individually defined, authority can pass to any branch of the descent group. When, however, one segment of a descent group successfully makes a claim of seniority over the other branches, because, for example, their founding ancestor was the senior of a set of brothers, then seniority becomes collectively vested in a group. All members of that group, irrespective of chronological age, become socially senior to members of other descent groups, and retain their seniority from generation to generation. Such is the origin of royal families in many African societies.

The same device of extending the seniority principle from individuals to groups within a descent group can be applied through fictional kinship to entire societies. Many African societies, for example, are made up of a definite number of clans which are historically distinct descent groups. One of the clans is defined as the royal clan from which the king must be chosen (although frequently the choice of the king from among the eligible princes is made by a body of elders drawn from the commoner clans). The status of the royal clan is legitimized by an origin myth that the society grew out of a set of brothers (or sisters), one of whom was senior to the others, and was therefore the founder of the royal clan.

Sometimes the process of centralization of power is triggered or greatly accelerated by the introduction of a technological innovation, especially in weaponry. Firearms have played that role when introduced by Europeans into stateless societies. By trading firearms, Europeans enabled hitherto powerless groups to capture power, and helped constitutional monarchs to become ruthless tyrants. A few firearms, even primitive muzzle-loading ones, in the hands of well-chosen henchmen have often proven sufficient to alter drastically the balance of power in bow-and-arrow societies.

Legitimation of Power

The organizational details of states have varied enormously, but the bag of tricks used to attain and keep power has been rather limited. One of the most universal features of developed states is that their ruling class seeks to justify the *status quo*. Almost invariably, ruling classes attempt to legitimize their superordinate position by some kind of ideology beyond "might is right." According to Max Weber (1968), there are three main types of legitimizing ideologies: the *traditional*, the *charismatic*, and the *rational-legal*. The traditional type of legitimacy justifies itself on the basis of precedent and custom; the charismatic type on the basis of the personal qualities of the ruler, or, in modern Communist terminology, a "cult of personality"; and the rational-legal type on grounds of bureaucratic procedures and efficiency in achieving certain aims.

These three types of legitimacy are far from exhaustive. Some ruling groups, for example, have rationalized their position on racial grounds; the Watuzi of central Africa believed that their tall stature was a qualification to rule; the Europeans of South Africa based their claim on their lack of skin pigmentation; the Nazis in Germany thought that Aryan blood was a mark of superiority. The interesting fact is not so much the specific rationalizing ideology, but that any at all should seem necessary. Why cannot ruling classes be content simply to rule and to enjoy the fruits of exploitation?

Many social scientists, particularly those who are the product of the Western liberal tradition, reply that if any political system is to endure, it must rest on the consent of the governed, on broad consensus about basic aims. That proposition is both wishful thinking and pious nonsense. Although the amount of consent from the governed that a regime enjoys varies widely, many long-lasting, stable governments, such as those of slave societies or contemporary South Africa or the Russian system both before and after the Revolution, have been naked tyrannies enjoying very little consensus and consent. It is true that widespread terror is an unstable and unwise way to govern, which seldom lasts more than a few years, but steady coercion and exploitation have been the normal rather than the exceptional ways of running a government.

Even regimes that have been more than averagely oppressive, however, have generally sought to rationalize the *status quo,* very often through a theory that the oppressed classes really benefit from their oppression, or more insidiously yet, that the government through "representative" institutions expresses the "will of the people." Some of these social myths seem relatively successful in fooling the masses; other much less so. Both "bourgeois" and "people's" democracies belong to the relatively successful examples of mass mystification in modern times, but, in the past, religious rationalizations have most often been an "opiate for the masses," to use Marx's phrase. (Little did Marx realize that the very success of his brilliant indictment of bourgeois society would make socialism the opiate of the proletariat in the countries where a new oligarchy rules in the name of the working class.)

The consensus theory of society and of government assumes that legitimizing ideologies have to fool nearly all of the people nearly all of the time. They demonstrably do not, but even if they only fool some of the people all of the time, and all of the people some of the time, they serve some purpose for the ruling class. The consensus assumption is quite superfluous.

If a government can successfully ''win the battle for the minds and hearts of the people,'' to use that overworked *cliché*, all the better for it. But the fact is that no government needs to (and probably none ever succeeds anywhere near completely for more than a few months). What is needed for stable government is not active consent, but passive acquiescence; not consensus, but behavioral compliance. Whether a citizen agrees with his government's policies matters far less than his conviction that compliance with the government will entail fewer unpleasant consequences or produce more benefits for him than defiance. The hallmark of most governments is despotism tempered at its best by inefficiency, corruption, and nepotism. The response of the average citizen is to cheat on his taxes as much as he dares, but otherwise to keep his nose clean, so long as he is not either driven to desperation by brutal oppression, or led to optimism by an ineffectual and vacillating government. The wisest tyranny is that which tyrannizes moderately.

Surplus Appropriation

Besides a legitimizing ideology, ruling classes generally share the characteristic of funnelling off surplus production away from the primary producer and for purposes of which he typically does not approve. This is the main source of conflict between rulers and ruled, and it is the main reason why legitimizing ideologies are invented, either to hide that basic fact of government or to try to convince people that it is in their interest to be plucked. Rockets to the moon, we are told, contribute to the progress of science and hence to the welfare of humanity; the bombing of North Vietnam kept the world safe from the Red (or Yellow) Peril; concentration camps purified the Reich of the corrupting influences of World Zionism; the building of pyramids, battleships, royal palaces, or other expensive toys of the ruling class proclaims the greatness of a nation; and so go official fairytales.

Not only do all ruling classes charge "management fees," but, by and large, the more technology has enabled to increase the size of the surplus produced, the more voracious the ruling class has been. In most of the states found in simpler agricultural societies, much of the little surplus that is gathered in labor and taxation is redistributed in the form of feasts or other mass-participation rituals, rather than used to keep the ruling class in opulent leisure. In the more advanced agricultural societies, the economic gap between the rulers and the ruled grows immense. The surplus, instead of being wasted in collective revelry is sunk into costly wars, which are often quarrels between the ruling classes of various states, and the conspicuous consumption of the elite. Shaka, king of the Zulus and conqueror of South-Eastern Africa in the early nineteenth century was a bloodthirsty tyrant, but, aside from the size of his harem, his life style was not appreciably different from that of his subjects. Emperor Shah Jahan, the seventeenth century ruler of India, imported marble from Italy to build the Taj Mahal as a grave for his favorite wife, and, had not his son imprisoned him, he would have had a replica of the Taj in black marble built for himself as well.

In advanced industrial societies this trend has been partly reversed. Productivity has reached such dizzying levels that the standard of living of the average citizen has increased enormously. In the words of an American president, the United States is rich enough to afford both guns and butter, both fragmentation bombs for the peasants of Vietnam and television sets for its ghetto dwellers. At the elite end of the scale, there comes a point where the expenditure of yet more money brings virtually no improvement in one's standard of living. Also, egalitarian ideology makes it seem in bad taste in both capitalist and socialist countries to make a vulgar ostentation of wealth, so that the rich and the powerful indulge in much conspicuous austerity, or, at least, in inconspicuous consumption, such as good and expensive education for their children, art collections, study trips, and the like. The economic gap between the poor and the rich has narrowed to some extent in industrial societies. High productivity and advanced industrial technology have both raised the economic floor of the poor and made the rich the victims of the diminishing returns of money beyond a certain level.

The great "arsenal of democracy" has, for the last quarter century, been much more of an arsenal than a democracy. The United States spends (in both absolute and relative terms) a greater amount of money on "defense" than does almost any other country, East or West. One year of the American defense budget would have kept the Egyptian Pharaohs wallowing in sybaritic luxury for several dynasties. Even the contemporary industrial states remain vast machines for siphoning surplus production from the producer and to benefit the rulers and bureaucrats. In fact, industrial states do so on a scale and with an efficiency far greater than their predecessors. The main difference is that geometric increases in productivity have enabled industrial states to cover the fleeced flock of their citizenry with the blanket of social security.

Monopolization of Violence

Ruling classes, in addition to fleecing their subjects and trying to indoctrinate them, have also invariably attempted to claim a monopoly of the means of violence necessary to coerce them. Stateless societies raise armies for external war, and these citizen armies are usually composed of all able-bodied male adults. States, on the other hand, have more or less professionalized armies used both for external war and for internal repression. More developed states have, in addition, specialized police forces devoted exclusively to internal repression, principally the repression of any violence that does not emanate from the government itself. (This is what police forces call the maintenance of "law and order," a phrase that covers the repression of both criminal violence and political opposition.)

The more developed states also maintain a vast apparatus of institutions designed to confine the movements of those who threaten the established order: prisons, concentration camps, labor camps, reformatories, rehabilitation centers, or whatever euphemistic term is used.

The bigger and the more developed the state is, the more efficient and encompassing the apparatus of coercion and violence. The level of the technology of violence, surveillance, and control seems a better predictor of police methods and practices than the political complexion of the regime. Even the few countries that boast a tradition of *habeas corpus* and police restraints have class-biased and violent police forces. It is true that all police forces are trained not to be wantonly violent, since wanton violence is bad policy. The best professional police force is one that always makes the threat of violence credible enough not to have to use force publicly. Parsimony in the actual use of violence combined with a readiness to resort to it in the face of opposition is the hallmark of an efficient police force.

The size and complexity of a state's police and prison system is a good index of its need to repress counter-violence, which is, in turn, a measure of the failure of the ruling class to indoctrinate the ruled. The existence of a state necessarily creates a conflict of interest between rulers and ruled; and conflict calls forth violence and counterviolence. "Law and order" is, in effect, the result of the ruling class using its superior means of violence to suppress both the criminal and the political violence of those who have an interest in challenging the *status quo*.

It is conventional in "democratic" countries to draw a sharp distinction between criminals and political opponents, and to stigmatize as "dictatorial" or "totalitarian" those states that suppress both. "Democratic" states claim to suppress political opposition only if it is violent; yet even "democratic" states suppress nonviolent political opposition if it constitutes a real threat to the class in power. Thus, strikes are stopped by court injunctions; troops are called in to operate harbors and trains; states of emergency are proclaimed suspending civil liberties; unarmed students protesting foreign wars are shot down by the National Guard; minorities peacefully protesting racial discrimination are savagely beaten by the police; and draft-dodging pacifists are jailed, as are those who refuse to pay what they regard as unjust taxes or to obey unjust laws. Violence, in short, is applied to all those who violate laws, and laws are passed, interpreted, and enforced by the ruling class. No state has ever tolerated political opposition, violent or otherwise, that threatened the interests of the ruling class.

The kind of opposition tolerated in "bourgeois" democracies is that in which two or more sectors of the elite alternate in office after the ritual of elections without changing in any significant way the establishment position of any one of them. The United States is, perhaps, the prototypical example of a political difference that does not make a difference. The Republican and Democratic Parties are really clubs that distribute patronage to different sectors of the ruling class. Parties or groups that do advocate significant changes, such as the Communist Party, have been persecuted despite the fact that their insignificantly small size and appeal never made them a realistic threat. Other bourgeois democracies, such as those of Western European states, have initially had more class polarization in political parties, but, to the extent that previously revolutionary parties have been drawn into the parliamentary game, they have ceased to be revolutionary. Socialist parties became "bourgeois reformist" (much as did the former "right wing" parties caught in the game of populist rhetoric), and developed a new elite of intellectuals and trade union bureaucrats with as much of a stake in the *status quo* as the older elites.

In short, all states, or at least all states that have gone beyond the most rudimentary stages of organization, are basically alike in the following respects: they are run by and for the benefit of their ruling class, which uses its power to extract surplus production from the masses; the ruling class tries to make the masses believe that the system works for the greatest good of the greatest number, but fails at least partially to convince the masses of its benevolence; to the extent that consent is lacking, the ruling class coerces compliance by trying to monopolize the means of organized violence.

Power, Conflict, and Revolution

Tension and conflict between rulers and ruled always exist, in more-or-less acute form, but only under special conditions do they erupt into violent revolution or civil war. Rarely do revolutions succeed. (By revolution here, we mean only the expressions of class conflicts between the rulers and the ruled, which result in fundamental institutional change, and we exclude *coups d'état,* "palace revolutions," and the like, which result only in a change of personnel but not in structure. For the latter type of phenomenon, we shall use the term "rebellion.") Revolutions tend to break out (and occasionally succeed), as the historian Crane Brinton (1957) noted, when several sets of factors coexist: when the government is viewed as oppressive but weak and vacillating; and when economic and social conditions are improving fast enough to convince people that the system can be changed but not fast enough to satisfy them. The latter phenomenon has become known as the "revolution of rising expectations." The former was commented on by Pareto (1963), who stated that an elite that was both rigidly impermeable to the more able elements of the lower classes and squeamish in the use of violence was lost. Both the French and the Russian Revolution, for example, fit that pattern.

Revolutions also happen when oppression is so thorough that people are driven to despair. Put in a situation where they feel that they have little to lose, people will rise at the risk of their life. Such explosions are more common than the conventional treatment of revolution recognizes, and the reason why such revolutions are deemed to be rare is that they almost invariably fail, and thus are called "uprisings" or "revolts" rather than revolutions. Peasant and slave revolutions have mostly been "revolutions of despair," rather than "revolutions of hope," and they have almost invariably been crushed. Uprisings of the "death commandoes" in Nazi concentration camps are another example of this kind of desparate action in the face of overwhelming odds.

Under the best of circumstances, the odds against the success of a revolution are long, unless the revolting group has access to or itself constitutes the means of organized violence. The formula for successful revolution should be: do not start one unless you can count on the support of at least some of the army. The more oppressed and disinherited a group is, the lower its probability of success, despite numerical superiority. Slaves and peasants are the great losers of history. For example, of the hundreds of slave revolts in the United States, Brazil, the West Indies, and other parts of the Western Hemisphere, only one succeeded, that which made Haiti independent. The ruling class of any state is invariably much better organized for violence than the oppressed, and the more advanced the technology, the truer this is. Revolution in advanced industrial societies like the Soviet Union, Japan, Germany, Britain, or the United States has been rendered obsolete by the technology of transportation, communication, information sorting, and violence. The expense of the technology and the expertise needed to run it put it beyond the reach of the oppressed.

The only revolutions at all likely to succeed in the contemporary world are "wars of national liberation," and even they are succeeding principally in the most technologically backward parts of the world; namely, in Africa and Asia where the poverty of the countries involved and the cost of crushing the movements undercut the profitability of classical political imperialism. Where the vital interests of industrial states are at stake, wars of national liberation are crushed easily enough, as shown by the Hungarian and Czech experience in the Soviet bloc, the Basque movement in Spain, and many others.

Even in Africa and Asia, the spectacular demise of European colonialism after World War II should not be interpreted as evidence for the inevitable success of "wars of national liberation." Apart from the fact that the war itself had badly shaken and weakened the colonial powers, "decolonization" was, in good part, a nonviolent process and the result of a conscious decision of the ruling class of the colonial countries. They correctly saw that the economic and political future of Europe was in Europe itself, and that it would be foolish to fight costly colonial wars, especially when economic neo-colonialism was such a cheaper alternative to obsolete political colonialism. In India and nearly all of Africa (except Algeria), "independence" was achieved peacefully.

Where colonial powers decided to fight it out, they clearly won in two cases (the British in Malaysia and Kenya), and they clearly lost in two other cases (the French in Indochina and Algeria). Of the latter two instances, however, only Indochina can be pronounced a clear military victory for the nationalist movement. In Algeria, the outcome was a military stalemate, much like the second Indochina war fought by the United States as the neo-colonial successor state to France. DeGaulle's political settlement of the Algerian war was a belated recognition that the economic interests of France were not linked with political domination, rather than an admission of military defeat. Perhaps the best proof that a colonial power obstinate and stupid enough to fight colonial wars can bring matters to an indefinite stalemate is Portugal. Portugal, the poorest, weakest, and most archaic and corrupt of the European colonial countries fought three colonial wars to a stalemate (Guinea, Angola, Mozambique) for more than a decade. True, Portugal lost swiftly against India in Goa, but that was an international war against a regular army, not a war of national liberation. The disengagement of Portugal from her "overseas provinces" came more from the political changes brought about by the 1974 military coup in Portugal than from military defeat in Africa.

THE IRON LAW OF OLIGARCHY

Another feature common to nearly all states is that their ruling classes are minorities, and indeed often very small minorities. This phenomenon was called the "iron law of oligarchy" by Michels (1949). Part of the reason for this phenomenon is economic: few societies can produce enough surplus to maintain more than a small proportion of its population in luxury and, hence, any ruling class has an interest in restricting access to it, so as not to have to spread the fat of the land too thinly. However, economics alone do not explain everything, for the iron law of oligarchy operates even in the affluent bourgeois societies that produce so much as to be able to spread the surplus to broad strata of the population, and in the Communist societies whose ruling class maintains (or affects) an austere standard of living.

Ideology, obviously, makes very little difference. The most unashamedly despotic societies are as oligarchical as the self-styled democracies. Nor is there much to choose between the Western "bourgeois democracies" and the Eastern "people's democracies." The latter accuse the former of empty parliamentary formalism and the former call the latter totalitarian. In both cases, the term "democracy" is a clear misnomer: both systems are dominated by the will of a few thousand top-level bureaucrats, officers, industrial and financial managers, politicians, and technicians—not by the will of the people. The people are a vehicle for the propagation of ideology and a conveyor belt for the transmission of orders from the top. Democracy is a legitimizing myth, equally so under capitalism and socialism. It is the political opium of the twentieth century.

If economics accounts for only part of the iron law of oligarchy, and ideology for scarcely anything at all, what then is the root cause of the phenomenon? The answer lies in the nature of power and organization. First, the coordination of complex activities, and especially of interdependent activities, can most efficiently be achieved if power is unequivocally vested in a single line of authority. Second, the exercise of power generates yet more power; as with money, power produces monopoly. The powerful tend to become more powerful and fewer and fewer. Organizationally, then, the centrally organized state has a competitive advantage over the loose confederation, and the pyramidal power structure holds an edge over collegial or collective modes of decision making. It is no coincidence that, in the absence of a highly centralized civilian government, the military can so easily accede to power; nor that once the military have captured the machinery of the state, they can typically be dislodged only by losing a war to a foreign armed force, or by internal dissidence within the military.

The only effective rival to the military is a civilian bureaucratic state that is itself highly centralized, and in which the military and police are simply the specialized and centralized organs for the dispensation of violence. Indeed, it is doubtful that any modern bureaucratic state can be overthrown except through external defeat. No Communist regime has ever been overthrown; the Fascist and Nazi regimes were destroyed by external armed forces; and the bourgeois industrial bureaucracies have an equally good longevity record. All share, despite ideologies of mass participation and popular mandate, highly centralized and pyramidal power structures.

KNOWLEDGE AND POWER

Besides controlling the means of organized violence, ruling groups, especially in complex industrial societies, also control the flow of information. There is nothing new in the notion that knowledge is power, but the larger and the more complex a state becomes, the more strategic location in bureaucratic hierarchies gives one an advantage in gathering intelligence and in making use of it. That is one of the main reasons why, once a bureaucracy is established, its power tends to grow steadily. In a bureaucratic organization, the lines of communication and, hence, the flow of information are vertical, and the administered are in an atomized state of "pluralistic ignorance." I may know a bit more about the state of my own finances, for example, than I care to tell the Bureau of Internal Revenue, but the Bureau knows immensely more about the finances of 200 million people than anyone outside the Bureau can ever hope to learn. (The only contenders are credit-rating agencies, but they are far inferior because they lack the vast apparatus of coercion and sources of revenue of the Federal government.)

Not only is the flow of information in bureaucracies vertical (with a minimum of horizontal communication), but it is overwhelmingly upward. All bureaucracies are secretive; that is, they collect intelligence, both overtly and covertly. Once the intelligence is collected, they "classify" it as secret, supposedly in the interest of "national security." That is, all bureaucracies maintain and increase their power by centralizing not only power but also information. A bureaucracy, then, is a vertical organization in which orders flow downward and information upward. These two opposite flows feed on each other to

make the discrepancy in power between administrator and administered ever greater.

Bureaucracies of modern states almost invariably tend to become
ever more complex, powerful, self-serving, and secretive. This trend
is heavily dependent on the ability of modern states to collect and
retrieve information efficiently and rapidly, and to keep the public
from access to that information. That is why in complex industrial
societies, intelligence-gathering agencies increase exponentially.
Even the most intricate spy system in an agrarian society is childishly
simple compared to the maze of investigatory agencies (both public
and private) which mushroom in modern industrial societies. Furthermore, as is well known, intelligence agencies being themselves
bureaucratically organized, show a propensity practically equal to the
military to become autonomously powerful, to the point of threatening
their own hierarchical superiors outside the agency. This propensity is
countered by the supreme power creating mutually competitive intelligence agencies in the hope that they will use their power to contain
each other rather than to control the state.

The history of the cancerous growth of the FBI, the CIA, the
competing military intelligence agencies, and the investigatory
branches of the innumerable federal agencies (such as the Customs
and the Internal Revenue,) is a case in point. These agencies theoretically have limited and minimally overlapping jurisdictions, but, as
everyone knows, the FBI, an allegedly internal secret police, needs
little excuse to operate in Mexico; and the CIA, a supposedly international spy ring, is also a vast domestic operation. Nor is the American
case unique. Capitalist states like the United States and Japan rely
somewhat more on private enterprise (private detective agencies,
credit rating agencies, and industrial espionage) than socialist countries, but, in all, secret information-gathering is centrally organized
and enormously enhanced by modern computer technology.

A corollary of this state of affairs is that knowledge, including
science and technology, is not neutral. It is almost invariably biased on
the side of the powerful. The more knowledge exists, the more it will

concentrate in the hands of the powerful. In that sense, the scientific establishment, including the universities, research institutes, and even "independent" professionals, is almost inevitably ancillary to the ruling class. Although knowledge can be used against the powerful too, in practice, the capability of the citizenry to use knowledge against the government is extremely limited compared to the governmental capacity to use it against the people. It follows that the recent explosion in information retrieval technology has enormously increased the potential for truly totalitarian government. Given past trends, it would be naively optimistic to expect that the powerful, out of the kindness of their hearts, will not make use of that potential, legally or illegally. Modern states all engage in intelligence-gathering by means that are criminal in terms of their own definition of crime.

POWER AND TECHNOLOGY

States also differ a great deal from each other. Two of the most important sets of differences have to do with the level of technological development, and with the degree of ethnic pluralism of a state. The link between forms of government and technology has been extensively studied by Lenski (1966, 1970), Marsh (1967), Andreski (1964, 1968), and others. The emergence of the state, as we have seen, largely coincides with the development of agriculture. With agriculture, people stay put, which makes their governance much easier, and they begin to produce a surplus, which makes their governance worthwhile.

The most common type of rudimentary state, as exemplified by many African kingdoms, ancient Greek states, early Rome and others, is a conglomeration of unilineal descent groups united for purposes of defense, ritual life, and public works. Government is often, though not always, monarchical, and the constituent descent groups are usually represented by senior male members. This might be termed the "king-in-council" type of government: the monarch, typically a *primus inter pares*, rules with the advice and consent of a council of elders who represent the various lineage groups.

Power is restricted by custom, but the person of the king often assumes quasi-divine status and is surrounded by elaborate taboos (Frazer, 1890). Most of these states do not have currencies, hence taxation is typically in the form of labor for public works or agricultural produce stored in public granaries, partly to support the king's court, but also for ritual distribution at feasts or as insurance against need. The king's court may include thousands of retainers, servants, slaves, and courtiers, and there may be hundreds of title holders, but relatively few of these offices require specialized technical competence. Bureaucracy is at most embryonic. Such states sometimes have the beginnings of a professional army in the form of a king's bodyguard (often made up of low-status slaves or mercenaries), and when they do, this typically leads to a much more despotic form of government than in those states that rely on citizen levies.

Many of these elementary states have some form of domestic slavery, as well as elaborate status differences between their free citizens, but despite great status differences, power is frequently decentralized for a variety of reasons. Though the king's power may be theoretically absolute, it is usually circumscribed by the customary power of his vassals, by traditions or local autonomy, and by the limitations of his technical resources to impose his will. Because of poor and slow communications, a rudimentary accumulation of surplus (often in the form of perishable agricultural produce), and a small and lowly professionalized army equipped with simple weapons, the scope of control of the central government is often effectively limited.

The advent of more intensive and advanced forms of agriculture marked a drastic change in the organization of states. The "great civilizations" have often been characterized by highly centralized and despotic forms of government with a number of interrelated similarities in the economic and political spheres. Improved agricultural technology and production increase the size of the surplus that can be extracted from the peasants and they make commerce and handicraft production possible on a far larger scale. Sharply rising production facilitates a far more complex and efficient state apparatus, which can, in turn, be used to increase production further. Indeed, part of the new agricultural technology, especially terracing and irrigation, requires large-scale political supervision.

Allowing for substantial differences between the "great civilizations" of the Old and the New World, complex agricultural states are characterized by most of the following traits: irrigation; manuring and terracing; use of wind and water energy; use of pack or draught animals; urbanization; long-distance commerce and markets (and frequently the use of money); extensive handicraft specialization including an advanced metallurgy; and extensive transport and storage facilities. In terms of state organization, these technological innovations both require and facilitate several new developments, the most notable of which are true bureaucracies, that is, full-time specialists in administration with some technical expertise, sizeable professional armies with specialized training and weaponry, and large systems of public works involving the construction and maintenance of terraces, irrigation canals, roads, harbors, mines, palaces, tombs, and a variety of other projects aimed at increasing production or consuming the surplus for the benefit of the ruling class.

Government becomes increasingly divorced from kinship organization, and increasingly specialized, complex, powerful, and encompassing. Slavery grows from a small-scale domestic institution into a large-scale state enterprise to man the mines and galleys, build the roads and pyramids, and so on. Where slavery is not sufficient to maintain the public work system, corvée labor is organized. Tax collection, instead of being a customary system of tribute paying, becomes systematized and is entrusted to specialized bureaucrats who develop the art of squeezing the peasant just short of killing him. Tax collection becomes a cornerstone of statecraft.

The means of violence, by becoming increasingly based on trained expertise, specialized weaponry, and complex organization, are increasingly beyond the reach of the ordinary citizen. Armies now have regular officers and trained men, often social outcasts who are not squeamish about killing civilians. A mixture of intrigue, sycophancy, bribery, loyalty, and expertise determines access to positions of power, rather than customary criteria of seniority and kinship.

Not only is the efficiency of government greatly increased, but so is its scope. In more rudimentary states, most of the daily activities of ordinary citizens are a matter of indifference to the state, provided that the citizens fulfill a few basic obligations and do not violate the laws. In a more complex state, the government attempts to control a much wider range of activities, especially in the economic sphere. The peasant is told what to plant, the merchant what prices to charge, the artisan what metal alloys to use. Even in seemingly trivial matters, people's behavior is controlled by prohibitions and injunctions. For example, sumptuary regulations dictate what members of various status groups must wear by way of clothing and jewelry. Some states have even attempted to control the domestic behavior of their citizens, such as age of marriage, birthrate, and sexual behavior, but most ruling classes have been content with securing preferential access to their nubile female subjects.

Industrial Societies: From Coercion to Manipulation

It should be noted, however, that the scope of control possible in advanced agricultural societies is far from absolute. Genuine totalitarianism becomes a realistic possibility only in industrial societies. Even the best spy system is a poor substitute for computerized information retrieval systems, for bugged telephones, for lie detectors, for subliminal television messages, for programmed indoctrination, for market research, and for the infinity of control techniques at the disposal of the industrial state. In the past, most despotic governments have had the saving grace of relative inefficiency. Modern industrial technology, generally hailed as the great emancipator from the drudgery of physical labor and the scourge of epidemics, is also a frightening leap backward in human freedom. Indeed, the sophistication of the modern technology of control, by enabling the state to control not only action but also thought, has drastically affected the basis of control of modern states. Modern states continue to rely on violence as the ultimate mechanism to insure compliance, but there has been a dramatic shift toward techniques of manipulation in order to achieve control. Heretics are sent to insane asylums instead of being poisoned or burned at the stake. Student radicals are co-opted into the bureaucracy, instead of being sent to Siberia.

It is interesting to note that, despite slight differences in techniques, the advanced Communist and capitalist countries are remarkably similar in their increasing shift from naked coercion to covert manipulation. Modern regimes no longer liquidate their opponents; they co-opt them. They no longer hang their criminals, they rehabilitate them. They no longer excommunicate their heretics, they reeducate them. They have enough carrots at their disposal to enable them to spare the stick. In the United States, for example, blacks are no longer lynched; they are sent to "job opportunity programs." Radical intellectuals are no longer witch-hunted by Un-American Activities Committees; they are appointed directors of ethnic studies programs or administrators of the war on poverty. In the Soviet Union, too, Party sinecures and insane asylums have largely replaced the Stalinist labor camps and the NKVD torture cells.

In the affluent industrial societies, the consequences of compliance can almost always be made far more attractive than the remotely possible rewards of defiance. It makes sense for the starved peasant to revolt, even against staggering odds, but it makes very little sense for the university professor to do so, especially when ritualized criticism in the classroom has been defined as part of his professional role. Indeed, modern states have become so sophisticated in their manipulation of dissidence that they have institutionalized and ritualized the role of the rebel. Thousands of intellectuals are being paid to dissent, to be devil's advocate or maverick in universities or research institutes, in the expectation that their creative criticism will enable the government to improve their manipulative programs. Police officers invite young radicals to "rap sessions"; Jesuits read Mao Tse Tung; Red Chinese officials analyze the *Wall Street Journal*. The American government finances the Rand Corporation to study Soviet ideology, and the Soviet Union supports Institutes of American Studies. They all seek control through understanding, and, for the first time, they begin to respect the social sciences as capable of making a contribution to their technology of manipulation. Technology certainly accounts for far more differences between states than ideology. Ideology largely affects the style of government, not its actual form.

Ethnic Pluralism:
The Problems of Imperialism

Another important way in which states differ is in their degree of ethnic homogeneity. A multiethnic empire raises different and more complicated problems of control than a homogeneous nation-state. This is not to say that nation-states are free of class and other conflicts; but a common language and culture are frequent bases of political solidarity in a state. Once nationalist feelings are aroused in a multiethnic empire, the state faces problems of survival not found in more homogeneous states. Since ethnically pluralistic societies are typically ruled by one ethnic group at the expense of the others, the government is viewed as alien, and its problems of legitimacy are compounded. Since at least 90 percent of the world's states are not nations, but multiethnic conglomerates, the problem of ethnic dissidence is extremely widespread.

Nationalism, as history has repeatedly shown, may have a great deal of grass-root appeal, but it is, like most political movements, led by an elite. Nationalist leadership is typically composed of the would-be ruling class of the subordinate ethnic group, were it to achieve political independence. The fundamental problem of maintaining the unity of the plural society thus consists in reaching a *modus vivendi* between the ruling ethnic elite of the empire and the subordinate ethnic elites of its constituent ethnic groups. A range of solutions presents itself. At one extreme the ruling elite may try to wipe out the conquered elites physically, to decapitate the social pyramid of the vanquished people, as the Spaniards did in their American colonies, or as the West Pakistani tried to do with the Bengali more recently. This "final solution" is not likely to be successful, because the conquered ethnic groups still have to be governed and can most effectively be administered through officials of their own ethnic group. Thus, in most cases, a new subordinate elite has to be created for purposes of administrative convenience, and this new subordinate elite is a likely source of nationalist leaders.

At the other end of the spectrum of solutions is what the British have called the "indirect rule" system. Essentially, this consists in utilizing the conquered ruling class as agents of colonial administration on behalf of the conquerors. The conquered elite is stripped of any ultimate power, but retained in its privileged status, *vis à vis* the mass of their fellow ethnics. Native customs and institutions are left undisturbed, and the various ethnic groups are given a broad measure of local self-government, so long as the interests of the dominant ethnic group are not threatened. The British, for example, did not interfere with the caste system in India, and ruled most of their vast empire through a system of native maharajas, emirs, and chieftains, all duly under the final authority of British governors and the Colonial Office.

The advantages of indirect rule are obvious enough for the system to have been independently invented and applied in a great many empires. Indirect rule is a cheap and convenient way to rule conquered territories since, except for the superimposition of a new supreme ruling class, it freezes the *status quo* and does not entail the creation of any new governing apparatus. By turning the conquered elite into colonial puppets, indirect rule also has the multiple advantages of depriving the foreign subjects of potential national leaders; of assuring, if not the loyalty, at least the compliance of the conquered elites by protecting their economic and social privileges; and of accentuating class divisions among the conquered who often come to see their own privileged stratum as their exploiters rather than their ultimate colonial masters. The conquered elite thus find themselves in the position of go-between between their own subjects and their colonial overlords. Their position is extremely vulnerable—if they are not pliable enough they are summarily replaced, if they are too pliable they are detested by their subjects. This vulnerability and expendability makes them the reliable tools of the colonial regime, in exchange for which they are allowed to retain some of their class privileges.

A third solution to the ruling of plural societies is to absorb, assimilate, and co-opt the conquered ruling classes into the conquering one. This may be done either on a wholesale or on a selective basis. Sometimes conquerors attempt the cultural assimilation of the entire conquered ethnic group, a policy that has recently been called "ethnocide." The policy of "Russification" under the Czars was an example of such an attempt, albeit a largely unsuccessful one. Alternatively, assimilation may be a reward selectively granted to a tiny minority of the colonial subjects, as the Portuguese have practiced in their African colonies (or "overseas provinces" to use the Portuguese euphemism). Wholesale cultural assimilation is, in effect, an attempt to depluralize the empire and to create a new larger nation-state. Selective assimilation of the conquered elite, while retaining the pluralism at the base of the social pyramid, creates a homogeneous elite drawn from several ethnic groups, so that the potential leaders of nationalist movements define their interests in class rather than in ethnic terms. The Hapsburg and the French colonial empires are examples of policies of selective co-optation and assimilation of conquered elites, but, in both cases, the process was too selective to prevent the disintegration of the multiethnic conglomerate.

Whatever the policies of the colonial power, the secret of longevity of multiethnic empires is to prevent the rise of elites that see their interest more in ethnic than in class terms. Such potential nationalist leaders must either be wiped out or be sufficiently rewarded and co-opted to identify with their fellow class exploiters from the dominant ethnic group, rather than with their fellow ethnics against the colonial ruling class. The great error of colonial ruling classes is that they fail to realize that co-optation of the subordinate native elites, if done at a sufficient pace and on a sufficient scale, is very likely to succeed. Their downfall is often due to their failure to assimilate nationalist elites in time, and their tendency become a rigid caste proclaiming their racial or cultural superiority. In the successful management of the conflicting loyalties of class and ethnicity lies the art of statecraft in plural societies, a problem which the ruling class of nation-states does not have to face.

On the technological dimension, the general evolutionary trend toward larger, more complex, and more centralized states exercising ever-widening control over their citizens is clear. On the ethnic dimension, the trend is not as uniform. There have been several great cycles of formation and disintegration of large and multiethnic empires. The last four-and-a-half centuries of Western history alone have seen the rise and fall of the European empires in the Americas, of the Asian and African "second" empires of the same European states, and of the Hapsburg and Ottoman Empires in Central Europe and the Near East. The only vast colonial empire that survived two world wars and a revolution is the Russian one. A characteristic of multiethnic empires is that their disintegration is often as meteoric as their formation. Just when nationalism appears to be *passé*, it resurges with sweeping passion. The general rule about political behavior is that while people usually resent being told what to do, they resent it even more if they are being ruled by foreigners.

In the last two chapters, we have examined how man elaborated culturally in his biological propensities to aggression, hierarchy, and territoriality to create dominance-ordered hierarchies and political systems of extraordinary complexity. In Chapter Two, we suggested that aggression was the product of resource competition, mediated through territoriality and hierarchy. Let us now return to the problem of the distribution of material resources.

ADDITIONAL READING

The sociological literature on politics overlaps in good part with that on social stratification. In addition to the titles listed at the end of the previous chapter, Weber (1968) and Simmel (1950) stand out among the older writers. Eisenstadt's reader (1971) contains many excerpts from the timeless classics. Wittfogel's *Oriental Despotism* (1957) and Coulborn's anthology (1956) deal with complex agrarian societies. The great comparative work by Moore (1967) and Brinton's classic on revolution (1957) are well worth reading. In the last quarter-century, political anthropology has developed quite fast. One of the earlier works in that tradition is the collection edited by Fortes and Evans-Pritchard (1940). The Wallerstein anthology (1966) and Worsley's book (1970) are good on colonial societies. Orwell's brilliant fable, *Animal Farm* (1946), and his gloomy version of the future *1984* (1949) stand out, together with Huxley (1932), Marcuse (1966), and Ortega y Gasset (1932), as some of the most thoughtful indictments of modern industrial societies produced by contemporary writers.

7

Economics: Forms of Exploitation

Conventional economics define economic activity as that which has to do with the production of goods, and services. Such a definition, however, is deceptively simple, for the distinction between economic and noneconomic behavior is often far from clear-cut. In money economies with which economists usually deal, the criterion of what constitutes an economic activity is usually whether the good or service has a "market value." Thus, when a prostitute has sexual relations with a client, she contributes to the Gross National Product and she is earning income. On the other hand, when the housewife engages in the same activity with her husband or her lover, she is not earning income. She may have received a box of chocolates from her partner, but the chocolates are not wages, and the activity is not economic. Similarly, when Winston Churchill or Dwight Eisenhower painted a landscape, they were not engaging in an economic activity, but when Pierre Renoir or Pablo Picasso painted, their activity was indeed economic.

Even in money economies, however, payment for goods or services does not necessarily have to be in money for the behavior to be called economic. Thus, if I give a student a rent-free room in exchange for an hour of household work a day, I have entered an economic contract with that student. If my son, who also lives in my house, helps me in the garden or empties the garbage, this is not an economic relationship. In the first case, there is an explicit exchange of goods and services according to a mutually agreed rate, and one side of the exchange is contingent on the other. In the second case, all these conditions are lacking.

To call an activity economic is not to say that it is purely economic. The prostitute may satisfy masochistic urges or support a heroin habit as well as earn money. Or, I may rent a room to a student because I like him and want to do him a favor. Conversely, to say that an activity is noneconomic is not to say that it does not have certain economic aspects. The housewife's intercourse with her husband is presumably not contingent on her receiving a box of chocolates, and, hence, her behavior is not economic, but the acquisition of the chocolates by the husband obviously involved an economic transaction. Likewise, when Winston Churchill painted a landscape, he did not intend to sell it (so far as we know); yet he is now in no position to prevent his heirs from cashing in on the market value that his paintings have acquired by virtue of his fame, if not his talent.

In these examples drawn from Western societies, there is not much ambiguity in designating an activity as economic or noneconomic. That is so because in money economies, and especially in industrialized money economies, the distinction between what is economic and what is not is relatively sharply drawn. In most societies, this is not the case. Let us take the example of the institution of bridewealth found in a great many societies of Africa and elsewhere. In many societies, no marriage is considered legal until a certain quantity of goods set by custom (often livestock, metal objects, or some such standardized, nonperishable item of capital wealth) has been transferred from the lineage of the groom to that of the bride. Western missionaries and others have interpreted this institution as a commercial transaction in which women are degradingly traded against cows, sheep, or whatever. This ethnocentric interpretation is derived from a Western conception of chattel slavery.

It is true that the institution of the bridewealth involves the exchange of one valuable consideration against another, and thus has an economic aspect. But it is much more than an economic institution. The economic consideration, while important, is a warranty for a legal contract ensuring the legitimacy of the marriage and the offspring. Without bridewealth payment, the children are illegitimate, and may not inherit or even claim membership in the lineage of their father in a patrilineal system. If anything can be said to be "purchased" it is much more the right to claim jural authority over the future offspring of the bride, than the sexual and other services of the woman. Provisions for the partial or complete return of the bridewealth in cases of divorce or barrenness clearly indicate that the bridewealth is above all a legal warranty. Yet, it would be absurd to deny the economic aspects of bridewealth. For example, payment of bridewealth is one of the factors that allow rich men to be more polygynous than poor ones.

Another example of a form of behavior that involves both economic and noneconomic factors is the potlatch of the natives of the Northwest coast of North America. The potlatch was essentially a competitive display of wealth for prestige. Rivals would invite each other to lavish feasts at which great quantities of food, blankets, copper plates, boats, and other valuable items would be consumed, displayed, and wantonly destroyed. The invited rival had to reciprocate the feast on an even grander scale, or be declared the loser in this frantic prestige game. Like the many instances of conspicuous consumption for prestige purposes in Western societies (e.g., the competitive building of battleships or moon rockets between states), the potlatch has no economic rationality. While the motivation for the institution is not economic, conspicuous consumption on such an enormous scale had, of course, important economic consequences.

There are, thus, many activities which, though fraught with economic consequences, are not primarily economic in intent. It is therefore useful to distinguish between a broad category of *economic activities,* and a much narrower concept of *economic behavior.* An economic activity is any pursuit which contributes to the material subsistence of an individual or group. The hunter stalking an antelope or the peasant plowing a field engages in an economic activity.

Economic behavior, on the other hand, involves additional and
specific elements, namely, an exchange of goods or services according to a rational calculus of gain or loss. All societies obviously engage
in a great deal of economic activity, but economic behavior is characteristic only of the more differentiated societies. The range of behavior
that is purportedly economic tends to increase at the expense of other
forms of behavior as a society becomes more complex and differentiated.

The Four Economic Sectors

A common distinction related to that between economic behavior and
activities, is that made between a *subsistence* and a *market* economy,
or between the subsistence and the market sector of a mixed economy.
Economic behavior, as we have just defined it, is largely restricted to
the market economy, but economic activities are found in both types
of economy. There are very few (if any) economies left today that are
based purely on subsistence. Even the simplest hunting-and-gathering
economies have increasingly felt the encroachments of the market:
they barter goods with agriculturalists, or even have to work temporarily for them in order to obtain such valuables as metal objects which
they themselves do not produce. Pure market economies are equally
rare. Only the most advanced industrial societies approximate pure
market economies, but even in industrial countries some food fad-
dists, gardening enthusiasts, and other harmless eccentrics insist on
growing their own vegetables or raising their own chickens. Most
economies, then, have both a subsistence and a market sector, with a
tendency for the latter to expand at the expense of the former as the
economy becomes more complex, and especially as it becomes industrialized.

    This simple dichotomy between market and subsistence economy
does not cover the entire range of what we have called economic
activities. Long ago, Veblen (1899) stressed the importance of conspicuous leisure, conspicuous consumption, and conspicuous waste in
the achievement of prestige. We may thus speak of a *prestige* or

ceremonial economy which has little relationship to either subsistence or the market. The gains to be derived from these economic activities are psychic rather than material, yet the sometimes extravagant scope that they take can have far-reaching economic implications. Whole industries, for example, can develop around the production of goods to be consumed on ceremonial occasions, such as firecrackers on the Fourth of July. The example of the potlatch also falls under this category of prestige or ceremonial economy, as would the economic activities surrounding entertainment of guests, religious festivals, and rites of passage, such as weddings and funerals.

Finally, one should add a fourth economy, which might be called the taxation, or the *surplus-siphoning*, economy. In all politically centralized societies, the primary producers (in the first instance, the peasants) not only consume, sell, or spend what they produce; they also get a substantial share of it taken away by those in power. The product of taxation is used largely to support the luxurious style of the ruling class, to build and maintain public works, and to wage war.

Looking at these four economic sectors jointly, it is clear that all societies, even the technologically simplest ones, have at least an economy of subsistence and an economy of prestige. Even the smallest scale and technologically simplest societies have ritual celebrations in which food and other goods are ceremoniously and communally consumed and exchanged for reasons other than material sustenance (Mauss, 1954). Communion rituals, such as still exist in the contemporary religions of industrial societies, are nearly universal. There is hardly any society in which the ingestion of food is not to some extent ritualized, surrounded with taboos, and laden with religion and social significance; and yet food consumption is also the most fundamental and indispensable form of economic activity in which any society can engage.

In societies where the level of technology allows the accumulation of some surplus, the prestige economy can assume vast proportions, and can indeed serve as an economic leveler. The potlatch of the Northwest American Pacific Coast is a textbook example of how maintenance of a prestigious rank often involved economic ruin. There are many such examples, however, where the acquisition of prestige involves such heavy ritual expenditures as to prevent the accumulation of capital for any strictly economic ventures. This is the case in many Indian groups of Mexico, Guatemala, Peru, and Bolivia where, to gain prestige, a man must pass through a series of politicoreligious offices (*cargos*), each one of which entails a heavy economic burden to pay for food, drink, music, fireworks, and donations to the church during elaborate fiestas which often last for the better part of a week (Cancian, 1965; Colby and van den Berghe, 1969). Such groups typically have strong norms against the accumulation of wealth, and exert strong pressures for people to accept these *cargos*. Obviously, these lavish fiestas are wasteful in terms of economic rationality, and they hinder economic development, much to the chagrin of "progressive" technicians, politicians, and social scientists. However, the prestige economy is also a powerful economic leveler and hinders the growth of social stratification based on wealth.

In many African societies too, the prestige economy serves as a mechanism of redistribution of wealth; though in a rather different form. In much of Africa, even in the highly centralized societies, the assumption of power traditionally involved the obligation of hospitality and generosity according to one's means. Prestige was acquired not through the accumulation of wealth, but rather through its distribution in the form of largesse to wide groups of kinsmen, clients, and other dependents. A man's power and prestige were measured by the size of his clientele and the openness of his hospitality. Wealth was thus used not to create more wealth as in a capitalist system, but to consolidate power by creating obligations and by binding people to a dependent relationship.

As societies become larger, more complex, more politically centralized, and more stratified, the taxation economy assumes a growing importance. A larger proportion of the surplus is appropriated by the ruling class to support it in luxury and to maintain the machinery of violence (army and police) necessary to its survival. The sector of the economy based on the expenditures of the ruling class and financed by taxation (in produce, labor, or currency) becomes increasingly autonomous of the subsistence and prestige sectors, and grows much faster than the other two. This trend continues all the way to the most advanced industrial societies. The subsistence sector (except for the housewives' unpaid services, which are still not considered gainful employment) has become totally negligible in the United States and in other highly industrialized societies. Not only has the number of farmers declined to around one-tenth of the population or even less, but they generally produce for the market and buy their lettuce, apples, and eggs at the supermarket. As for the prestige economy, it does not entirely disappear. We still throw lavish parties, weddings, funerals, and other communal rituals, and we ritually exchange gifts and cards at Christmas, anniversaries, and similar occasions. But the vast majority of the people have far more taken away by taxation than they spend on entertainment and donations. Even much of the prestige economy is taken over by the state or by the business corporations. If one's position calls for lavish entertainment, the tab is picked up by the "expense account," or even a special entertainment allowance, as a distinct part of the perquisites of office.

The market economy only begins to rise to prominence in the more complex agrarian societies, and even there, the early forms of long-distance trade, mining, large-scale artisanal production, and market-place transactions are typically subservient to, and closely controlled by, the state (Polanyi, 1957; Bohannan and Dalton, 1962). Only with the general use of money, can a true market economy be said to exist. By general use of money, I mean that most goods and services are convertible in money, and that money becomes a truly generalized means of exchange. Generalized money is quite different from the special purpose currencies found in many relatively undifferentiated societies. A cow, for instance, if it can only be used for purposes of ritual sacrifice and bridewealth payment, is not generalized money. It can only become so if it can also be exchanged for labor, land, guns, or whatever. Market economies typically appear in the complex agrarian societies, and continue to grow at the expense of the subsistence and prestige economies in industrial societies. This is so much the case that modern economists concerned with industrial societies can afford to take only the taxation and the market economies into account, and to call these two sectors "the economy."

It is the hallmark of highly complex economies that "everything becomes commercialized" and that "money becomes the measure of all things." Western societies represent extreme examples of this trend, but non-Western societies, such as Japan, undergo a similar evolution as their economies become more differentiated. There is nothing intrinsically Western about economic behavior. Any society becomes "commercialized" as its economy develops. Many forms of behavior that are clearly noneconomic in simple societies become economic in complex agrarian or industrial societies. Hospitality and conviviality, for example, are universal phenomena; but only in more economically advanced societies are they commercialized in the form of hotels and restaurants. The celebration of religious festivals is also universal, but it takes a highly industrialized society to reach the degree of commercialization that Christmas has attained in the United States, and increasingly, in Europe.

The old cliché about prostitution being the world's oldest profession is, in fact, wrong. (The priesthood is without question the oldest specialized activity, not prostitution.) The commercialization of sex is a relatively late development that coincides roughly with the rise of agrarian and urban civilization. Entertainment in the form of music and dance became commercialized at roughly the same time as sex, the higher class courtesan being often an accomplished musician and entertainer as well, much as our modern cinema starlets. It takes an extremely complex society, however, to commercialize sheer human company (without sex) as examplified by the "escort services" provided by enterprising business firms in the United States. The saccharine smile of the airline stewardess offering fake hospitality in the pseudointimacy of a jumbo airliner is probably the ultimate step in the transformation of a human relationship into a calculated economic transaction: "We sincerely hope that you have enjoyed your flight and look forward to serving you again on your next trip." (Loosely translated this means: "Thank Boeing this flight is over. My feet are sore and you bums give me a pain.")

Exchange and Rationality

Two essential elements of economic behavior are *exchange* and *rationality*. The generality of exchange in social life was discussed in detail by Marcel Mauss (1954), who said that gifts and other forms of exchange were based on three interrelated obligations: to give, to receive, and to reciprocate. Many forms of exchange are highly ceremonial and ritualized, and cannot be described as economic behavior. Thus, exchanges of women between kin groups, or the gift-giving obligations between members of an American family at Christmas, or the giving of chocolates or flowers to the hostess at a dinner party cannot be meaningfully described as economic transactions.

Only when one of the determining conditions of whether an exchange is entered into or not is a deliberate calculation of the relative value of the goods and services involved, can one properly speak of an economic transaction. It is this calculus of gain in the exchange of goods and services that I shall call "rationality." This is not to say, however, that only economic considerations enter into an economic transaction. Indeed, *pure* economic behavior is the exception rather than the rule. Almost invariably, transactions that are in part economic also involve other motivations. Thus, whether I buy from A instead of B may be dictated by many nonrational considerations, such as A's ethnicity, religion, character, and physical appearance, as well as by such rational factors as price, service, and location. Yet my behavior continues to be economic so long as the nonrational factors do not significantly override the rational ones. Presumably, my liking of A is not so strong that I would buy from him at any price. If it were, then my "buying" from him would fall in some noneconomic category of behavior such as ritual exchange, or bribery, or tribute payment. The more common situation is one where, rational economic factors being equal or nearly equal, actual behavior is largely determined by noneconomic considerations. Generally, in industrial mass societies, a wider range of behavior tends to approximate the model of economic rationality than is the case in agrarian societies. A more abstract way of stating this trend is: The more complex a society's system of production is, the more economic behavior tends to become dissociated from other forms of behavior. For that reason, the relatively simple models of economic theory that are premised on the rationality of economic behavior and make little or no attempt to incorporate nonrational variables fit complex industrial societies best and are practically worthless in simpler subsistence economies. All societies have economies, of course, but only in a few societies do people tend to behave in the way economists assume they will.[1]

Even in highly industrial societies, however, there remains an important residue of nonrational factors in economic behavior. If one examines the American economy, which presumes to be the most efficient and rational in the world, one finds that such nonrational considerations as race and sex have an enormous effect on such basically economic factors as wages. The impact of race and sex discrimination of the American economy remains of staggering proportions, even after one controls for other important economic and social variables, such as productivity and education. Nonwhites and women earn much less than white men, and they tend to concentrate in occupations where their productivity is far below their potential. Recent efforts to reduce the effect of race and sex discrimination have sometimes resulted not in equality of opportunity, but in reverse

[1] Of course, I am not suggesting here that economists do not know that people frequently behave in ways which are not economically rational. Rather, in order to build models of economic behavior which are simple enough to be workable, they deliberately choose to ignore non-rational factors. The value of the abstract model is purely empirical: how closely does it *approximate* (and thus *predict*) actual behavior while remaining simple enough to be manageable?

discrimination, so that we are now beginning to experience the novel phenomenon of the overpaid incompetent member of a minority group hired for noneconomic reasons. In both instances, the motivations have little to do with economic rationality and efficiency. An attempt to correct irrationality can easily result not in rationality but in reverse irrationality.

Economic behavior, then, even in highly industrialized societies, is seldom purely rational. Nor must it be supposed that rationality is confined purely to the economic domain. In all societies, a good deal of the people's behavior can be predicted on the basis of what they perceive to be their self or collective interests, and to that extent human behavior has an element of rationality, but definitions of interest include many noneconomic factors. For example, it may be rational to bribe an official to obtain security even though one may be economically the loser.

Exploitation

The model of economic behavior that we have so far presented, based on an exchange of goods and services according to a rational calculus of loss or gain, has at least one serious limitation: it does not take into account *power differentials* through which relations of production are mediated. The implicit assumption in our attempt to define economic behavior has been that the partners in the exchange are equally free to enter the economic relationship and that their decision to do so will be determined by their respective calculus of gain. It is obvious that many economic exchanges do not follow that model, because of the disparity in power between the parties involved. Thus the *peón* on a Latin American *hacienda* is nominally entering a labor contract with his *patrón* whereby, in exchange for the right to use a plot of land, he obligates himself to furnish so many days a year of work. In theory, the *peón* is exchanging his services for the crops produced by his *patrón's* land. He may even be theoretically free to leave the *hacienda*. In fact, however, the unavailability of land, the

control of his *patrón*, debts, ties of ritual kinship, and many other
factors reduce the *peón* to a captive position in which his freedom of
action is much more limited than his *patrón's*.
Disparity of power reduces the free-enterprize theory of classical
economics to a fiction. It was one of the great contributions of Karl
Marx to economic theory to have incorporated the dimension of
power, or "relations of production" as he called it, into his economic
analysis. In stratified and politically centralized societies, many
economic relations, and certainly most of the basic ones, are mediated
through power relations, and this in turn is the root source of
exploitation. Exploitation is basically the use of power for gain.

In the example chosen above, of a prototypical feudal relationship,
even conservatives would recognize the presence of exploitation. An
even more extreme example would be the chattel slavery that existed
in the West Indies and the United States. There, no pretense at all was
made of the slave being a free economic agent, and by no stretch of the
imagination could the master–slave relationship be described as a
contract. To use again our previous distinction between economic
behavior and activities, the slave laboring in the cotton fields is
engaging in an eminently economic activity, but his utterly captive
condition precludes economic behavior on his part, except in the
broadest and nearly meaningless sense that he is exchanging his labor
for his physical survival.

Economic exploitation in modern industrial societies, both
capitalist and socialist, is less blatant but no less absent than in
agrarian societies. It has assumed new and more complex forms rather
than disappeared or significantly diminished. Indeed, it is far more
widespread than in many simpler societies, though perhaps somewhat
less ruthless than in many advanced agricultural societies. The history
of social evolution is in good part a history of the evolving forms of
economic exploitation, which is, in turn, closely related to the development of forms of political organization. Indeed, it is organization
that makes exploitation possible, and counterorganization of the
workers that sets limits on exploitation.

In hunting-and-gathering societies, there is a lot of economic activity, but relatively little economic behavior as we have defined it. The division of labor, except for a few religious and magical roles, does not extend beyond age and sex specialization. Such societies, being unstratified and politically uncentralized, do not know exploitation internally, though they often encounter it in their external contacts with more powerful neighbors. Within the family, power relations are well defined, with a clear hierarchy of adults over children and men over women, but, if the family can be described.as a tyranny, it certainly does not make much sense to call it economically exploitative. The family is the basic unit of both production and consumption. Both men and women play important and complementary roles in food-getting activities, the men doing the bulk of the hunting, and the women most of the gathering. Children until age six or thereabouts are primarily consumers, but start contributing to the domestic economy as soon as they are physically capable of doing so. The collected food is shared along principles that come close to the Communist maxim of "to each according to his needs; from each according to his capacity," though there is perhaps some tendency for men to get a greater than proportional share of the meat they hunt.

The main way in which such societies enter into specific economic relations and encounter exploitation is in their contacts with other more complex societies. The vast majority of hunting-and-gathering societies have been in sustained contact with more economically developed societies with which they have traded for thousands of years. The most rudimentary form of trade is the so-called silent one: the hunters leave a certain quantity of meat or other collected products in a customary spot; this is later picked up by the partners in the silent trade who, in return, leave behind agricultural or manufactured products. Continuation of the trade is subject to mutual satisfaction with the exchanges. In that sense, the exchange cannot be said to be exploitative, although the "terms of trade" tend to be unfavorable to the hunters. Thus, certain essential products, such as salt or metal weapons, which are easily and cheaply obtained by agriculturalists who are well connected with long-distance trade circuits, have great scarcity value to isolated hunters and therefore fetch a relatively high price. In the last analysis, however, a good bargain is subjectively defined, and, in the absence of any coercion or dire and pressing needs, every bargain made is almost by definition a good one.

Often, relations between hunters and agriculturalists are much closer than sporadic barter. We have seen for instance, that the Pygmies not only exchange products with their Bantu neighbors, but also offer their labor against food and have ritual ties to the agricultural villagers (Turnbull, 1961, 1965). Such a dependence relationship has been described as "serfdom," and indeed the Bantu regard the Pygmies with amused condescension and in a quasi-proprietary manner as "their Pygmies." However, the anthropologist Colin Turnbull, who studied them best, raises the interesting question of who exploits whom. In sheer economic terms, he claims, the Pygmies are the winners. Their labor is sporadic and inefficient, and there is enough food in the forest to give them the option to regain their independence whenever they choose. Pygmy excursions into Bantu villages are more in the nature of a lark to obtain luxuries than of an economic necessity.

Much different, however, is the relationship between Bushmen and Bantu in the Kalahari region of Southwestern Africa (Silberbauer and Kuper, 1966). The Bushmen live in a harsh, arid, semidesertic environment, and their precarious habitat is constantly encroached upon by hunters with firearms who exterminate the big game, by herdsmen whose cattle overtax the scanty pasture, and by agriculturalists afflicted by a population explosion. Destitution forced many Bushmen into real economic serfdom; they became cheap laborers for their neighbors in exchange for food, either on a temporary or on a permanent basis.

Pastoralist societies are also, in general, relatively free of exploitation, although some pastoral societies practice slavery. The main exploited "class" in most pastoral societies, however, is nonhuman; namely, the livestock. Even though cattle or other livestock has often been regarded as a form of capital, its ownership in nonmonetized economies has seldom led to severe social and political inequalities. Cattle raids and epidemic diseases produce rapid fluctuations in livestock ownership, and so does the institution of the bridewealth, which in most pastoralist societies is paid in livestock. The sex ratio of one's children has a randomizing effect on the social distribution of livestock: daughter's bridewealth brings in livestock while sons' brides cost livestock. Livestock is thus an obvious form of wealth that can be accumulated, is relatively nonperishable, and has the endearing property of reproducing itself. But the distribution of wealth in pastoralist societies resembles more the vagaries of a slow-motion poker game than the relentless capital accumulation and class formation of agrarian and industrial societies.

Another feature of livestock raising is that it is neither labor-intensive, nor land-intensive. This means that the economic premium on either land or slave ownership is not great. Although a lot of land is needed, pastures are usually held in common; and when new pastures are needed, they are frequently acquired by the force of arms at neighbors' expenses, rather than purchased. Sometimes also, peaceful agreements are reached between agriculturalists and pastoralists, such as that, after the harvest, herdsmen may pasture their livestock whose droppings are used as fertilizer by the farmers.

In general, pastoralists are far more concerned about *use* than about *ownership* of land, and their form of land use is specialized, limited, extensive, and generally communal. Thus, the premium put on transforming wealth in livestock into land ownership is minimal or nonexistent. Pastoralists, being nomads, move over land as groups in temporary and cyclical occupation, rather than become rooted proprietors of land. Similarly, the economic incentive for slave ownership is minimal, as the members of the extended family are typically sufficient to pasture and protect the flocks. Thus, even though most herdsmen are quite bellicose and frequently take prisoners, in only a few pastoralist societies does slavery play an important economic role. War captives are typically ransomed, killed, or released if men, or absorbed into the victor's family if women or children, rather than made slaves. Where slavery exists, as, for example, among the Tuareg of the Sahara, it tends to be of the benign "domestic" type.

In short, pastoralism does not favor the accumulation and concentration into few hands of any of the three basic means of production: land, labor, or capital. The main form of wealth is livestock, ownership of which is subject to great and largely random fluctuations due to the vagaries of disease, predation, raiding, and bridewealth payments. While great differences in livestock holdings may exist between family groups at any given time, these differences are sufficiently unstable to militate against the formation of a rigid class order. Pastoralist societies tend to be relatively egalitarian in class terms. It should be noted, however, that pastoralist societies often have a sharp sexual division of labor, the males having in nearly all cases a monopoly of livestock-tending. In a few cases of pastoral groups in the high altitude areas of the Andes, women do some pasturing of flocks (Flores, 1968), but generally livestock is men's business. Also, many pastoralist groups are rigidly stratified by age.

All the above remarks, it should be stressed, apply only to "pure" pastoralist societies, not to the many groups that combine livestock breeding with agriculture. At the industrial end of the spectrum, the Texas cattle baron is not a pastoralist. He is a manufacturer of beef in an industrial order.

Agriculture and Surplus Production

The great evolutionary leap forward (or backward, as many ecologists, ethologists, nutritionists, and others have argued) in techniques of production came with agriculture. Pastoralism is not fundamentally different from hunting; it is basically a form of predation made more easy and reliable through the taming of the prey.[2] But with agriculture, man, the errant carnivore, becomes a sedentary omni-

[2]It should be noted that pastoralism does not antedate agriculture in social evolution, and indeed in some cases is a more recent development. As a form of production, however, pastoralism had far fewer revolutionary consequences than agriculture in comparison with a hunting and gathering economy.

vore, or even a reluctant vegetarian. There is little wonder that, with agriculture, all the fundamental aspects of man's existence are radically altered: his ecology, his diet, and—most importantly for our purposes—his social organization.

The Neolithic Revolution, as the dawn of agriculture has been called because it generally coincided with the development of polished stone tools, probably happened independently or semiindependently some 6000 to 8000 years ago in half a dozen regions of Asia and Africa, and a couple of millenia later in Europe and the Meso-American and Andean area. It caused the world's first population explosion. Even the simplest type of tropical slash-and-burn agriculture can support human population densities at least 10 times as great as is possible under pure livestock breeding, and 20 or more times as great as in a hunting-and-gathering economy. Intensive irrigated agriculture with the use of natural fertilizers can produce human densities of hundreds or even thousands per square mile, compared to less than one in practically all hunting-and-gathering economies, or typically between one and five for pastoralists.

Man insured his proliferation by becoming omnivorous, or, in the case of poor agriculturalists, almost exclusively vegetarian. From a precariously surviving tropical and subtropical predator, man was transformed by agriculture into a devastatingly prolific mammal, biologically the most successful and ubiquitous of primates.

Besides a geometric increase in population density, agriculture had several other far-reaching consequences. Agriculture, being both labor- and land-intensive, puts an economic premium on the ownership and control of these two means of production. Since land is now permanently occupied and intensively used, there is an obvious incentive to claim exclusive proprietary, or at least usufructuary, rights over it. It is true that many agricultural societies have communal systems of land tenure, whereby ownership or usufruct is vested in large descent groups, or held in trust by the ruler. Some agricultural societies even provide for periodic reallocation of land according to need, as for example in the Inca Empire. And in many agricultural societies, land is not a commodity that can be bought, sold, or alienated to outsiders. Notwithstanding these facts, the concern over the occupation or ownership of land, and the legal definition of rights concerning land are far more developed in agrarian societies than in pastoralist or hunting- and gathering ones.

Furthermore, as agricultural techniques become more elaborate, and as tillable land becomes scarcer because of the population explosion produced by advancing technology, land tenure systems become increasingly complex. Most of the cases of societies that hold land communally and that have few if any notions of land ownership as distinguished from usufruct are *simple* agricultural societies in the tropics. The ''slash-and-burn'' type of agriculture, using the hoe or digging stick as basic implements and lacking the plow and draft animals, only permits moderate population densities as tropical lands typically have to lie fallow for long periods after use. In such relatively extensive types of land use, precise boundaries and rights are of much less consequence than in advanced agricultural societies where techniques of irrigation, fertilization, crop rotation, and plowing, make for high population densities and intensive usage of the last scrap of arable land. In such advanced agricultural societies, land tenure laws define in minute detail ownership, usufruct, rent, sale, water rights, mineral rights, tresspass, rights-of-way, boundaries, measurements, and pasture and hunting rights.

While agriculture makes land much more valuable than under pastoralism or hunting and gathering, and although every improvement in agricultural technology increases the value of land, the economic exploitation of land also requires *labor*. Only in the last century and a-half, the development of agricultural machinery made possible by industrialization has reduced the importance of labor as a factor of production; but we are considering here agrarian societies, not the agricultural sector of industrial societies. Until the industrial revolution, the profitable control of land was intimately linked with the control over the labor to work it. Even the most technologically developed agrarian societies, using the wheel, draft animals, plows, irrigation, and wind and water as sources of power, did not substantially reduce the need for labor, nor even the roughly eight or nine to one ratio of peasants to nonpeasants. They merely increased labor productivity, and thereby the size of both the population and of the surplus that could be extracted from the peasants.

In advanced agricultural societies, therefore, land tended to become alienated into the hands of the few, well beyond their capacity to work it themselves. This control over land, to become profitable, implied in turn a control over the labor to cultivate it (or, alternatively in some cases, the development of large livestock-breeding estates as in the Enclosures movement in Britain, or the large Latin American *haciendas*). The labor force of most advanced agrarian societies is in some sense unfree. If it does not consist of outright slaves, as was the case in parts of the Roman Empire or in the plantations of American colonies, it is often largely made up of serfs, or *peones*; that is, of peasants who not only lack land they may call their own, but who are unfree or unable to leave the land they work for the owner.

In the past couple of pages, we have differentiated between "simple" and "advanced" agricultural societies, a distinction based largely on the complexity of the technology used. Although there is no hard and fast division between these two categories and although some societies, as for example, the Inca Empire, fall somewhere in between, agricultural societies do nevertheless tend to fall into two broad technological levels.

The "simple" agricultural societies (sometimes called "horticultural") are concentrated principally in sub-Saharan Africa; pre-Columbian America, especially the Amazonian, Caribbean, and North American plain areas; the Micronesian, Polynesian, and Melanesian islands; and a number of the smaller "tribal" societies of the South and South-East Asian mainland. These areas are predominantly tropical, with generally poor, fragile soils that cannot sustain continuous cultivation. These lands are cultivated in cycles, by cutting down and burning the wild vegetation the ashes of which constitute a natural fertilizer; growing one or two crops on the cleared site; and letting the land go fallow to recuperate its fertility over periods of up to 15 or 20 years. The basic implement is some form of hoe, "foot-plow," or, simplest of all, a wooden digging stick with a fire-hardened tip. Such societies typically use no wheeled transport, no draft animals or animal-drawn plows, and no wind or water energy except for sailing (e.g., they have no wind or water mills). They often make use of natural fertilizers and of crop rotation, and some of them resort to rudimentary forms of irrigation; but large-scale irrigation systems, aqueducts, terracing, and other elaborate construction works are not known.

This level of agricultural technology permits only moderate popula-tion densities, typically in the range of 5 to 20 per square mile in the tropical savannahs, or even less in the rain forest zones. Many such horticultural societies, though not all, have substantial differences in prestige and power between social classes; have a fairly well differen-tiated division of labor, with a dozen or more craft specialties; are organized in states, though generally small ones; and know small-scale domestic slavery. Yet the surplus production too is limited to produce vast differences in wealth between social classes, and to support large public works. Some of these societies, like the Yoruba of Nigeria, are urbanized, have organized markets, and engage in long-distance trade with other societies. A few even use standardized items, such as cowrie shells or copper crosses, as currency; and have been literate, such as the societies of the Western Sudan in Africa. Gener-ally, however, cities, international trade, literacy, and currencies are more characteristic of the advanced agricultural societies.

Most anomalous, perhaps, are the indigenous civilizations of Meso-America and the Andes which, despite a technology far less developed in some respects than that of many sub-Saharan African societies, did produce enormous megalithic structures (palaces, pyramids, temples), vast public works (irrigation canals, aquaducts, causeways, roads, bridges), large urban centers, and great accumula-tions of wealth reflected in the luxurious life style of the priesthood and aristocracy. Yet all this was achieved without wheeled transport or draft animals, without a system of writing (of with only a rudimentary system in the case of the Mayas), with a metallurgy almost entirely devoted to sumptuary objects in precious metals, and with the simplest of agricultural implements (digging stick in North America, foot plow in the Andes).

With complex agricultural technology, in the societies sometimes called "agrarian" to distinguish them from the horticultural ones, a number of social and economic developments take place, or at least, play a much more prominent role than in horticultural societies. These societies, characteristic of China, India, Egypt, and Mesopotamia for 5000 or 6000 years, and of the rest of the Mediterranean basin, Ethiopia, Japan, Indonesia, and Europe for 1000 to 3000 years, are urbanized, literate, densely populated, politically centralized, despotic, exploitative, and highly stratified by wealth as well as by power and prestige. The technology is sufficiently productive to maintain the ruling class in luxury and to support vast statal and religious projects, but not sufficient to raise the great mass of the peasantry much above the subsistence level. Artisanal crafts are far more developed than in simple agricultural societies, both in numbers of craftsmen and in their specialization. The land is typically alienated from the peasantry, which is kept in servile or semiservile status and taxed just short of starvation to support the urban ruling class, priesthood, merchant class, and to a lesser extent, the craftsmen and domestic servants who serve the rich and the powerful.

Besides the proliferation of artisanal production, much of it to satisfy the demand of the upper strata for luxury goods, and of service occupations, likewise devoted to the enhancement of the life style of the urban elites, complex agrarian societies are also characterized by the large-scale extension of commerce, both internal and external. This, in turn, means the existence of a substantial merchant class; of established trade routes, both maritime and land-based; of currency and the use of precious metals for commerce; and of well-policed and well-regulated market places. Some of these features are found in incipient form in some of the more developed horticultural societies (e.g. in West Africa), but they only assume full importance in complex agrarian societies.

Despite the growth of crafts, services, and trade in agrarian societies, the privileged urban classes seldom exceed 10 to 15 percent of the total society, even if one includes in them, besides the aristocracy, the priesthood, and the merchants; the artisans, soldiers, servants, concubines, and prostitutes who are their retainers. These societies still cannot afford to maintain more than a small minority of the population in idleness or luxury. They must rely on a vast labor force to produce a surplus because even the best agrarian technology is still very labor-intensive, and they must be ruthlessly exploitative of the many to squeeze out enough surplus to keep up not only the luxurious life style of the elite, but the state and military apparatus that does the squeezing internally and the plundering externally.

In short, the main differences in economic structure between horticultural and agrarian societies are twofold:

1. In agrarian societies the ruling class has far greater control over both land and labor as basic factors of production. Agrarian societies typically have landless, servile peasantries.
2. In addition to the primary sector of the economy (agricultural production), the secondary and tertiary sectors (handicraft production and commerce and services) assume a greatly increased importance.

Essential conditions for these developments to take place are improved transportation and communication. Agrarian societies must maintain a secure transportation system by land, river, and sea to move troops for internal repression and external security, and to permit the easy flow of goods and of labor for public works. Commerce and control require good transportation, and good transportation facilitates commerce and control. The same is true of communication, hence the link between complex agrarian societies and literacy. The accumulation of accurate knowledge made possible by literacy is a powerful help to the governing class. Until the last century of world history, literacy has always been a privilege and monopoly of the ruling and priestly classes. (Literacy extending to even half of the population came earliest in Japan, followed in the late nineteenth century by Western Europe and North America. Eastern Europe and some of Latin America achieved it in the twentieth century. For much of Asia and nearly all of Africa, it has yet to be achieved.)

Another interesting feature of agrarian societies is the relative powerlessness of their merchant classes. The merchant classes are privileged in terms of wealth, but they rarely control government. More typically, they are at the mercy of the ruling class. Agrarian states generally try to control the economy through tariffs, subsidies, tolls, taxes, licenses, set prices, and the granting of monopolies. Trading is typically a state-granted privilege, arbitrarily revocable, and obtained and maintained by courting, cajoling, flattering, and bribing officials. The merchant class itself often responds to this state control by policing itself and organizing in monopolistic guilds in order to defend its interests in this complex *modus vivendi* with the ruling class.

The predicament of the merchant class in agrarian societies is that it is too wealthy not to be an obvious target for the rapaciousness of the ruling class. Yet, as a major producer of wealth and source of credit, the merchant class is indispensable to the rulers, and hence cannot with impunity be robbed out of existence. Thus, the merchant class frequently exists on precarious sufferance. This phenomenon of "weak money" is especially pronounced when the merchant class consists of a closed caste of foreigners, or of a religious minority, as it frequently does. The Jews of medieval Europe, the overseas Chinese in South-East Asia, expatriate Indians and Lebanese are all classical examples of "pariah capitalists" who have alternatively thrived and been persecuted in agrarian societies.

With the growth of commerce and of a monetized economy in agrarian societies, the stage is set for *capitalism*, the beginnings of which are found in the more complex of the agrarian societies. Indeed, the essence of capitalism is treating *time* as a marketable commodity. Capitalism consists basically of lending money for interest. Money lending and usury, characteristics of agrarian societies, gradually develop into large-scale credit and banking for the financing of palaces, the construction of public works, the outfitting of ships, and other ventures. To the extent that the merchant class becomes a capital-lending class, it gradually gains power at the expense of the traditional ruling class.

The peasant is always left holding the short end of the stick. In addition to the control of his landowner, he also falls under the grip of the moneylender. More complex and interesting, however, is the relationship between the ruling class as a consumer of wealth and the mercantile capitalist as a lender of wealth. In the latter phases of the European agrarian regimes, for example, from the sixteenth to the eighteenth century, the aristocracy became increasingly indebted to the rising bourgeoisie. The noble Electors who contended for the post of German emperor, for instance, had to turn to banking houses like the Fuggers to finance their election, thus putting the bankers in the position of kingmakers. For the French aristocracy too, the bourgeoisie was the goose that laid the golden eggs. For some time, the geese were content with buying titles of nobility with their golden eggs, but when they saw the futility of that, they seized power.

The great limitation of agrarian societies was technological. Though a vast improvement over the technology of horticultural societies, agrarian technology made only a limited use of energy other than human and animal. Wind was used for sailing, milling, and irrigation, and water energy was used for milling and a few other rudimentary purposes; but none of these techniques radically increased the productivity of labor or the speed of transportation. Except for printing—a late invention in Europe (mid-fifteenth century), but a much earlier one in China—nothing of revolutionary economic or technological consequence happened for several millenia. Horses galloped no faster in the eighteenth century than in the third millenium B.C. Sailing vessels were faster and bigger, but not radically so. The main technological improvement was in killing, with the development of firearms, but productivity increases were relatively slow.

Gunmaking, however, had not been an entirely destructive enterprise. For several centuries, deathdealing had been the mother of invention, to the point that, by the late eighteenth century, European metallurgy had improved sufficiently to build a steam engine. As every eighth grader knows, the use of steam as a source of energy suddenly multiplied severalfold the productivity of labor and unleashed the Industrial Revolution. But it was not technology alone that created the industrial society; rather it was the marriage of machine technology with capitalism that ushered in the modern production system. As Marx lucidly noted, capital, rather than land or labor, now became the key factor of production to control. Surplus could now be achieved far more rapidly by buying machinery and hiring people to operate it than by squeezing rent out of peasants.

Industrial Societies

The advent of the industrial revolution thus immensely increased the scope of capital as a factor of production at the expense of land and to a lesser extent, of labor. Investment in more complex and expensive machinery, and increasingly in machine tools (i.e., in machinery to produce yet more machinery), multiplied the uses of capital beyond anything conceivable in an agrarian society. Moreover, the little capital produced in agrarian societies was largely used in nonproductive ventures: to support the conspicuous consumption of the elite, to build prestige projects like temples, tombs, and palaces, or to finance military expeditions. With the development of industry, capital became invested predominantly in productive enterprises that, according to the "multiplier effect," would generate yet more capital. Industry, in short, enormously accelerated capital growth.

Industrial capitalism also profoundly transformed the nature of imperialism, as Lenin (1969) noted over half a century ago. Imperialism, or the conquest of one nation by another, is an old pattern of human history. With the mercantile capitalism of Europe in the six-teenth, seventeenth, and eighteenth centuries, various capital-rich countries had established vast colonial empires: Portugal and Spain first, followed by Holland, France, and Britain. Early capitalism had already transformed overseas conquest into a business proposition. Capital was used to set up monopolistic and state-chartered com-panies, like the famous East India Companies of Britain, France, and the Netherlands. These commercial ventures would outfit vessels, monopolize trade, establish plantations, and even set up semiprivate colonial governments in a designated part of a given country's over-seas empire.

Starting in the sixteenth century, and increasingly in the seven-teenth and eighteenth centuries, the mercantile capitalism of Europe had made imperialism a worldwide system of exploitation of the economic resources of the colonies for the benefit of the "mother-country." The intricate relationship between industrialization and imperialism is clearly illustrated by the history of Japan and the United States. Japan, the only major non-Western power who, through a policy of isolationism, avoided being sucked into the vortex of European colonial expoitation, was also the first non-Western country to industrialize, with only a half-century time lag compared to Europe, and at least half-a-century's head-start over much of the colonized world. Japan's "economic miracle" was due, in good part, to the political stroke of having avoided becoming a colony of Europe. Besides Japan, the only country outside Europe that appreciably industrialized in the nineteenth century was the United States, who, though an outgrowth of European colonialism, gained its indepen-dence three-quarters of a century before it industrialized.

Industrialization greatly intensified the expoitative relationship be-tween Europe and the rest of the world, which had begun with mercantile capitalism. To the extent that a country was colonized, it was prevented from industrializing, and thus from improving its standard of living. Conversely, holding colonies was an important impetus to the industrialization of Europe. The essence of modern

European imperialism (and, in a more economic form, of United States imperialism) is the complementary relationship that exists between the industrial country as a producer and seller of manufactured products, and the colonies as both producers of cheap raw materials and agricultural products, and as consumers of manufactured goods.

Industrial capitalism generated two insatiable needs: first, it required an ever-growing amount of raw materials, such as metals, energy sources, and fibers; and second, in the face of chronic overproduction, it always needed new and expanding markets. So overriding were these two needs that the Industrial Revolution unleashed that last great assault of European imperialism, the one that engulfed Africa in the 1880s. Hitherto, Africa had been for Europe almost exclusively a source of slaves to operate the plantations of its American colonies. Until the Industrial Revolution, Africa had not seemed rich enough to be worth invading. Now, the intense competition for raw materials and markets between the European countries made them turn to seemingly less attractive real estate, if only as a preemptive move to prevent other countries from grabbing it.

The economic policy of colonial powers was remarkably similar. They were concerned with each other's competition, and from the beginning of European colonialism in the sixteenth century, attempted to maintain a strict monopoly of trade between each of them and their respective colonies. Some of the weaker colonial powers, such as Belgium, had "free trade" agreements imposed on them by the others; and the decadent colonial powers of Spain and Portugal had their shipping preyed upon by Dutch, English, French, and Danish privateers. But the prevailing rule was that each European "mother country" traded only with its own colonies. Also, the industrial nations of Europe were concerned about the possible competition of incipient industries in their own colonies. Thus, it was consistently the policy of Europe to prevent industrialization in the colonies, and to keep the latter as suppliers of cheap raw materials and agricultural products. Great Britain, for example, was worried about the great industrial potential of India, especially in the textile industry.

It was no accident that the industrialization of Asia and Africa began only after the demise of colonialism in the post-World-War-II era. Latin America, which has been semiindependent for a century and a half, is considerably better off than Asia and Africa, though still lagging far behind Europe, Japan, and North America. Still today, the relationship between "developed" and "developing" countries (to use the United Nations euphemism for the rich and the poor countries) continues to be ruled by unequal terms of trade and economic dependence, now generally called neo-colonialism.

It is against this background of colonial exploitation that the claim of modern capitalism to have equalized opportunities, leveled wealth, and democratized politics must be considered. As Lenin (1969) noted, the relative improvement in the condition of the working class of industrial countries was in good part the product of colonial exploitation. In a prophetic stroke of Marxian revisionism, Lenin thus attributed the failure of class polarization to take place in industrial societies to the increasing polarization between poor and rich nations. The welfare state of the more progressive bourgeois democracies rests in part on the abject misery of two-thirds to three-fourths of humanity. Even the proletariat of capitalist countries, went Lenin's argument, stood in the position of oppressor *vis à vis* what today we call the Third World.

Of course, industrial capitalism is not entirely attributable to colonial exploitation, nor vice versa. Portugal, the oldest European colonial power, remained the economic backwater of Western Europe despite its vast empire. Sweden, Europe's wealthiest country, industrialized without overseas colonies. While industrial capitalism was a worldwide system of exploitation that knitted the world together in a vast network of unequal economic ties to a much greater extent than had ever been the case before, it was also to a large extent an endogenous process of the industrializing countries.

Initially, even in the industrializing countries, the blessings of industry seemed mixed indeed. Millions of impoverished peasants flocked to overcrowded cities where they became a miserable, exploited proletariat. Appalling sanitary conditions, a mushrooming population, industrial pollution, rural exodus and decay, child labor, the inferno of steel mills and coal mines—all contributed to a picture of monstrous, inhuman exploitation of the many for the benefit of a small class of *nouveaux riches*. Furthermore, the old petty bourgeoisie of small merchants and traditional craftsmen seemed destined to sink into the proletariat because of the relentless tendency of capitalism toward monopoly. Marx predicted, plausibly in his time, that the rich would get fewer and richer, and the poor would multiply and find themselves in an increasingly abject condition, until desperation would drive them to revolution.

Although such conditions still exist in a few of the more primitive capitalist countries, such as South Africa, they no longer prevail in most of the industrial countries, capitalist or socialist. Marx was quite right about the monopolistic trend of capitalism, a trend that still continues, and which, ironically, found its ultimate expression under socialism, in the form of the single monopoly of the state. Marx's most serious error, however, is that he conceived of the economy as what modern game theorists call "a zero-sum game"; that is, a game in which A's gain is necessarily B's loss. He failed to foresee the enormous growth in the size of the total cake which industrialization would eventually bring about.

It was only since the turn of the twentieth century that the rise in the standard of living of the entire population of industrialized countries began to be evident. Along with ever-growing production came great strides in hygiene and medicine, a declining birthrate, mass literacy, reformist legislation, labor unions, universal suffrage, and a few social revolutions (e.g., the abortive Paris commune of 1870 and the successful Mexican and Bolshevik revolutions).

An obvious solution to the chronic problem of overproduction in industrial countries (which Marx saw as one of the major weaknesses of capitalism), is to increase consumption, which in turn means to increase wages, which in turn is made possible by rising productivity. The sweatshop of the early nineteenth century slowly gave rise to the consumerism of the mid-twentieth century. Capitalism survived thanks to the growing affluence of the working class, to the bourgeoisification of the proletariat, and to the insatiable propensity of wider and wider segments of the population to consume more and more.

So profound have these changes in the capitalist system of production been, that some authors prefer to talk of the contemporary affluent societies, whether capitalist or socialist, as "postindustrial," or "postcapitalist" (Dahrendorf, 1959). Compared to agrarian societies, or even to the early phases of industrialization, contemporary industrial societies are vastly better off economically. The poor of the United States are not only economically better off than the poor of, say, India, but they are considerably better off than about 90 or 95 percent of the population of India. The economic gap between rich and poor countries is so vast that there is practically no overlap in income distribution between them. An American definition of abject poverty would be an annual income of $2000 for a family of four; in India, even after reducing the dollar amount to allow for a much lower cost of living, such as income would put one in the top 10 percent of the population. The urban middle class of India lives under far inferior economic conditions than American families on welfare, and the Indian middle class is relatively far smaller than the American middle class.

Only through the most myopic fixation on consumption criteria, however, does the economic cornucopia of "postindustrial" societies lead to sanguine conclusions about the progress of mankind. First, over two-thirds of mankind live in the "proletarian nations" of the Third World, and the general tendency seems to be for the economic gap between rich and poor countries to become wider rather than narrower. Much of the world, especially Asia and Africa, stagnates in poverty and disease. Second, the affluent (and effluent) countries are contaminating the ocean and the atmosphere, consuming irreplaceable resources, degrading the fauna and flora, and generally contributing to making our planet unfit for human habitation at an ever-accelerating pace, while the population explosion of the poor countries raises the spectre of massive and chronic hunger. (Vast stretches of Africa have experienced chronic famines for decades, and the situation is no better in South Asia and parts of China.)

Third, while our technological capacity for destruction is now truly planetary, our restraint in the use of aggressive force shows no improvement. The calculated savagery of American bombings in Vietnam in the absence of any threat to the United States, for example, was fully comparable to the Nazi *Blitzkrieg* of the 1940s. Indeed, one of the achievements of the postindustrial society is the ability to produce both T-bone steaks and atomic missiles. As C. Wright Mills (1959) put it, the Welfare State has become a Warfare State. One of the byproducts of the "industrial–military complex" is a permanent war machine of unprecedented magnitude and destructiveness.

Fourth, even within the affluent countries, the benefits of abundance are unequally distributed. The pie is bigger, but the slices seem to have remained about as unequal as they were several decades ago (though less unequal than in agrarian societies because of the bulging middle class).

Fifth, advanced industrialization, especially automation, cybernetics, and computer technology create the overwhelming problem of the redundance of labor. During early industrialization, there was a need for a lot of cheap, unskilled labor to operate machines. Now, the need is for fewer and fewer, highly trained, and highly paid technicians. The unskilled worker or the worker with obsolete skills will increasingly join the ranks of the chronically unemployed kept in involuntary idleness on "welfare" rolls. Unemployment shows every sign of increasing in the advanced phases of capitalism.

Lastly, economic affluence does not appreciably alter the distribution of power and the nature of tyranny. Unlike wealth, which can be almost indefinitely created, power is a zero-sum game. If power over people is control over their behavior, then A's gain is B's loss. Modern industrial states do not seem to be any less oligarchical than agrarian states, and advanced technology greatly increases the scope of control of the ruling class.

The Convergence of Capitalism and Socialism

In the nineteenth century, socialism was seen by many as the great hope for the liberation of mankind. Now we know better. We know that Marx's diagnosis that power derived from ownership of the means of production was wrong. The real issue is not who owns capital, but who controls it. It is nonsense to speak of "people's capitalism" because millions of shareholders own some productive capital. Everybody knows that General Motors is run by its few top echelon managers, not by its millions of shareholders. Similarly, the socialist fiction of communal ownership of the means of production is a thin disguise for the tyranny of the Party *apparatchiks* (bureaucrats). In both cases, a small minority rules and democracy is a legitimizing myth. Socialism, in practice, turns out to be state capitalism.

The "convergence" theory of socialism and capitalism is usually cast in the optimistic perspective that characterizes American social science. The usual version of the theory is that capitalist and socialist countries as they evolve, will merge somewhere in the middle into a benevolent welfare state, free of the inequalities of capitalism and of the authoritarianism and dogmatic rigidity of communism. Communism will become increasingly liberalized, pragmatic, and flexible as it grows affluent. Capitalism will gradually accept more and more state control of the economy and cradle-to-the-grave social security.

There is little question that the similarities in the political and economic structure of industrial societies, whether capitalist or socialist, are more fundamental than the differences. The legitimizing ideologies differ, but in both cases democratic ideology is a façade for oligarchic rule by bureaucratic and managerial elites. The social stratification of both systems is quite similar: occupational prestige and rewards, income distribution, educational ladders, and other attributes of class correspond closely. Both systems exhibit an approximately equal blend of achievement and ascription, of mobility and rigidity. The nominally "free" economy of capitalist countries is somewhat more flexibly state-controlled than planned socialist economies, but in both cases the major economic decisions are taken by bureaucrats and managers rather than by risk-taking entrepreneurs. Both systems are equally aggressive and imperialistic, and maintain equally sizeable military establishments while claiming to be peace-loving. Both have elaborate police forces, and both have developed political regimes ranging from the ruthlessly dictatorial (Hitler, Stalin) to the relatively liberal (Tito, Roosevelt).

If capitalism and socialism are indeed merging into a single type of mass society, it is more in their deviation from their stated ideals than in their achievement thereof. Both systems have state-planned or at least heavily directed economies, despite the capitalist myth of "free enterprise." Both systems are heavily militarized, despite protestations of pacifism. Both systems have developed mammoth-sized and increasingly centralized administrative and managerial bureaucracies, despite ideologies of federalism, decentralization, grassroot democracy, and withering away of the state. Both systems profess to believe in the equality of people, but perpetuate gross differences in income, prestige, and power according partly to achieved, partly to ascribed criteria. Both systems, in short, are authoritarian, bureaucratic, hierarchized, mass societies.

Another question frequently raised is whether the industrial society is linked to Western culture, and whether we may expect a cultural homogenization of the world as industrialization spreads. Japan, the most industrialized non-Western country, is generally taken as the test case. Some argue that Japan is becoming Westernized or even Americanized, while others maintain that Japan remains culturally very different from the West and true to its own traditions. In terms of basic political and economic structure, Japan is indeed similar to other industrial bureaucratic mass societies. It has deliberately adopted and adapted Western technology, bureaucratic and military organization, and educational systems. In addition, American cultural influence made itself felt during the military occupation after the Second World War, and the mass media diffuse certain cultural traits, for example, musical or dress styles associated with "youth culture."

Notwithstanding all these Western influences, and the undeniable structural similarities between all industrial mass societies, the prospect of Japan, or indeed any other industrializing non-Western country, such as India or Egypt, becoming replicas of the West is extremely remote. Industrial societies will probably become somewhat more like each other than will agrarian societies, because the economic integration of the world throws them into constant contact with each other, but cultural and linguistic diversity will persist for the foreseeable future.

Various societies and eras have defined economic goals and problems for themselves. For nineteenth-century European capitalism, it was how to keep expanding production, securing cheap raw materials, and finding markets. For postrevolutionary Russia and post-Meiji Restoration Japan, it was how to catch up with Western Europe and the United States. Ironically, now that perhaps one-third of mankind has achieved a standard of living securely above the level of desperate want and starvation, we are thrown right back at the starkest problem of survival as a species on our planet. We are becoming aware that if we project the trends of the past couple of centuries into the next one or two, the future is too horrible to contemplate.

ADDITIONAL READING

In addition to the works of Weber, Veblen, and Marx already cited, which deal with large-scale complex societies, there is a growing literature in economic anthropology, extensively surveyed by Cook (1973) and Dalton (1969). One of older classics in that tradition is Mauss, *The Gift* (1954) which analyzes various forms of non-monetary exchanges in small-scale societies.

Bohannan and Dalton (1962), and the Polanyi reader (1957) examine the economic systems of agrarian societies while the Firth collection (1967) is more general. Smelser (1963) and Parsons and Smelser (1956) represent attempts by functionalist sociologists at tackling economic phenomena from a broader perspective than that adopted by economists. Frank (1967) documents for Latin America, Lenin's thesis (1969) that capitalist development in some countries keeps other countries underdeveloped.

PART
III

The Better Things of Life

8

Religion
and Magic

The universality of religion and magic in human societies has preoccupied critical minds for millenia and sociologists for over a century.
Many of the early classics of sociology and anthropology dealt with
religion, notably the works of Weber (1930, 1951, 1952, 1958),
Frazer (1890), Durkheim (1915), and Malinowski (1948). To say that
religion and magic are universal is not to state that there are no
atheists, but rather that in all societies one encounters religious and
magical beliefs and practices. Specialists in these beliefs and rituals
are also found in nearly all societies, and the priesthood is without
question the world's oldest specialized profession.

Religion and magic share a concern with the supernatural—a class
of phenomena that cannot be experienced through the senses or
through instruments. The existence of these phenomena cannot be
either proven or disproven through experimentation, the logic of
causal inference, or any of the canons of scientific inquiry. The
distinction commonly drawn between magic and religion is that the
former constitutes a deliberate attempt to manipulate the outcome of
specific events through ritual, and the latter involves prayer, propitiation, or supplication to supernatural powers, but no direct attempt at
manipulation. Thus, an invocation to goddess earth asking for a
successful crop is a religious act; burying charms in one's fields to
ward off evil spirits is a magical act; posting scarecrows to chase away
birds is a scientific act.

Paradoxical as it may first seem, the sociological study of religious phenomena has often been pursued by nonreligious persons. The seeming paradox disappears, however, when one considers that looking at religion as another set of social facts to be explained implies skepticism about the theological answers of any given religion. The comparative study of religion implies benevolent neutrality toward all religions, and thus skepticism concerning the dogmatism of any of them.

Religious sociologists have often denied the existence of a conflict between faith and science, claiming that the two operate at different levels, and hence are not contradictory. Yet, in practice, sociological and religious outlooks, while not logically incompatible, make strange bedfellows. Thus, the practicing Catholic sociologist would have difficulty in making the obvious association between Eucharist and other forms of ritual cannibalism among, say, Amazonian Indians. When the theological and the sociological outlooks meet under the skullcap of the same person, the two are typically compartmentalized to continue coexisting.

Theories of Religion

One of the most influential early sociologists of religion was Durkheim, who, in his masterful *The Elementary Forms of the Religious Life* (1915), developed the most explicitly sociogenic theory on the origin of religion. Durkheim essentially turned the Book of Genesis on its head. It was not God who created man in his image, suggested Durkheim, but rather the reverse. Basing his monumental work on the study of totemism among Australian aborigenes, Durkheim concluded that the totemic plant or animal associated with a given clan is really nothing more than a "collective representation" of that social group. Much like the flag is an emblem of a country, the totem is not sacred because of its physical properties, but because it symbolizes the social group that honors it.

Durkheim viewed totemism as the most "elementary form of the religious life," and from there extended his analysis to what he saw as more developed forms of religion, such as pantheism, polytheism, and monotheism. In all societies, says Durkheim, a clear distinction is made between two spheres of life—the *sacred* and the *profane*. The profane are the mundane affairs of daily life explainable in natural terms. The sacred deals with the mysterious supernatural forces that control human destiny. But what are those supernatural forces? Clearly, society itself, answers Durkheim. For, although society is the product of human interaction, human behavior is also controlled by its own collective creation. Society is more than the sum of the individuals who compose it. It becomes through its "collective consciousness" and "collective representations" an entity *sui generis,* a force independent of individuals, which powerfully shapes and controls individual behavior. Man, seeking to explain that mysterious force of his own unwitting creation, invents God, a collective representation of society. Prometheus invents God to explain his shackles (which he has forgotten he has himself put on).

Religious life, continues Durkheim, consists of basically two sets of phenomena—*beliefs* and *rituals*. Both the shared beliefs and the shared rituals of a common religion serve to reinforce the social solidarity of the society. The great rituals of sacrifice, communion, and rites of passage, performed in practically all societies, bring together their members in common participation, reaffirm common beliefs and symbols, and recement the bonds of solidarity between people. Religious ritual, in the last analysis, is a collective reaffirmation of the community of believers, of society itself.

Malinowski (1948) took a different tack from Durkheim's. To Malinowski, the universality of religion is explained by the need that people have to find answers to fundamental problems and security in their endeavors. Men, he suggests, resort to supernatural explanations when natural ones fail. Where science does not provide answers, religion and magic come in. To the physicist, thunder and lightning are the result of electrical discharges; to the peasant, they are divinities. In a classic illustration drawn from the Trobriand Islanders of the Pacific among whom he spent several years, Malinowski (1948) pointed out that lagoon fishing, relatively safe and predictable, is devoid of magical rituals, while open ocean fishing, risky and unreliable, is replete with it.

Malinowski's notion of magic and religion as covers for ignorance was not unlike the old evolutionary scheme proposed by Durkheim's master, Auguste Comte. Comte suggested that humanity progressed from religious to metaphysical to scientific explanations, thereby leaving religion with a contracting domain, and leading to a gradual secularization of society. We shall return later to the important issue of whether industrial societies are getting more secularized. Suffice it to say here that Comte, himself, relapsed into the religious stage, suggesting that sociology was the new religion of society, and its practitioners its priesthood.

Marx's ideas about religion were more prosaic and less general than Durkheim's or Malinowski's, but no more pious. Marx was primarily concerned with the way in which religion seemed to buttress the *status quo* and consolidate class exploitation in complex societies. To him, religion consisted of a set of myths manipulated by the ruling classes to keep the masses satisfied with their humble lot. The promise of rewards in the hereafter distracts from the reality of injustice and exploitation in the present. It is undoubtedly true that religion has often been a conservative tool in the hands of the privileged, but it has also been a revolutionary force. Also, since religion is found in unstratified societies, and thus antedates class exploitation, Marx's theory can hardly explain the origin of religion. In fairness to Marx, however, it must be said that religion was not of central concern to him, and he therefore never made more than passing references to it. Both Durkheim's and Malinowski's theories account better for the universality of religion. All three are in the grand social science tradition of religious skepticism. Whether religion is a code name for society itself, a smokescreen for ignorance, or mystifying opium for the masses, all three made it plain that they did not believe in it.

Whatever the source of the "supernatural impulse" in man, there is little question that it is a fundamental aspect of human behavior, that it is interlinked with almost every other aspect of human society, and that, as far as we know, it is unique to man. Not all people are religious, but man is a religious animal.

The Priesthood

Not only is religion found in all societies, but there are certain broad similarities found across a wide spectrum of religions. In all or nearly all religions, one finds both a body of *beliefs* and a set of *rituals*. Although religion is for everybody, few if any religions seem to be able to survive without a specialized body of priests who claim preeminent knowledge of the sacred lore and custody over the practice of the rituals. Even religions like Judaism and Islam, which claim not to have a priesthood in the sense of a sacralized class, put great stress on the special knowledge of the spiritual leaders. Religion, then, is almost invariably accompanied by professional specialization, and more specifically, by specialization in more-or-less esoteric knowledge.

The close historical link between the priesthood on the one hand, and knowledge, science, and literacy on the other is evident. If religion is basically an attempt to answer important and difficult questions for which there are no demonstrable solutions, it is hardly surprising that priests should base their claim to special status on their ability to provide the answers, and should attempt to preserve a monopoly of that claimed knowledge. Entry into a priesthood is seldom widely open. Access to it is limited by birth (in the case of hereditary castes), by difficult and lengthy training, by exacting tests of character, or by a combination of these. Priestly status always confers privileges which, at a minimum, free the priest from the necessity of earning a living through physical toil, and at a maximum, identify the clergy with the ruling class as in states that are called theocratic. Whether the clergy is synonymous with the ruling class, or whether it is merely a subordinate but privileged segment of the upper strata, priests are invariably far better off than the run-of-the-mill peasant or worker from whom they derive their physical sustenance.

Diverse though religions may seem to be in their specific beliefs, they do however share certain broad characteristics. Most of them, whether nominally pantheistic, polytheistic, or monotheistic, recognize a hierarchy of supernatural forces under a supreme deity who is generally credited with the creation of the world. Nearly all religions have an "origin myth"; that is, an articulate account of how the physical world and mankind got started. Not surprisingly, many societies trace their origin to an ancestor couple, of divine or semidivine descent. Royal families often claim divine or semidevine origins in an attempt to imbue their political power with supernatural sanction (Frazer, 1890). The divine right of kings is probably one of the most common independent inventions in world history. In Japan, Egypt, and Inca Peru for example, the king or emperor claimed divine descent. In the Christian and Muslim traditions, political power has until recently claimed divine sanction. Most traditional African monarchies have imbued the person of the king with sacred qualities.

Rituals

Similarities in ritual are also found across societies, far beyond those explainable by historical diffusion. The most striking common religious rituals are *sacrifice* and *communion*. In a vast range of historically unrelated societies, plants, animals, and humans are ritually killed, cooked, and consumed, with an amazing identity of basic meaning attributed to the ritual. The act of ritual immolation imbues the sacrificed object with sacredness, and the act of communion suffuses that sacredness to the body of believers. Communion is a ritual for sharing the qualities of the supernatural. As human sacrifice is the most valuable offering, ritual cannibalism is frequently the ultimate form of sacrifice, independently practiced in most parts of the world, including, symbolically, in Christian ritual. Indeed, the orthodox Catholic who is bound by dogma to reject the symbolic interpretation of Eucharist, is a self-confessed cannibal, since he believes that Jesus who has both a human and a divine nature is physically present in the host.

Nearly all religions are also closely linked with the *rites of passage*, which punctuate the social ages of people in nearly all societies. Rites of passage may sometimes be secularized, but in the vast majority of cases, they are religious rituals. Birth, initiation, marriage, and death, as important moments of social existence are almost always sanctified. Even in as secularized an event as an American college graduation ceremony, there is generally a vestigial invocation to divine guidance. The milestones of human existence call for religious ritual: the human animal becomes fully human only after being consecrated into the community of believers. And, of course, death, the most anguishing and universal of all human problems, always calls for a religious solution. Some conception of the prolongation of another form of life after death seems to be the universally human reaction to the dissolution of the flesh. In all societies, man considers himself far too important to accept the idea that he will utterly cease to exist. Man, with his conscious sense of destiny, refuses to accept the biological fact of death.

DIVINATION

Along with consciousness of destiny, comes a powerful urge for prediction and control. Divination is almost invariably one of the specialized functions of the priesthood, and frequently it constitutes a well-defined specialty within the priesthood. Magic, the attempt at supernatural control, is also a nearly universal specialized craft practiced by persons endowed with supernatural powers. A distinction is usually made between malevolent and benevolent magic, and to each type correspond distinct social roles, the former stigmatized, the latter honored. Sometimes the roles of diviner and witch are combined, sometimes not. Medicine is commonly associated with withcraft, and even modern Western psychiatry has more in common with the medieval exorcism of demons than psychiatrists are willing to admit.

(What, for example, is the *id* of Freudian psychiatry if not a little personal demon?) Even in as secularized a science as metereology, jocular associations with divination is still a living part of our folklore. The American farmer with an agronomy degree from his land-grant college may still resort to the services of a water-witch with a forked stick before deciding where to sink a well (Vogt and Hyman, 1959).

FEASTING

Religion is not only awe-inspiring; it is also fun. The great religious rituals of mass participation are typically occasions for very mundane diversion. Indeed, in most preindustrial societies, religious festivals are the main source of collective merrymaking. The greatest congregations of people occur at the religious festivals or places of pilgrimage, and, where people congregate, they not only pray, but trade, exchange views and gossip, fraternize, entertain themselves, eat, drink, and fornicate. Much of music and the theater has its origin in religious ritual. The great sacred pageantry is almost invariably accompanied by music and theatricals. The marketplace and commercial fair is also a common accompaniment of great religious festivals. Gluttony, drunkenness, sexual license, and other forms of sensual indulgence, which may be severely censured at other times, are often tolerated or even prescribed on religious occasions.

Anyone familiar with religious celebrations in the Indian parts of Meso-America or the Andes, for example, knows how heavy drinking is a socioreligious obligation at fiestas, a fact that translates into a high rate of chronic alcoholism among both anthropologists and Indians. Religious fiestas also call for the preparation of massive amounts of special and scarce foods such as meat, beyond the reach of the regular peasant diet. Similarly, a relaxation of sexual morality is a common accompaniment of religious feasting. Otherwise chaste women may be religiously obligated to prostitute themselves, as in the "temple prostitution" of ancient Greece and Rome, or couples may have to copulate in public to insure the fertility of crops, or the fumes of alcohol and the aura of excitement may lead to a generalized orgy.

Even religions like Christianity and Islam, which stress austerity and fasting, punctuate deprivation with revelry. During Ramadan, for instance, Muslims break the daytime fasting with nightly meals that far exceed ordinary fare. Or, in the Catholic tradition, the fasting of Lent is preceded by the feasting of Carnival.

Religion and Politics

Another important feature of religion is its close association with politics. Separation of church and state is barely 200 years old as an idea, and is still incompletely applied in most contemporary states. The norm throughout history has been for the state to be religiously legitimized, and for the clergy and the ruling class to be either one and the same as in theocracies, or at least closely associated. It is true that many states have incorporated people of more than one religion, but almost invariably one of two things happened: either one religion has been firmly entrenched as the official state religion with superior status, or contending religious communities have been engaged in protracted and violent conflicts. In only a few modern states has the state been a religiously neutral arbiter between peacefully coexisting religious groups. Even the twentieth century, which prides itself on religious tolerance, has known many bitter and prolonged religious conflicts: between Muslims and Hindus in India and Pakistan; between Jews and Muslims in the Near East; between Catholics and Protestants in Northern Ireland; and between Christians and Muslims in the Philippines, to mention just a few examples.[1]

---

[1] Many "religious" conflicts have, in fact, complex underlying causes, which often include competition for scarce resources between groups that are unequally placed. Thus, the conflict in Northern Ireland has an important class dimension, and much of the bitterness between Arabs and Jews boils down to the question of who has a right to live where. Nevertheless, religion (or "race" or ethnicity) is commonly chosen as the most important criterion of primordial affiliation. It may well be true that much of the bitterness in the Northern Irish conflict is, in the last analysis, a question of class discrimination rather than religious differences, but in practice, polarization takes place along religious, not class lines.

Religious pluralism is one of the most precarious bases of political organization. The state is almost always associated with one religious group, that of the ruling class. Other religious communities may be tolerated, so long as they remain small and do not threaten the political order, but even then, they have often been victimized and persecuted, as with Jews in Europe. Commonly, religious groups are prime contenders for political power, and the victory of one means the defeat of the other. In medieval Europe, for example, the contest was between Christians and Muslims, and it came to an end only after countless crusades and holy wars, with the final expulsion of the Moors from Spain in the late fifteenth century. As soon as Christians and Muslims stopped fighting each other, the Reformation created a new religious split between Catholics and Protestants. In the seventeenth century, the history of Western European states, especially Britain, France, Germany, and the Netherlands, was a nearly continuous struggle for supremacy between contending Christian sects.

It is hardly surprising that religion is so often linked with political hegemony, and hence is so frequently the source of bloody conflicts. Since political power is legitimized in religious terms, it follows that those who do not share the religious beliefs of the sovereign are not only heretics but potential traitors. Political loyalty is defined in terms of religious conformity. If swearing on the Bible is the test of truthfulness in court for example, by implication Buddhists or Hindus are beyond the pale.

Ethnic and Universal Religions

In one important respect, however, religions differ. Most of the world's religions are what might be called "ethnic religions"; that is, they are so closely linked to a particular society that its practitioners are not eager to spread the faith. Proselytism may be a totally foreign idea to them. For example, religions in which the ancestor cult or totemism plays a central role are obviously particularistic. If you do not belong to the clan that is identified with a totem or that makes offering to a particular set of ancestors, you are by definition outside the religious community.

Some religions, and a few of the most spectacularly successful and sanguinary ones, have been universalistic in their outlook. Christianity and Islam are obvious examples. All people are equally eligible to adopt the tenets of the sole true faith and to achieve eternal salvation. Therefore, the true believer must work toward the conversion of infidels until the whole of humanity embraces the true faith.

The ideal of universal human brotherhood preached by proselytizing religions has often been contrasted with their extraordinary intolerance and brutality in practice. There too, the paradox is only apparent. Although proselytizing faiths accept the admissibility of all, they also proclaim a monopoly of truth, which relegates those not in the fold to the status of infidels, valuable only as potential converts. As military conquest is the swiftest way of spreading a religion, it is little wonder that the sword and the cross, the crescent, or whatever should so often go together. Few religions have achieved marked and lasting success through patient and peaceful preaching. Militant sects that have taken to the sword have swept enormous regions of the globe with lightning rapidity. One need only think of the spread of Islam in the seventh century, and of Christianity from the sixteenth through the nineteenth century, during the period of European colonial expansion.

This is not to say that the militant, proselytizing religions have always converted infidels by force. Sometimes they have, but, more often, association with the ruling power has been a sufficient incentive for conversion. Religious conversion is seldom the result of purely religious motivations. Mundane self-interest typically achieves conversion with greater speed and ease than evangelizing efforts. Thus, for example, after the colonial conquest of Africa, becoming a Christian was virtually the sole means of access to Western education, since most schools were controlled by Christian missionaries. In some colonies, the only way for an African to acquire postprimary education was to enter a seminary. Much of the success of Christianity in Africa is attributable to the monopolization by missionaries of the educational system, and hence of access to nearly all positions of power and affluence. Even when no cynical calculus of gain enters religious conversion, the sheer prestige of the ruling class exercises a halo effect on its faith. One way for the conquered to become more like the conqueror (and to share some of his privileges) is to join his faith.

Both Christianity and Islam with their credo of equality and ease of conversion have been great cements of empire. Conversion has been a great channel of upward mobility, an effective mechanism for elite co-optation in multiethnic empires, and a unifying ideology for otherwise heterogeneous states.

Religion is often associated with conservatism and with the established order. We have just stressed the link between almost any established political order and an official religion. Religion provides legitimacy for the state and for the privileged classes, and the state plays the role of defender of the faith. Even Napoleon, who cynically asked how many divisions the Pope had,[2] insisted on being crowned emperor by the Pope,[3] thus sealing his betrayal of the French Revolution.

However, to stress the conservative role of religion is to give undue emphasis to only one side of the coin. Religion has also been a great source of change in human history. The oppressed and the dispossessed are not always content to adopt the faith of their oppressors. Frequently they rebel, and rebellion often takes a religious cloak. Some Marxists might argue that religious conflicts are generally class conflicts in disguise. Without having to commit oneself to a position that relegates religion to the role of a derivative phenomenon, it is clear that many, if not most, religious reform movements are in important respects movements of social protest aimed at changing conditions in this world at least as much as in the next one. Most religions that started on Indian soil, such as Buddhism, Jainism, Sikhism, and many Hindu reform movements, were in part protests against the caste system. The Reformation was a protest against papal authority and the worldliness and corruption of the Catholic Church.

[2]The anecdote, interestingly, is also attributed to Joseph Stalin.
[3]In the end, he grabbed the crown from the Pope's hands, and crowned himself.

MESSIANISTIC MOVEMENTS

Situations of foreign domination are especially likely to spawn religious movements with revolutionary implications. Throughout the colonial world thousands of sects variously called "nativistic," "revivalistic," "messianistic," or "millenarian" have emerged (Sundkler, 1948; Worsley, 1957). These movements have had a number of features in common. Overriding the many differences of detail, their common political theme has been the liberation of colonial people from foreign rule through the coming of a messiah who would herald the arrival of the golden age. Usually led by a charismatic leader who is regarded as the envoy of God, these sects are often nationalistic, otherworldly, puritanical, and militantly egalitarian and antiwealth. Most of them are ephemeral; they are either crushed by force, or disintegrate through the death of the prophet or through internal factionalism.

A few, however, have been spectacularly successful, notably Christianity, which started as a messianistic sect in a remote colony of the Roman Empire. The great monotheistic religions of Judaism, Christianity, and Islam, with their messianistic tradition, have each spawned hundreds of these millenarian movements, particularly in colonial situations.

While messianistic movements often have revolutionary ideologies, they seldom succeed and, to the extent that they do, they typically cease to be revolutionary. Respectability is the price of survival for millenarian sects. They become more bureaucratic and hierarchical; they reinterpret their prophecies in a more pragmatic direction; and they tone down their attacks on the *status quo.* Sometimes, they become the new established church, as did Christianity in Rome after the conversion of Constantine.

SYNCRETISM

Another common phenomenon when different societies come in contact is religious *syncretism,* or the fusing of elements of different religions into a new one. Practically all new religions are syncretistic in the sense that they blend elements of preexisting belief systems and rituals. Islam, for instance, is syncretistic of both Judaism and Christianity, and Christianity bears the mark of the many "mystery" cults that flourished in the Eastern Mediterranean during the Hellenistic period.

Sometimes, however, a religion that remains officially the same is profoundly modified when transplanted to a foreign environment. One of the most striking examples concerns the case of Roman Catholicism in the heavily Indian parts of the Andes and of Meso-America. The indigenous population was ostensibly converted to Catholicism in the wake of Spanish conquest, and, for the last four centuries, the Indians have called on Catholic priests to perform their rites of passage, such as baptism and marriage. But the actual belief system and ritual life of these Indian groups is a complex syncretism of the Catholic and the pre-Colombian, in which, for example, deities of the native pantheon are identified with Catholic saints. This syncretism still persists after several centuries of attempts by the Catholic church to stamp out "idolatry." The official church has to tolerate syncretism or be altogether rejected.

Secularization

One of the great processes of change in the last two centuries has been called *secularization*, or the removal from the religious sphere of institutions that had been traditionally connected with it. Its intellectual roots are to be found in the eighteenth-century French philosophers of the Enlightenment whose verbal assaults against the *Ancine Régime* did not spare the Catholic Church. Many of these ideas became incorporated in the Constitution of the United States, the first state in Western history to have explicitly established the principle of separation of church and state in its constitution. The precedent has now spread to most European countries, both socialist and capitalist.

Not only was political power increasingly separated from religion in many states. Education too, once a monopoly of the church and a privilege of the few, became both democratized and secularized. In socialist countries, all education is lay and state controlled. Most Western European and American countries continue to tolerate religious schools, but run a parallel system of state schools at all levels, which in many cases has overshadowed the religious schools. Similarly, the rites of passage have become more-and-more secularized. High school graduation and the acquisition of a driver's license are becoming more significant symbols of adulthood than Bar Mitzvah or Confirmation. In most countries, one can get married civilly without the blessing of a priest.

In the arts as well, the diminished importance of religion is evident. Traditionally, much of music, painting, sculpture, and architecture was devoted to the glorification of God (or his representative, the king). The medieval cathedrals soared loftily from the sea of puny houses of the people who erected them. In Manhattan, it is St. Patrick's Cathedral that is dwarfed in a forest of skyscrapers. Bach was a church organist: Leonard Bernstein is a jet-set entrepreneur. Van Eyck, da Vinci, and Murillo painted chaste madonnas: Renoir, Matisse, and Gauguin wallowed in luscious nudes.

The extent to which contemporary societies have become secularized, however, must not be overstated. First, it is probably a mistake to view secularization as the logical and inevitable consequence of the development of an industrial, technological civilization. It should be seen as a Western historical phenomenon that spread to other parts of the world through the political and economic hegemony of Western powers. If religion is fundamentally an attempt to answer unanswerable questions, then it will be with us for an indefinite future, and it is not at all inconceivable that the trend toward secularization might be reversed.

Second, secularization is often not as thorough as official ideology would have us believe. No state has managed to stamp out religion, much as some have tried. Some revolutionary countries, such as Mexico and the Soviet Union, have resorted to bloody persecution to eradicate religion, but have so dismally failed that they had to revert to a more tolerant policy. Poland, after a quarter-century of Communist rule, seems no less religious than Spain, which still recognizes Catholicism as the official faith. In Spain, the association of the Catholic Church with the corrupt Franco dictatorship seems to have kept Communism alive, while in Poland, persecution of the Church by a Communist dictatorship subservient to Soviet interests has made the Church a rallying center of Polish nationalism.

Many highly industrialized states, like West Germany and Belgium, have far from complete separation of church and state. In West Germany the state collects taxes on behalf of the Catholic and Protestant Churches, pays official salaries to ministers of religion, requests religious information from its citizens in many of its state offices, practices an informal religious quota system in its civil service, and even establishes religious segregation and teaches religion in the "state" schools. In Belgium the state subsidizes the Catholic schools and pays their teachers, in the same way as it does in its own parallel system of "lay" schools. In Israel only religious marriage is recognized by the state and being Jewish confers privileges of immigration and citizenship not granted members of other religions. The United States, for all its tradition of separation of church and state, still has people swearing on Bibles in courts, mentions God in its oath of allegiance and on its coins, has a chaplain recite prayers to open sessions of Congress or to inaugurate a President, and pays ministers of religion to serve as chaplains in its armed forces.

Finally, the extent of secularization that a country is said to have achieved hinges on how restrictive one's definition of religion is. Many authors have noted the similarities between religions and ostensibly secular ideologies like nationalism or Communism. Some have even spoken of "secular religions," and have compared conflicts like the Cold War to wars of religion in previous centuries. Perhaps we could apply the label "mystification" to both religions in the narrow sense and to the secular ideologies of more recent vintage, and conclude that the level of mystification used by the ruling classes to legitimize their power remains roughly constant, and that secular ideologies serve just as well as religious ones for that purpose. If religion is the opium of the masses, Marxism-Leninism, Fascism, and nationalism is their heroin.

Interestingly, the attempt by radical thinkers to dispense with religion was often couched in quasi-religious terms. The French Revolution tried to substitute the cult of Goddess Reason for Catholicism. The positivist scientists of the nineteenth century spoke of Nature in such teleological terms as to make it a very good substitute for God. Auguste Comte, after proclaiming the triumph of Science over Religion and Metaphysics, and after enthroning Sociology as the queen of sciences, conceived of sociologists as of a new priesthood presiding over the happiness of mankind, and of Sociology as a new religion of society. Patriots make Mother Country their goddess, and sacralize its symbolic paraphernalia: flags, national anthems, soil, blood. The luckless infantryman who stops a bullet in the swamps of Vietnam is a martyr in the cause of freedom. When his corpse is feeding the maggots, he is said to have spilled his blood for God and Country, or, as the case may be, for the triumph of that Communist millenium, the Great Proletarian Revolution.

Even magic, which may be thought to have yielded to science in its claims to influence the course of events, is not all that clearly in retreat in industrial societies. Is the Saint Christopher medal on the automobile dashboard any different from the Pygmy hunter's amulet to ward off the evil spirits of the forest? Is not the gambler who blows on the dice for luck performing as much of a magical act as the Trobriander performing rites before an ocean fishing expedition? Card reading, palmistry, tea-leaves reading, horoscopes, and other forms of divination continue to be practiced in the most industrial societies. Water witching continues to be firmly believed in by many thousands of American farmers (Vogt and Hyman, 1959).

If there is a conclusion to be drawn from all this, it is that God is not dead, nor about to be for the foreseeable future. Supernatural thinking is both a consequence of man's cerebral development and of his intellectual limitations. Man is intelligent enough to seek answers to all problems, including the most fundamental ones for which he has not been able to find natural answers. Or, if he thinks he has found natural answers, his *amour propre* makes him reject them. As a being conscious of his destiny, man finds the thought of his own extinction utterly abhorrent. Religion is, in the last analysis, man's attempt to assuage the mental agony that his thinking provokes. He invents a God more powerful than he, so that he can share His immortality.

ADDITIONAL READING

Several of the early sociologists and anthropologists, especially Durkheim (1915), Frazer (1890), and Weber (1930, 1951, 1952, 1958) were vitally concerned with religion. Malinowski (1948) gave a classic interpretation of the relationship between science, magic, and religion. Worsley (1957) is an excellent account of messianistic movements in the Pacific, and a critique of Weber's concept of charisma. Sundkler (1948) deals with religious syncretism and messianism in South Africa. Of the great religious classics, the *Bhagavad-Gita* offers one of the most coherent alternatives to the dualistic Judaic-Christian-Muslim world-view, and probably the one most compatible with modern scientific thinking.

9

Arts
and Sciences

Defining art broadly as the pursuit of beauty, and science as the pursuit of knowledge, both activities are universal in human societies. There is an ethnocentric tradition in Western scholarship that sees science as having been invented in seventeenth-century Europe, and that restricts the definition of art to the European concept of *l'art pour l'art* (art for art's sake). To be sure, that tradition recognizes that beauty can be found in other cultures, but it somehow claims for the West a monopoly of the conscious and gratuitous search for beauty, and makes an invidious distinction between the artist and the artisan. Similarly, Western historians of science admit that the growth of science in modern Europe had roots in Greece, Egypt, Rome, and the Arab world, and they perhaps grudgingly admit that the Chinese also invented a few things (often several centuries before the West, as was the case with printing). Nevertheless, many Western scholars still seem to believe that the scientific ethos of knowledge as a desirable end in itself, the scientific logic of induction and deduction, and the scientific methods of observation and experimentation are Western inventions. The Western scientific outlook, they believe, is now spreading to the rest of the world, but the West remains the fountainhead of modern science. They rather immodestly explain this through the evident superiority of Western science.

The Universality of Science

Let us imagine a different scenario from the well-known one of European colonial expansion. If Portugal, a puny country of perhaps two million people, and Spain with perhaps five or six million people only recently unified after long wars of reconquest against the Moors, could conquer nearly half of the world in the sixteenth century, it is not unreasonable to assume that China, the world's biggest and oldest nation-state, possessing a technology generally superior to that of the West, could have done at least as well. At that time, China had around 200 million people; its ships were much bigger than anything the Portuguese could build; printing with movable type was long known; and the Ming Dynasty was a period of strong political centralization. The edge of China over the West, numerically, technologically, and politically, was considerable.

In fact, China very nearly conquered the world just before the West did so. A half-century before Portuguese sailors timidly began to venture down the coast of West Africa, Admiral Cheng Ho, in the first decade of the fifteenth century, led several massive naval expeditions that took him to Africa, with hundreds of ships and tens of thousands of sailors and soldiers (Eberhard, 1960). The combined fleets of Christopher Columbus, Magellan, and Vasco de Gama would have been a puny reconnaissance party compared to Cheng Ho's mighty armada.

The reasons why China chose not to conquer an overseas empire are complex. Piracy along the Chinese coast made navigation risky, and inland trade routes were secure. In any case, the Chinese decided that these massive naval ventures did not pay. Let us assume, however, that the imperialist designs of the Emperor would have prevailed over good commercial common sense, and that the Chinese would have decided to conquer the world. Would it not, then, be safe to assume that science would now be universally recognized as a Chinese achievement? Would not acupuncture be taught at Harvard Medical

School as the dominant school of scientific medicine? Would not Freud be regarded as a quaint Viennese witch doctor whose outlandish ideas would never have come to anybody's attention had it not been for the brilliant monograph of a Peking anthropologist on "Child-Training Practices Among Tyrolian Mountaineers"? Would not the imaginative but altogether fanciful ideas of that Viennese witch doctor be used in anthropology courses as a classical illustration of the prescientific mentality of the West? Does it not suggest a deranged mind to believe that sons want to kill their fathers because they want to copulate with their mothers, when the father of sociology, Confucius, discovered long ago that filial piety and respect for paternal authority is the basis of all social order? Freudianism might have become a faddist cult among a few counter-culture dropouts at Peking University, but no self-respecting psychiatrist could take him seriously.

We need not pursue our pleasant fantasy of a Chinese-dominated world much further to see how puerile and ethnocentric our Western monopolistic claims on "modern science" are. To the extent that the Western outlook does indeed dominate the world, it does so, not because of intrinsic superiority, but because of political and military domination. To be sure, it takes a certain level of social organization and of technology to achieve large-scale domination. It is also true that Western science, starting in the seventeenth century, helped give the West an increasing technological edge in production and weaponry over the rest of the world. But it must not be forgotten that much of the European colonial conquest took place *before* the "Scientific Revolution," and that economic and technological development in the West was both the result and the cause of colonial expansion.

All societies have a body of empirical knowledge about the world—verified by experience, culturally transmitted, and learned. That is, all societies have science. This body of knowledge is often codified in cosmologies, historical narratives, legends, and other standardized accounts wherein verifiable fact is intertwined with fiction and ideology, but this is true in the West also, notably so in the social sciences. Certainly, if we claim a social science for ourselves, then we must grant one to every society. Curiously, even anthropologists, who have been preaching relativism for at least 40 years, have difficulty in conceiving of their own discipline as only one among thousands of what they call "folk systems" when they deal with their "natives." Through a supreme act of ethnocentrism, anthropologists add the prefix "ethno" to much of what they do in nonliterate cultures. The study of Bach scores is musicology, but the study of Zulu choral singing is *ethno*musicology; an account of Napoleon's wars is history, but Usman dan Fodio's conquests in Northern Nigeria are *ethno*history, and so on.

Obviously, all music, all science, all history, all food is ethnic, in the sense that it is linked with an ethnic group. The hamburger and milk shake at the drive-in restaurant are no less ethnic than the sweet-and-sour pork at the Chinese restaurant. If the Yoruba wood carver working on a mask for the next Gelede festival is doing ethnic art, so was Michelangelo when he painted the Sistine Chapel. If we must call the medicine practitioner among the Navaho a witch doctor, then we should extend the courtesy to the Harley Street gynecologist or the Massachusetts General Hospital brain surgeon.

My argument is simply this: all cultures have an empirical view of the world, valid according to certain criteria, and none has a monopoly of "scientific truth," whatever that may mean. There is no universally valid criterion whereby our view of the world should be called science, and everybody else's "ethnoscience" or "folk systems." The prefix "ethno," as it is so commonly used in anthropology, is not only a redundancy, but an invidious one.

The Universality of Art

What is true of science is equally true of art. Here the invidious distinction is between artists and artisans. Within a given society, the distinction has validity. Clearly, the blacksmith who spends all his time fitting horseshoes is not operating at the same level as his colleague who is making the wrought-iron gates for the cathedral.

What is untenable, however, is the notion that complex societies have artists producing "great art," while simpler societies only have artisans producing "tribal art" or "folk art."

Western ethnocentrism in art is still deeply ingrained in our culture, as witnessed by what we do with the art objects we exhibit. For a long time, much of the so-called primitive art was exhibited in museums of natural history, or in ethnographic museums, or in heterogeneous warehouses for the plunder of empire like the British Museum. We admit a few select Asian cultures in our national art museums, but not the masterpieces of Africa or Melanesia. These land, at best, in anthropology museums or in segregated museums of "primitive" art, or, worse yet, as a small section of *curiosa* in a museum of natural history, along with stuffed birds and pinned beetles.

In one respect the Western conception of art and of science is unusual, though not unique. In most cultures knowledge and beauty are pursued not as abstract ends in themselves, but to serve some other purpose. This was generally the case in Western cultures as well until the nineteenth century. Western artists and intellectuals then began to make the extraordinary claim on their society that they were entitled to be supported in comfort, and to be free to do whatever struck their fancy, irrespective of whether anybody else thought it served any purpose or did any good. Such an extravagant demand for unbridled parasitism is seldom accepted at face value, even in affluent Western societies. Most Western scientists work on applied research for corporate sponsors, such as the military establishment or industrial concerns. Those who do "pure" research often have to justify their existence by teaching, and much of the money spent on "pure" research is given in the belief that, sooner or later, the findings will be of some practical use. As for art, the professional artist still has to please patrons if he is to make a living from art. Thus, theory notwithstanding, the position of the Western scientist or artist is not very different from that of his colleagues in other societies. It is, therefore, the height of absurdity to restrict the definition of either art or science to its rarefied, pure form, which exists only in the wishful thinking of the practitioner.

SPECIALIZATION IN ARTS AND SCIENCES

In the least differentiated societies, arts and sciences are not specialized activities. Science, in the broadest sense of accumulated wisdom and experience, is closely correlated with age, and the old typically fulfill the function of imparting their knowledge to the young. Except, however, for some specialization in medicine, that oldest and most universal of sciences, simple societies do not have professional scientists. As for the arts, they are practiced to some extent by everybody, though some are recognized as better than others. Everyone plays music, sings, and dances, and some form of music is a cultural universal or near-universal. Some form of plastic art is also found everywhere. At a bare minimum, it takes the form of personal adornment, such as the use of cosmetics, jewelry, decorated clothing, tatooing, body painting, or mutilations. But even such seemingly utilitarian items as pottery jars, baskets, or weapons seldom fail to display some concern for beauty and adornment. Even in classless societies where there are no professional artists, almost every item of current consumption shows some attempt to transcend its strictly utilitarian use and to be aesthetically pleasing.

In slightly more complex societies, such as many of the agricultural societies of Africa, one begins to find artisanal, and, by the same token, artistic specialization. The village blacksmith, potter, or weaver is both an artisan and an artist. He produces to satisfy both material needs and aesthetic tastes. In the field of science, the transmission of knowledge through education often begins to leave the family sphere, and the phenomenon of schooling appears. Age groups of children are taught by their elders (not necessarily their parents or even relatives) all they need to know to become good citizens. These "initiation schools," as anthropologists call them, are fundamentally no different from our Western schools.

EDUCATION AND SCHOOLING

Once more, we find the ethnocentric practice of using a special term to designate institutions in "primitive" societies that are not significantly different from our own. If Africans have "initiation schools," then, so do we, and the word "initiation" becomes a redundancy. In the typical "initiation school," children are physically segregated from adults, and are also separated by sex. They are taught by adults a mixture of empirical knowledge, moral precepts, and "tribal lore," and they graduate to adult status by going through initiation rituals, otherwise known as "rites of passage."

All of these features are found in Western schooling systems: the spatial segregation of children from adults, the age and often the sex segregation of the children, the teaching by adults, the content of the teaching, and the rites of passage.

Much Western school education is moral and mythological, rather than factual. Even in the secularized schools where religion is not taught, courses on ethics, civics, or "social studies" provide a code of moral precepts. History is typically taught as nationalistic mythology ("tribal lore") bearing only an occasional resemblance to facts. Conformity is rewarded, and critical, iconoclastic thinking discouraged. Discipline and respect for authority are stressed. At the end comes the rite of passage in the form of the graduation ceremony, complete with invocations to the gods, incantations by the elders, and the masquerade of caps and gowns. Except for longer duration and a greater emphasis on technical knowledge, the educational system of industrial societies differs little from the "initiation school" of simple agricultural societies.

MASS AND ELITE PRODUCTS

The transition from the simple, stateless agricultural society, to the complex, stratified, agrarian state marks important changes in the institutionalization of arts and sciences. Each bifurcates by social class into an elite and a mass variety. With the centralization of power and the siphoning off of surplus production for the benefit of the ruling class, the latter are able to patronize specialists in arts and sciences. Artists provide entertainment and luxury goods for the court and the nobility. Court musicians, jesters, acrobats, dancers, actors, courtesans, and other entertainers develop artistic traditions to please the increasingly fastidious tastes of their patrons, and the gap in both style and content between the "great tradition" of the court and the "little tradition" of the peasantry widens.[1] The material forms of art also become increasingly specialized and elaborate. To the village black-smith who makes hoes for peasants has been added the goldsmith who does filigree jewelry for the court; the cobbler is supplemented by the saddle-maker; the potter by the porcelain decorator; and so on.

Entirely new forms of art develop out of ruling-class demands for the decoration of their mansions, palaces, temples, and tombs. Architecture, painting, sculpture, rug and tapestry weaving now employ full-time specialists in the keep of the wealthy and the powerful. Much of the competitive display of power and wealth in the ruling class is channelled into artistic production, especially in great monuments that satisfy the yearning of the powerful for immortality. Many of the greatest artistic achievements of mankind have been purchased at the cost of untold misery and suffering on the part of the peasants who have had to defray these extravagant projects, but the lot of the artists has typically been one of relative comfort and privilege. The professional artist has very seldom been of the ruling class, for members of the ruling class with artistic pretensions did not have to become professionals. However, the artist's lot has characteristically been far more comfortable than that of the average peasant. The artist in complex agrarian societies has generally enjoyed the status of a lesser courtier or, at least, of a privileged servant.

Knowledge and the Priesthood

Specialization of knowledge also grows substantially with the development of complex agrarian societies, and much of that growth is

[1]The terms "great tradition" and "little tradition" have been extensively used by anthropologists and historians, especially in reference to India. These two terms differentiate the art tradition, not only by social class, but also geographical spread. The "little tradition" shows much more local variability than the great tradition which is, by definition, the tradition shared by the ruling class of a large state. The term "little tradition" has inevitably acquired pejorative connotations, but I am using it without derogatory intent.

linked with the priesthood. Most priesthoods became classes of specialists in knowledge, and they tried to maintain monopolistic control of their stock in trade by restricting access to knowledge. That is, they made knowledge esoteric, and they Sanscritized their trade by such devices as using a dead or foreign language incomprehensible to the masses, or by restricting the spread of literacy. Occasionally, priesthoods have so successfully manipulated the power that esoteric knowledge gave them that they managed to become the ruling class of theocratic states. However, the clergy has generally been a subordinate sector of the ruling group itself. Conflicts between church and state over secular power have been common, which indicates that the clergy, through its control of esoteric knowledge has often been a dangerous contender for the secular ruling class.

The history of medieval Europe illustrates well the temporal power of the Catholic Church and the way in which the clergy tried to monopolize knowledge as an instrument of power. By using Latin until the middle of the twentieth century, the clergy maintained its supranational unity in a vast multiethnic domain, and effectively made its knowledge esoteric to the masses. The clergy taught the masses only what it wanted—the catechism and little more. Until the Renaissance, the clergy maintained a virtual monopoly on literacy, and the monasteries were practically the sole repositories of the fund of knowledge legated to the West by the Greco-Roman tradition. Even the nobility were often illiterate until the sixteenth or seventeenth century. The universities were completely under Church control, and such secular education as the clergy offered was virtually limited to its own ranks and to the nobility. By the eighteenth century, religious secondary schools began to open their doors to the bourgeoisie, but mass education and literacy had to wait until the nineteenth century. The seventeenth century marks the first real glimmers of success in the secularization of knowledge, a process bitterly opposed by the Church. Even Newton, one of the towering scientific minds of seventeenth-century Europe saw himself as a theologian, as much, if not more, than a physicist.

Fundamentally, the same set of linkages between church and state, and between both of these and the development of a "great tradition" in the arts and the sciences has prevailed in most of the complex agrarian societies. In the vast area under Islamic influence, from Indonesia to Morocco, political power has been religiously legitimized, and religious leadership has been the monopoly of a literate class of learned men (*imam*) versed in religious, legal, and secular knowledge. That class also controlled the Koranic universities and schools and used a classical Arabic dialect, incomprehensible to the peasants, as a sacred language common to the literate and ruling class. In China the Mandarin tradition of learning grounded in Confucian philosophy was much more secularized and open to the lower classes. The ruling bureaucracy, whatever its class origins, was by definition a literate group whose monopolistic control of power and knowledge rested in good part on an extraordinarily complex written language. It took practically half a lifetime of leisure to learn how to read and write sufficiently well to pass the qualifying examinations for a bureaucratic position.

The surplus production made possible in complex agrarian societies led to the development of arts and sciences by specialists for the enjoyment and benefit of the powerful. This pattern is in sharp contrast to the unspecialized character of, and the more equal and universal access to, art and science in unstratified societies. What of industrial societies?

Arts and Sciences in Industrial Societies

Industrial societies, it seems, have undergone a process of secularization of the arts and the sciences, and of democratization of access to education. Both of these processes preceded the Industrial Revolution, and thus cannot be said to be necessary consequences of it. Furthermore, whereas we have a number of instances of complex agrarian societies that developed in at least partial independence of each other, we basically have only a single historical case of industrialization. This case diffused from Europe to other parts of the world, much of that diffusion being due to the political domination of European countries *before* the industrial age. Therefore, causal inferences are almost impossible to draw. We can observe only what happened in Europe, starting in the seventeenth century.

Just as the Protestant Reformation had shaken the doctrinal authority of the Church in religious matters, men of sound common sense and enough curiosity to observe the world around them began to challenge Church theories about the nature of that world. Step by step, from Copernicus and Galileo to Darwin, Catholic cosmology came tumbling down. By the eighteenth century, many of the leading minds of Europe had become converted to the anticlericalism and the inquisitive, skeptical, irreverent spirit of the French *philosophes*. With the French Revolution, the grip of the Church on education was broken. Napoleon's educational reforms, establishing a system of nonreligious state schools, spread throughout much of Europe in the wake of his conquests. By the second half of the nineteenth century, the countries of Western Europe were on the way to achieving primary education and literacy for the masses, a system of lay secondary schools for the middle classes and a network of scientifically oriented, lay universities for the intellectual elite.

Japan, which by the seventeenth century had already achieved a literacy rate far higher than Europe's, modeled many of its post-Meiji Restoration educational reforms after the German and French systems, and fully kept pace with the industrial nations of the West in terms of mass education. It still remains the only non-Western country to boast a practically 100 percent adult literacy rate. By the early twentieth century, the United States extended the European notion of mass primary education to the secondary-school level, and eventually, after the Second World War, to the university level.

The philosophy of mass education, and especially of a common public education is, as we already suggested, not unique to the West. Many unstratified non-Western societies had long practiced it. It was, however, a departure from the restricted and esoteric conception of learning that had developed in medieval Europe and in other complex agrarian societies.

Lay education resulted in the secularization of both science and the arts, and opened those fields to the talented from all social strata. An increasingly technocratic society became increasingly reliant on formal education, and the principle of meritocracy gained ground. But did mass education make the industrial societies any more democratic and egalitarian?

MERITOCRACY

As wittily shown by Michael Young (1961), meritocracy is, in fact, a highly elitist notion, leading to a brand of oligarchy that is all the more resilient for being based on innate differences in talent and intelligence. Intelligence is an ability which in any large human group is distributed along a bell-shaped curve; that is, about two-thirds of the people cluster around mediocrity, 12 to 15 percent are rather dumb, and an equal number rather bright. Some 5 percent at each end are stupid or brilliant. Intelligence (or at least its measurement by tests that are necessarily culture-bound and class-biased) is affected by many environmental conditions, such as cultural stimulation in the home, and adequacy of diet. Severe dietary deficiencies, for instance, result in mental retardation. However, given an adequate diet and a reasonably stimulating social environment, intelligence is largely determined genetically.

In the affluent industrial societies, starvation has been virtually eradicated, and mass education insures at least a common basis of mental stimulation for the entire population. Although the home environment produces great class differences, especially in motivation and attitude to academic learning, there has been some equalization of environmental conditions. Therefore, individual differences in intelligence, as measured by tests (however class-biased and culture-bound these still are), can be expected increasingly to reflect inborn, genetic differences. If, then, selection for the higher positions in society follows strictly meritocratic principles, it could be expected that soon the social classes would be sharply stratified by intelligence. Initially, meritocracy would make for much mobility, since most class orders have traditionally hindered upward mobility of the lowly born gifted and downward mobility among the highborn nitwits. Soon, however, meritocracy would lead to a genetically based caste system.

Industrial societies are still far from being thoroughly meritocratic. The United States and South Africa are still racial caste societies (i.e., they are stratified according to skin pigmentation), a principle that bears no demonstrable relationship to intelligence or to talent of any sort. A debate currently rages in the United States around the neo-racist theories of Jensen (1969) concerning qualitative differences in intelligence between whites and blacks. Jensen's arguments are unconvincing because the racial discrimination existing against blacks makes it impossible to "control for class" in comparing racial groups for performance on intelligence tests. A genuine meritocracy would almost certainly lead to complete racial integration, because the evidence points towards the absence of *innate* differences in intelligence between racial groups.[2] But a genuine meritocracy would also quickly lead to inbreeding population groups stratified by intelligence, a system of inequality far more unshakable than the class tyrannies of the past because, for once, the basis of inequality would make some objective sense.

The American educational system is still very far from being meritocratic. In fact, it is much less so than many European, Asian, and African educational systems that are far more selective and intellectually elitist. In many ways, the American educational system has the worst of both worlds: it is socially elitist and intellectually

---

[2] The currently fashionable argument among white academic liberals that blacks need preferential treatment to compensate for past discrimination is in fact latently racist despite its benevolent pretense. Only a belief in the inferiority of blacks can lead to the conclusion that blacks cannot compete on the basis of merit, and therefore need the shelter of "benign discrimination."

egalitarian. The entire culture has powerful norms of antiintellectualism, and the ideology of American educators makes them go to great lengths in pretending that intellectual differences do not exist. In the end, the pretense does not fool anyone, but still, ''streaming'' of students by ability is ''undemocratic.'' Most of the streaming that still covertly goes on is by social class and race, irrelevant criteria at best. The truly bright child of whatever social class has to suffer the educational deprivation of being held back to the least common intellectual denominator of his school. By now, this ideology of intellectual egalitarianism has even invaded the universities, including the graduate schools.

This seeming digression on education and intelligence leads us back to the topic of this chapter. Can a society so heavily reliant on advanced science and technology survive with an educational system that is, in its basic philosophy, similar to those of extremely undifferentiated societies? The answer is, I think, negative, and the main reason that the system has worked at all is that the ideology of intellectual egalitarianism has been surreptitiously violated. Thus, we find a paradoxical situation. In Europe, education made no apology for intellectual selectivity at each school level. It was accepted that only the brighter students made it through university. Therefore, the entire system of higher education remained at a homogeneously high level. In America, the belief that everybody is entitled to higher education has led to a fantastic degree of stratification in quality within so-called higher education.

The ideological pressures toward intellectual egalitarianism, however, continue unabated, with the result that a Gresham's law of education set in: bad education chases away good one. Pressures for ''relevance,'' against grading, for giving preference to the ''culturally deprived,'' and so on, all result in levelling the whole educational enterprise downward. In effect, the entire society is becoming culturally deprived. By now, even Ph.D's from Harvard and Berkeley become intellectually suspect. Grade inflation and degree devaluation are so rampant that, where quality and competence still matter, evidence for them has to be sought outside the very system which claims to provide a valid basis of evaluation.

The remedy is obvious, though probably ideologically unpalatable. Education in a complex industrial society serves two radically distinct functions. On the one hand, it must equip every citizen with the minimum civic and intellectual baggage to function as a member of society. This is the function of all educational systems, even in the most undifferentiated societies. This type of education I would call the "initiation school" model. It should be unselective, either by social class or by intelligence (barring, of course, the feeble-minded who could not be expected to fend for themselves under any circumstances). The second type of education is that which imparts technical skills, and that kind of education, if it is to be efficient, is, by definition, elitist. Different people have different skills (and not only intellectual skills matter), and technical schooling should bring out the most from the gifted, whether in pottery making or in nuclear physics, in diesel engineering or gourmet cooking, in poultry farming or industrial management. The initiation school should make us good "generalists," whether as Zulus, Eskimos, or Americans. Technical schooling should make us competent specialists. The initiation school cannot attempt to do the job of the Massachusetts Institute of Technology, nor should that school try to convert itself into an initiation school for the "culturally deprived" who, alas, abound in America (and come in all skin colors). The refusal to dissociate these two radically distinct functions of education, and to carry through the logically very different consequences of each has led to an educational system which is both expensive and inefficient, intellectually egalitarian and socially elitist.

Perhaps the only level of technical education that still works to some extent in the United States is graduate education, and there the model is still essentially that of a medieval guild: the master craftsman teaches his apprentices. We run our public primary and secondary schools like initiation schools, and our universities like feudal guilds. Is it not time that we consider more viable alternatives?

ADDITIONAL READINGS

A whole specialty of sociology, called the "sociology of knowledge" devotes itself to studying the role of ideas and ideology in society, but it has concerned itself almost exclusively with Western societies. A classic in that tradition is Mannheim (1946). The sociology of science is usually considered a separate specialty from the sociology of knowledge, but it has also suffered from ethnocentrism. Kuhn (1962) and Ben-David (1971) do a good job of tracing the development of science in Western societies. Of the major sociologists who gave the arts a prominent place in their thinking, Sorokin (1937, 1941) stands out. The sociology of education has spawned an enormous literature, most of it quite pedestrian. Good accounts of higher education, both in America and elsewhere, are Ashby (1966), Jencks and Riesman (1968), Touraine (1974), and Burn (1971). Among anthropologists, the main contributions to the study of thought have been made by French scholars, especially by Lévi-Strauss (1966, 1970), and earlier by Lévy-Bruhl (1966). Young's piece of social science fiction on meritocracy makes for amusing reading.

10

Fun and Games

With the acquisition of a complex brain, *Homo sapiens* developed the need to keep himself amused. The capacity to be amused runs a wide individual gamut from Queen Victoria to George Bernard Shaw, but it is probably a safe generalization that most people would rather be amused than bored. Thus, it should come as no surprise that fun and games are found in all societies.

The Biological Basis of Play

The very universality of play in human societies raises again the question of its biological foundation. Play is far from being uniquely human, but it seems largely limited to mammals, and most developed among the more intelligent mammals, such as the primates and carnivores. This strongly suggests a linkage between play and intelligence. To be amused and to seek amusement as an end in itself, presupposes a certain level of mental development. Play, as many other aspects of our behavior, is governed in part by *Anlagen*, which we share with other primates, especially the very playful higher primates.

Another line of evidence pointing to the biological foundations of play is the fact that play behavior is far more developed in young animals than in older ones. Not only in man, but in monkeys, apes, cats, dogs, and other playful animals, subadults are far more inclined to play games than adults. Indeed, many of these animal games are tests of strength and an apprenticeship of skills that will later be used in earnest in hunting or establishing oneself in a dominance hierarchy.

Play, then, is a form of apprenticeship for life, another indication of its close link with intelligence.

Human behavior, in play as in many other activities, is different in degree but not in kind from that of other mammals. Humans, being more intelligent, are also more playful, and remain more playful longer in life than other primates. The adult gorilla or orangutan are deadly serious creatures, even though their young are constantly playing. Humans, on the other hand, retain some capacity and taste for games in later life, though appreciably less in old age than in youth.

The linkage between play and intelligence can also be observed in individual differences. The elusive quality known as a "sense of humor" seems closely linked with intelligence, a fact implicitly recognized in the double meaning of the word "dull." Indeed, it may well be that the linkage between play and age is mediated in part through intelligence. The mind of the child is far more active and inquisitive than that of the adult, and the decline of intelligence with age, while slow and gradual, is well documented. Holding age constant, it seems that less intelligent persons tend to take themselves and their fellow men far more seriously than the intellectually gifted. The better mind has a greater need to seek amusement and a greater capacity to find it, even in the most unlikely places.

Another characteristic of human fun and games is their gregariousness. It is scarcely surprising that, as a social animal, man should also seek amusement in the company of other humans. With the exception of gambling, which is relatively asocial, man seeks diversion in groups, or at least, the solitary form of a given game is considered inferior to the social one. Solitaire is not nearly as entertaining as poker or bridge; drinking, eating, and dancing are not much fun alone; a joke is no good without an audience; even the solitary exploits of hunting and fishing have to be endlessly told and retold to be fully savored (aside from the fact that few people go hunting and fishing alone). Fun, in short, is something to be shared, even if the fun is derived from suffering. Secretly pulling a fly's legs is a sordid and infantile little game; killing bulls to the *olés* of a Sunday afternoon crowd has captivated millions of people for hundreds of years. By and large, the more people, the merrier. There are a few forms of entertainment, like chess and love-making, which are best practiced *à deux*, but, in most societies, the main occasions for merrymaking are on a gargantuan scale: festivals, football games, rock concerts, and so on.

The human propensity to be playful is such that some sociologists have come very close to analyzing *all* human behavior as if it were a game. Perhaps the most influential proponent of this approach in contemporary sociology is Goffman (1959, 1963, 1971) who interprets behavior as a manipulative game of play-acting in which we "manage" the impression or image we create in others, and vice versa. While this approach makes for very amusing reading, and is, no doubt, a psychically and financially rewarding game for Mr. Goffman to play, it has the drawback of all approaches that endeavor to do too much of a good thing. If play becomes synonymous with behavior, it loses its value as a concept. Much closer to the mark is Huizinga (1955) who, while he clearly recognizes the play element in practically every aspect of culture, and even suggests that culture has its origin in play, nevertheless spells out the characteristics that differentiate play from nonplay. Huizinga defines play as a *voluntary* action, undertaken within clearly defined space and time *boundaries*, according to definite and binding *rules*. Play, furthermore, is an end in itself, is accompanied by a feeling of tension and of joy, and is consciously recognized as different from ordinary life; that is, "not for real." To see the whole world as a stage, then, is in a sense, to remove oneself permanently from it, to play God. Most of us do so only part of the time.

Huizinga goes on to develop an evolutionary theory of play; as culture develops, the play element in it retreats in importance. Since the nineteenth century, he claims, we are more deadly serious than ever, and even our way of killing is less playful than it once was.

Where are the good old days of ritual combat, of sporty, chivalrous wars, of dueling? Where are the redeeming graces of fighting guerrillas in swamps?

I find Huizinga's evolutionary argument unconvincing. It may be true that modern wars are more "for keeps" and less for fun than the cattle raids of the East African pastoralists, or the combat of medieval knights in armor, but then some wars in the remote past have also been in deadly earnest, indeed genocidal. Furthermore, even though our modern wars may be less playful than those in the past, they are still not completely devoid of ritual. Generals are still prone to think in terms of game theory, and to play what they explicitly call "war games" in the intervals between real shooting wars. The fact that war games are taken seriously by generals does not make them any less games. Many games are taken seriously by the players, and the tension is often intense. Adults find amusement in the earnestness with which children play cops and robbers, but is the behavior of Bobby Fisher playing chess any less serious?

The distinction between games and war is far from clear. Agonistic behavior is evident in many games. Sports that have become national rituals of mass participation like bullfighting, American football, ice hockey, boxing, and wrestling have acquired many characteristics of combat. That makes them not unlike the highly ritualized warfare of many "primitive" societies. Our politics, too, or at least the public part of our politics, such as elections, parliamentary debate, and the like, have also become increasingly ritualized and divorced from the real processes of competition for power. When we see a carefully groomed and made-up president give a press conference on television, we all know we are watching a theatrical performance, much more akin to watching *Hamlet* or *King Lear,* than to observing "real" political behavior.

Overall, then, it is doubtful that contemporary industrial societies are less playful than simpler societies. There may be less emphasis on play in one aspect of our institutions, but that is made up by an increase in playfulness in other domains. Religion, for instance, may become more internalized and less dependent on ritualistic mass plays, but then our politics are becoming more and more of a circus. Consider, for example, the election primaries of the two major American political parties: from pompon girls to popcorn vendors, a national convention is amazingly like a World Series baseball game. The play element in culture, to use Huizinga's phrase, seems more a constant than a variable in social evolution.

Play as a Profession

Where complex societies differ in degree from less complex ones, however, is in the degree to which play has become *professionalized*. Complex agrarian societies begin to develop the full-time specialization of professional entertainers, and the trend continues in industrial societies where entertainers run into hundreds of specialties and tens of thousands of individuals: football quarterbacks, jazz saxophonists, call girls, geishas, Shakespearean actors, ballet dancers, circus acrobats, animal trainers, masters of ceremonies on television shows, and many others. In addition, a number of occupational roles that were once not primarily thought of as entertaining have acquired histrionic dimensions, such as political campaigning and university lecturing.

The professionalization of entertainment is particularly evident in sports, where attempts to keep a sharp distinction between amateurs and professionals (e.g., in the Olympic Games, or between collegiate and professional football) are becoming increasingly unworkable. More and more play activity in industrial societies is vicarious: we watch other people who are paid to entertain us. We are increasingly being entertained, rather than entertaining ourselves. Indeed, the need for more and more entertainment in industrial societies is the direct result of a rapid increase in leisure time.

The professionalization of play obviously brings with it a sharp distinction between actor and spectator. At the village feast, a few professional musicians may get paid to provide instrumental music, but everybody joins in the dancing, singing, drinking, and merrymaking. The conductor of a symphony orchestra, on the other hand, would frown on his audience joining in the chorus of Beethoven's Ninth Symphony, much less humming along during the other three movements. The role of the symphony concert audience is to pay the admission ticket, to sit quietly, and to clap politely between pieces (but, please, not between movements).

In turn, this sharp distinction between audience and actor implies that what is play for the audience is work for the actor, and this makes for the most fundamental difference between participant and spectator forms of play. Cracking jokes for an audience in front of television cameras, or having sex 20 times a night with paying customers is not much fun for the actor.

What is play and what is not is thus not always a clear-cut matter, or, at least, it depends on the point of view or the person involved. When Laurence Olivier plays King Lear, he is a professional actor and an amateur king. When Richard Nixon made a television appearance, he was an amateur actor and a professional president.

Play and Social Class

With the professionalization of play there also came the linkage between play and social class. The beginnings of professional entertainment are found with the rise of centralized states and of social classes. In classless, stateless societies, some people are naturally more talented storytellers, comedians, acrobats, buffoons, or punsters than others, but they receive no rewards other than social approval and conviviality for their antics. Centralized power brings with it the king's fool, the court musicians, the concubines, and all the other menials whose reward for amusing the powerful is a social and economic status more secure than that of the mass of the peasantry. Yet their status also remains lowly enough that they can make no claim to power, though they often enjoy the special privilege of criticizing and ridiculing the powerful with impunity. The king's fool is really no fool at all: he is the intellectual-in-residence, who may be impertinent so long as he is amusing, a license not unlike that of contemporary academics.

The fact that the court has historically been the first center for the development of professional entertainers has also led to the frequent bifurcation of games, sports, and entertainment into a "high" and a "low" tradition. Certain forms of fun were more socially esteemed and deemed to be proper only for the nobility, while others were declared fit for the masses. Snobbery in the pursuit of pleasure generally increases with social complexity, as do other manners of invidious distinction. Certain games or sports become debased over time, as their popularity spreads to the lower strata (e.g., skiing and golfing in recent Western history), while other forms of entertainment originally deemed plebeian graduate into "high culture" as they lose their popularity (e.g., grand opera between the nineteenth and twentieth century). Generally, however, fun is sought in the company of one's social peers, though an occasional slumming expedition to see how the other side lives might be good fun as well. (Locales where the upper classes come slumming often become tourist attractions after they lose their snob appeal; for example, Pigalle and the Moulin Rouge in Paris. But then tourism is in fact an international form of slumming, wherein a satisfyingly close look at human misery can be achieved from the safety and comfort of an air-conditioned bus.)

The one major exception to seeking fun among one's peers is eroticism. The bed, at least as much as the 45 Colt, is the great equalizer. High status males, far from being adverse to having sex with lower status females, have frequently preferred them as sex objects to women of their own group. Insofar as sex has been played as a game (as distinguished from being merely an aspect of a serious, long-lasting relationship), class inequality between the partners has often lent it special piquancy. Of course, the nature of male domination is such that sexual games with social inferiors are often openly engaged in by upper status males, while the same behavior is repressed or at least clandestine among upper class women.

Modern industrial societies are still highly stratified and snobbish in their pursuit of pleasure. The specific form of what games are chic may change, but the principle of invidiousness remains. Almost every form of play has a whole scale of social gradations: from the $10 streetwalker to the $100 call girl; from the Las Vegas one-arm bandit to the Monte Carlo roulette table; from the Texas rodeo to the Spanische Hofreitschule.

Games, then, often reinforce social inequality. They also relieve the tensions caused by inequality. A great many societies have rituals that have variously been called of rebellion, of reversal, or of license. In these rituals, acts which, under normal circumstances would be condemned, become permitted under specified conditions (such as within a certain time span or between certain persons). Akin to these rituals are what anthropologists call joking relationships between privileged individuals, such as the king and his fool, an uncle and nephew, a grandparent and grandchild. These are relationships between individuals whose status is greatly unequal, and yet where the subordinate partner may with impunity steal from the other, insult him jokingly, engage in sexual bantering with him, and so on.

Joking relationships, as well as rituals of reversal or rebellion, generally challenge one or both of two things: rules of sexual morality and rules of authority. The European tradition of Carnival, especially in Germany, exemplifies both of these rule reversals. German Carnival, a clearly specified time period preceding Lent each year, is characterized by a relaxation of both sexual morality and hierarchical class relations. Members of different social strata who would normally address each other in the polite form may say "Du" during Carnival. Public ridiculing of authority figures is tolerated. Scanty costuming and the wearing of face masks to hide identity is widespread, and erotic games between strangers are not uncommon. Women, who are normally not expected to take the sexual initiative, may do so during Carnival.

Similarly, rigidly hierarchical organizations may have periodic rituals, such as the Christmas office party, during which sexual and hierarchical inhibitions are relaxed (often with the help of alcohol, an extremely common aid to communal revelry throughout the world). In some cases, roles may actually be reversed: men dress as women and vice versa; or officers obey enlisted men. It is clear that these rituals do not threaten the normal state of affairs. They merely release the tensions associated with it, and actually reaffirm norms by contrast. The one night when you may tell your boss off or flirt with his wife reminds you of the 364 days when you may not.

It is one of the characteristics of human intelligence that almost any kind of behavior can be made into a game or a play. One only needs a group of people to agree to a set of arbitrary rules, and a game is on. Many activities that are not games in themselves can be made more pleasurable by making them into games. For example, eating, drinking, or copulating are not games in themselves, but readily lend themselves to games. This being the case, one could expect an infinite variety in the kind of games played. In fact, the repertoire is relatively limited. Some games, like "hide and seek" and "catch," are so simple that it is safe to assume that they have been independently invented many times over. But other complex games like chess have diffused universally and are played according to amazingly similar rules. If there is one potent proof of the psychic unity of mankind, it is in the universal appeal of similar kinds of games. Many aspects of culture, such as religious beliefs, or art styles, are not easily exportable. Games, however, are. Who would think, for example, that such a "typically" American sport as baseball would appeal to people as different from Yankees as Japanese or Cubans? Yet it did. West Indian descendants of Africans play cricket with as much gusto as Englishmen. Hong Kong businessmen play golf as assiduously as Scotsmen. Chess, checkers, cards, and dice are all nearly universal games. If the law permitted it, bullfighting could become a thriving concern in the United States, as shown by the success of the sport in Mexican border towns catering to an American clientele.

Types of Games: Games of Chance

The basic kinds of games are limited in number, and remarkably similar across cultures. First, there are games of chance, in which the main motivation seems to be the desire to *affect one's fate*. A game of chance essentially pits oneself against destiny. Not surprisingly, games of chance are often closely linked with divination, and some games, such as dice, are directly derived from divination techniques. Many divination techniques are generated by mechanical devices that result in predictable statistical distributions of events. (Such, for example, is Yoruba Ifa divination, based on 256 "heads or tails" combinations of eight sequentially ordered seeds. To each combination attaches a set of verses which are interpreted by the diviner.) The main difference between divination and gambling is that in the former the person attempts to know his fate, and in the latter to affect it. However, the distinction is not all that clear-cut, since attempts to affect one's fate are often accompanied by predictive calculations of odds.

Gambling is the least social form of game behavior. The gambler may, and often does, pit himself against other gamblers, but an impersonal roulette wheel will serve just as well. The motivation for gambling is not so much gain, since compulsive gamblers continue to play at games where they know that the odds are against them. The motivation, rather, seems to be to gain a sense of control over one's destiny. That is why the amount wagered is often more than the gambler can afford to lose. Gambling for inconsequential sums has no kick to it, if gambling is your game. Of course, many people play bridge or poker for inconsequential sums, but these are games where the elements of skill and sociability are at least as important as the element of gambling, and they do not attract people whose primary motivation is gambling. Unlike the pure forms of gambling, which are highly asocial, the "friendly poker game" is an eminently sociable occasion in which the gain or loss of small sums or money is almost incidental to the whole pastime (Zurcher, 1974). Games of chance can involve not only money but even supremely important things such as honor (as in wagering the sexual favors of a woman one loves) or life itself (as in "Russian roulette," that ultimate form of gambling).

Games of Skill

Second, there are games of skill, usually subdivided into mental and physical. These games are by definition social, in the sense that one's skills must be pitted against those of others, but sociability is not their main object. The main motivation for competitive games of skill, from team sports, ritualized war, dueling, and prizefighting to chess, card games, and verbal jousting, is *dominance*. This is confirmed by the seemingly greater attraction these games have for men than for women. To be sure, women can be trained to want to compete as well, but ethnographic evidence indicates that competition in games of skill tends to be a predominantly male concern. (Gambling and the third main category of games, games of sociability, are extensively engaged in by both men and women.) While a lot more research into gender differences in play behavior is needed, my own observations in Africa, Europe and America seem to indicate that even as spectators at games of skill, women tend to behave differently than men. College men may drag their dates to football games, but men seem to go primarily to see the game and tend to become much more engrossed in partisanship than women who appear to come along more for reasons of sociability than for the pleasure of seeing beefy young men brutally bump into each other. Television audiences of sport events tend to be predominantly male as well, and this is true in many different countries.

Games of skill lend themselves quite well to being spectator games, unlike games of chance. Watching a roulette wheel becomes a bore after a few minutes, but a prizefight, or a basketball or soccer game can attract vast crowds willing to stand in long queues, fight traffic, and pay for exorbitantly priced tickets. Even chess, a game whose action is at best slow, can be watched with pleasure. (Of course a chess game can also be printed in a few lines without much loss of content, .

so the incentive actually to watch the game is much less than in, say, football.)

In games of skill, spectators vicariously identify with the dominance struggle of one of the actors or teams. A game of skill becomes much less enjoyable to watch if one could not care less who wins. Without identification with one of the parties in the contest for dominance, the game loses much of its salt. The Olympic Games are an interesting case in point here. Theoretically, the games are supposed to be strictly individual; yet the fact that they pit together thousands of athletes in hundreds of events makes spectator identification with individual athletes difficult. Therefore, much to the chagrin of Olympic Games idealists who understand very little about human behavior, the Games are almost completely redefined as a form of international warfare. We count gold, silver, and bronze medals by country, much as we might count scalps, shrunken heads, or downed jet fighters in a real war.

That dominance rather than sociability is the name of skill games is further shown by the fact that so many of them can be televised so well. To be sure, watching your *alma mater* play its annual football game against its arch-rival on television is not as good as being there. But it is still good enough to keep you chained for two hours to your set and to make you endure commercials. Sociability plays a role in ritualized dominance contests. It is not an accident that a team is more likely to win on home ground with a friendly crowd. However, games of skill find sufficient justification in the search for dominance that they can still be enjoyed with a minimum of sociability, even vicariously as a TV spectator in the solitude of one's living room. This is so true that live events have to be protected from the competition of television by bans on simultaneous broadcasting.

Among games of skill, the primarily physical ones vastly exceed in popularity the primarily mental ones. Many more people watch bullfights, soccer, or baseball than bridge or chess. Of course, physical action in sport is a far more visual spectacle than watching people move chess figures. But even for participants, there is a sense in which the direct physical fight for dominance is more immediately satisfying than its sublimated intellectual forms. Age is an essential factor: to participate in games where physical condition is a paramount condition of success is fun only for the short period when one is in one's physical prime. But intellectual games of skill can be successfully played much longer. The motivation for dominance is the same in both, and even games that seem primarily physical (like American football) are enhanced by their intellectual content as well.

There is, however, a sense in which physical dominance is primordial, and intellectual dominance derivative. We love a good fight, and, by and large, the more brutality and gore the better. One only needs to observe the behavior of children on school playgrounds. A fist fight (almost invariably between boys, not girls) will instantaneously attract a circle of spectators (who are themselves mostly male). Two boys (again much more often than girls) playing checkers in a corner of the playground, even though they, too, are symbolically fighting for dominance, will not attract nearly as much interest.

Games involving gore and tripe seem to be especially fascinating despite our pretenses to the contrary. North Americans, for example, affect squeamishness when watching Mexican bullfights, but relish seeing two men systematically beat each other's face into a bloody pulp in the ring, occasionally to the point of death. Bear-baiting, a favorite game in Europe until two or three centuries ago, is officially outlawed, but the teasing of animals in zoos, especially of large dangerous animals rendered impotent by incarceration, can still be observed with great regularity. Examples of gory games from other societies abound: dueling, ritual combat, headhunting, the Roman circuses, the Aztec and Toltec ball game in which the losers were executed. All these activities incidentally, are closely sex-linked: males engage in them far more than women, and with far more relish, both as participants and as observers.

Games of skill, then, appear closely tied to the human drive for dominance, and, thus, to aggression. In intellectual games, this drive is sublimated into completely nonviolent channels, but the competitive striving for superiority and dominance is no less intense for all its surface gentility. Bobby Fisher is much berated for the cold-blooded ferocity with which he is playing chess, but the amiable gentleman who plays for fun rather than for victory never becomes a grand-master.

Games of Sociability

Finally we come to the broad category of games wherein *sociability* is the main aim. As already suggested, sociability can also play a role in games of skill, especially among spectators, and conversely, gam-bling and skill competition may be secondary factors in games of sociability. Nevertheless, many games are played primarily for their sociability value. Thus, for example, playing strip poker in sexually mixed company is quite a different pastime than joining an illegal back-room poker game and playing for high money stakes. The rewards of sociability games are attention and approval. Sociability games are often closely tied to religion, art, and sensuality.

The prototypical sociability game is the great orgiastic religious festival so common in societies across the world. A key distinction between this and games of skill is that, in the latter, the boundary between the participant and the spectator is sharply defined. In the former, all persons in attendance are in some sense active participants. Even the anthropologist whose main purpose is to observe and record behavior is forced to take part in the drinking, the dancing, the eating, and the general merrymaking. (I speak here as one who has frequently been forced to imbibe nauseating alcoholic beverages against his will, an experience shared by many colleagues.) The great festival, inter-preted by Durkheim (1915) and Mauss (1952) as a ritual reinforcing "collective consciousness," has most of the characteristics of a game: its time and space boundaries are well defined; behavior follows definite rules that differ from those applying to the rest of the year (sometimes a greater austerity, sometimes a greater permissiveness). That it is taken seriously by the participants does not make it any less a game, for we have seen that many games are taken quite seriously. But festivals, however serious, are enjoyable.

Festivals are occasions for numerous social encounters, made all the more enjoyable through the performance of stylized forms of entertainment, mostly of a participatory nature. There are theatrical performances (both secular and sacred, such as religious services and processions, puppet shows, stylized story telling, juggling, and acrobatics); music and dancing (frequently led by professionals, but engaged in by most participants in the form of singing, clapping, shouting, and dancing); and an orgy of conviviality helped by an abundance of food and drink, the latter frequently alcoholic. At such festivals it is not uncommon to see gambling, divination, and games of skill, but the main object is sociability. Ties of friendship, kinship, or ethnicity are ritually reaffirmed through common participation in pleasurable activities. The festival becomes essentially a vast stage in which all participants act in a play for each other's benefit.

Games of sociability are not restricted to festivals; they are also engaged in on a smaller scale and at more frequent intervals. In Western societies, for instance, the dinner or cocktail party falls in the category of a ritualized game where conviviality is enhanced by alcohol, the consumption of food, the telling of jokes, and other forms of formal entertainment from witty conversation to the projection of slides about last summer's European vacation. An element of competition, potlatching, and social climbing may be present in these affairs, but the main object of the game is sociability. Eating, drinking, or sex are not games in themselves, but they can easily be turned into games in a congenial social setting where sensuality becomes an adjunct of conviviality. Solitary drunkenness is no game, but a contest of who can drink whom under the table is. Similarly, sexual intercourse in itself is not a game, but mate-swapping by spinning bottles is. Eating a hamburger at the corner drugstore is no game, but selecting a gourmet meal from a menu in French, by candlelight, in order to seduce your companion into bed is.

Play, we have suggested, is pretty much a constant in human history. Not only do all societies have games, but they have remarkably similar ones, clustering around one or more of the following: chance, skill, and sociability. The more differentiated societies professionalize games more than the simpler ones, but play behavior is universal.

Basically, we suggested three levels of explanation for the universality of play behavior. First, play probably has a biological foundation. It is not unique to man, and it is linked with the development of intelligence, with age (being more developed in the young), and, in the case of games of competitive dominance, with sex. Second, play seems to have psychological functions: it is pleasurable; relieves tension and tedium; and satisfies the drives for dominance, sociability, and control over the unknown. This psychological level of explanation appears linked with the biological one insofar as there seems to be a biological basis for dominance and gregariousness. Third, play behavior probably serves to reinforce social solidarity, to act out social tensions and conflicts in relatively harmless ways, and to reaffirm norms and values even when these are ritualistically violated.

If play behavior can be considered childish—and, philogenetically, this is the case—then *Homo sapiens* can be said to be the most childish of animals. His labile brain retains the inquisitiveness and the level of activity necessary to sustain a constant search for amusement. That same brain, as we have seen in the two previous chapters, drives him to seek answers to all his questions in knowledge derived from experience, if possible, and, if not, in supernatural explanations. Purged of his drives to dominate, conquer, exploit, and possess, man might be quite an amiable chap, a kind of brainy chimpanzee. Alas, he is not, which leads us to the melancholy conclusions of the last chapter.

ADDITIONAL READING

Generally, sociologists have regarded play and games as a trivial area, and have not studied it much, but, of late, the sociology of sport has developed (Edwards, 1973). For a broad historical and cultural treatment of the subject, see Huizinga (1955). The collection edited by Truzzi (1974) contains several studies of sports, games, and gambling. Piaget (1951) has written about the development of play in children, and Miller (1973) analyzes the relationship between the play behavior of man and other species. Herman (1967) and Cohen (1960) deal with gambling. Other general works are those by Robbins (1955) and Caillois (1961). The sociological approach developed by Goffman (1959, 1963, 1971) tends to analyze all social interaction as a manipulative game, and indeed to make play-acting synonymous with human behavior. Sipes (1973) examines the relationship between war, sports, and aggression. Millar (1968) analyzes play from a psychological perspective.

11

Conclusion: Can Things Get Better?

One of the most fundamental differences of opinion in the world has been between the optimists and the pessimists. And perhaps one of the main reasons why social scientists have such a poor record of prediction is that, while social scientists have belonged mostly to the optimistic tradition, the pessimists, more often than not, have proven right. Certainly most founding fathers of sociology have been incurable optimists. Comte, Spencer, and Marx all believed in their special brand of progress. Spencer believed in Evolution and Mother Nature; Comte in Positive Knowledge and Science; Marx in the Great Proletarian Revolution that would bring the classless, stateless society. Among the great sociologists, Weber emerges, among other things, as the outstanding pessimist. He was also one of the least wrong because he was too good a historian to make foolish prophecies, and too sensitive an observer of the turbulent politics of his time to have any illusions about the fundamental goodness of man.

Optimism and Pessimism

By and large, the pessimist has been the villain of the social science farce, and for extremely interesting reasons. Social scientists have had a vested interest in making themselves and others believe that they possess trained expertise to predict social events and to guide the course of human destiny. Believing, as they do for the most part, that thought can influence action, and hence the outcome of social events, they regard the pessimist as the bad guy whose thoughts help bring about manmade calamities. When the President's Council of Economic Advisers predicts rampant inflation, the stock market goes down and prices continue to go up. If the national chairman of the NAACP were to predict the spread of prison riots as a consequence of intolerable racism in penal institutions, he might help bring this about. When Hitler threatened war over the Sudetenland or the Danzig Corridor, he brought the greatest holocaust of human history one step closer. This phenomenon is known in social science as the "self-fulfilling prophecy": the very prediction of an event enhances the probability of its occurrence.

Although there is some validity in the notion of the self-fulfilling prophecy, the concept is often used one-sidedly to stigmatize the pessimists when they turn out to be right. The harbinger of bounty, when right, is praised for his clairvoyance, but the messenger of doom is scapegoated if his prediction is successful. The successful gloomy prediction, it is agreed, is not the result of the pessimist's expertise, but of his malevolence, which led him to make the prediction to provoke panic or incite violence. This double standard in applying the concept of the self-fulfilling prophecy implies that the optimist is a benevolent but powerless expert, while the pessimist is an omnipotent evil genius who manipulates events to make his sinister predictions come true.

In point of fact, sociologists have little to worry about their predictions being self-fulfilling. Few people are foolish enough to take sociologists seriously for their predictions, whether of glee or gloom, to have any perceptible impact on the real world. All the same, within the profession, the optimists, whether of the left or of the right, are the good guys, and the pessimists are the cynics and the bad guys. Hence, the popularity of optimism. Nothing succeeds like the prediction of success, if not, alas, in the real world, then at least in the profession. The issue of the self-fulfilling prophecy brings us to the problem of social engineering. The ubiquity of social change is obvious enough. Thus, it is foolish to claim that we are impotent to change things. We do all the time, with every single one of our actions. The issue is not whether we can change things, but whether we can change them according to our wishes, or those of our corporate sponsors. This is what sociologists call social engineering, and, potentially, social engineering means big money. So far, among social scientists, only economists have been taken at all seriously at the social engineering game.

There are basically two positions taken by sociologists on the issue of social engineering. The optimists of the left, believing in free will, think that accurate prediction will always elude social scientists because, as free agents, we can always defeat predictions and manipulation. Horrified by the spectre of totalitarianism, they fervently hope that the social sciences will never be scientific. Their central credo is the *self-defeating* hypothesis: they believe we have the freedom to invalidate predictions. The optimists of the right, on the other hand, believe that human behavior, though complex, is not intrinsically unamenable to scientific prediction and manipulation, at least in the aggregate, if not at the individual level. Being also great believers in Progress through Science, the optimists of the right still embrace Comte's vision of mankind's salvation through social engineering. Just as nuclear physics can move mountains, so can sociological faith move human masses to ever greater achievements.

Unfortunately, both positions are partly right and partly wrong. The optimists of the left are right in fearing the totalitarian and deleterious consequences of social engineering, but wrong in their optimism that free will shall forever prevent effective social engineering. The optimists of the right, on the other hand, are correct in believing in the possibility of predicting and controlling *aggregate* human behavior, but they are wrong in predicting beneficial consequences from such ability. In short, both groups are wrong in their optimism.

The Perils of Social Engineering

My contention is that it is relatively easy to change things in a controlled and predictable direction *for the worse,* but extremely difficult and unpredictable to do so for the better. Calculated attempts to change things for the worse are often successful, while meliorative schemes most frequently fail or even backfire. These sweeping statements must be buttressed by facts, but first, let us define what we mean by "the better" and "the worse." Let us stay clear of the subjective, elusive, and controversial concept of happiness, and stick to three easily measurable ("operationalizable," as my jargon-prone colleagues would say) ones. I shall call "for the better" any changes that produce greater *freedom* (defined as the range of actions a person may take without interference from others), greater *material welfare* (including not only level of consumption, but health and social security), and which reduce the level of *destructive conflict.*

The notion of destructive conflict needs some further definition. Not all conflict is destructive. Thus, I would not call a panel of undergraduates discussing, however acrimoniously, the merits of free love or abortion on demand destructive, unless they would start coming to blows and doing grievous bodily harm to each other. But the kind of conflict that leads to saturation bombings, gas chambers, lynching mobs, and holy wars is destructive. I will admit that the destructive conflict that develops in revolutions can sometimes eventually lead to an improved situation, but the cases are not nearly as numerous as optimists on the left generally believe. One of the great acts of faith of the left is blind adherence to a theory of history that felicity is to be achieved through catastrophe. Revolutions, however, only improve on previous conditions if the *ancien régime* was more than averagely tyrannical, and even then the price is often staggeringly high as shown, for example, by the French, Mexican, and Bolshevik revolutions.

Let us now examine some empirical evidence in support of the proposition that deliberate and predictable change for the worse is easy, but that meliorative attempts are difficult and problematic. In order to avoid sterile discussion as to what is good and what is bad, I chose two areas in which the overwhelming majority of people would agree with my value judgements, namely, armaments and racial or ethnic prejudice. I think I may safely assume that nearly all my readers will share my belief that disarmament and the eradication of racial and ethnic prejudices are desirable aims.

Disarmament

The history of concerted attempts by governments and private organizations to achieve mutual disarmament, or at least limitations of armaments makes most discouraging reading. The most massive and concerted attempts were made by the major world powers in the aftermath of two disastrous cataclysms, namely the First and the Second World Wars. The insanity of war, and the horrendous escalation in the destructive power of man were painfully obvious to victors and vanquished alike after the holocaust of the First World War. Yet, after many interminable conferences, the main concrete result achieved was an extremely limited agreement restricting the number and tonnage of warships according to a formula which more or less froze the naval *status quo* between major victorious powers. As to the attempt by the victorious allies to prevent the rearmament of their major foe, Germany, it was effective for a bare 15 years. Within 20 years, Germany had rearmed, Japan had grown as the dominant Pacific Ocean power, and the stage was set for another world war, on a scale three or four times as large as the first one.

The Second World War, as we all know, ended with the biggest bang yet. The American bangs called forth the Soviet counter-bangs, and in quick succession Britain, France, and China got into the act as well. By 1974, even India with its hundreds of millions of paupers got into the atomic club. The protracted attempts by the Soviet Union and the United States to put a brake to the costly and dangerous game have had the modest tangible result of an agreement to stop exploding thermonuclear devices in the atmosphere. They only did so at a time when they both no longer needed to test nuclear devices above ground in order to continue improving their destructive capacity. However, France and China still continue dumping radioactive debris on the world in order to develop their own *force de frappe* to match that of the superpowers. The prospect seems quite good that countries like India, Israel, South Africa, and Brazil might soon do likewise, each of course for its own good reasons, like conjuring the Communist, Arab, Black, and Yankee Peril respectively. Between the fall of 1972, when the United States and the Soviet Union signed the SALT treaty on the limitations of nuclear arms, and the spring of 1973, American nuclear warheads increased from 5890 to 7040 and Soviet ones from 2170 to 2260, according to the Stockholm International Institute for Peace Studies.

Most of us can be thankful, I suppose, for nearly thirty years without an atomic war, and it may be that the spectre of total annihilation is at last exerting some restraint on our inborn aggressiveness, but that is small comfort if one is luckless enough to live in Indochina, the Near East, or some other area of endemic war, however "conventional."

While disarmament can be said to have failed dismally–even modest limitations of armaments have been ineffective–the examples of armament races are numerous. Such limiting factors as may be found in these races seem to be attributable to available resources (and the willingness of the major powers to fight war by proxy), and not to human sanity. Even desperately destitute countries like India and Pakistan, whose history is a long chain of famines, epidemics, and natural disasters, gleefully engage in arms races. South Africa, Israel, Egypt, and the superpowers (the United States, the Soviet Union, and China) have all had escalating military budgets since the Second World War. Even relative peace is no obstacle to arms races, as shown, for example, by competing Latin American countries still eager to buy obsolete European warships, or the last generation of surplus fighter-bombers. Peace, then, is as elusive as ever.

Racism

The history of concerted attempts to eradicate or at least diminish racial, ethnic, religious, or caste prejudices is scarcely more edifying than the history of disarmament conferences. Perhaps the most massive efforts in that direction have been undertaken in the United States and in India, in both cases for roughly a quarter-century. In both countries, a modicum of progress has been made on the legal front, but racism and casteism are still massively present. In some instances, feelings of racial and caste membership have even been reinforced by such supposedly benign measures as discrimination in reverse and minority group quotas. Even if some objective indices of discrimination have diminished (e.g., differential income or education), it is doubtful that mutual group hostilities have been lowered, and it may even be argued that the "revolution of rising expectations" has created a deteriorating climate of race relations in the United States. In the last few years, Americans, both white and black, think more than ever in terms of racial categories, and indeed are constantly encouraged to do so, both by "progressive" leaders who talk of Black, Brown, Yellow, and Red Power, and by liberal reformists with their paternalist rhetoric of compensatory education and benign quotas.

There is abundant evidence that racial and ethnic hatreds can be easily and predictably increased. This was successfully achieved at the national level by Nazi Germany and by South Africa. In a few short years, Goebbels and his Propaganda Ministry had transformed a nation of 80 million relatively sane people noted for their high level of education, technology, and science into an unthinking and disciplined mass of militarists and racist bigots. It is true that Goebbels had an underlying basis of nationalism and anti-Semitism with which to work, but it is one thing to tell nasty little parlor jokes about Lazarus' long nose, and quite another to send six million people to gas chambers. The latter takes well-organized planning. Goebbels' achievement stands out as the most successful piece of social engineering that the world has ever seen. The Nazi anti-Semitic campaign, in its design and execution, was a true technological achievement of social psychology.

The South African government's policy of *apartheid* is not genocidal in intent, nor is its avowed aim to worsen race relations. The aim is to keep the nonwhite majority perpetually under white political domination and economic exploitation (van den Berghe, 1965). This is effectively achieved through a policy of rigid racial discrimination and segregation, which is hardly conducive to interracial amity and good will. Increased racial hostility is then invoked by the government as evidence for its theory that interracial contact produces conflict, even though the main source of the conflict is the police shooting people down or bashing them over the head.

Experimental evidence substantiates the same conclusions on a small scale. Many studies have shown that experience and contact between members of different racial groups resulted in some lowering of prejudices. But the changes were seldom dramatic, were generally situation-specific (e.g., a white served by a black salesman in the cosmetic department of a store might accept that black person in that department, but not in the food or clothing department), and were subject to certain conditions, such as equality of status and noncompetitiveness in the contact situation. In short, the findings are that, under egalitarian, nonthreatening conditions (seldom achieved in real life) intergroup contact tends to reduce prejudice, but neither fast nor dramatically (Allport, 1958).

This is in sharp contrast with what the experimenter can achieve in a well-designed hate-thy-neighbor campaign. In a striking experiment of this sort (filmed for television under the title "The Eye of the Storm"), an American schoolteacher managed within a single day to make her blue-eyed pupils strongly prejudiced and aggressive against her brown-eyed students, by telling them that science had proven the superiority of blue-eyed people over brown-eyed ones. The following day, she successfully reversed the pattern, telling her brown-eyed pupils that *they* were superior. Just by dispensing a few mild rewards and punishments, she was able to divide her all-white class into two hostile groups of vicious little racists. She had, in fact, engineered instant bigots.

Our friends, the optimists of the left, have a reasonably plausible explanation for the sorry state of mankind, which is more than what the optimists of the right have to offer. Inequality, war, and other manmade plagues of humanity, they tell us, are the inevitable results of the class interests of those in power. There is a flourishing armaments industry because selling arms is good business and, furthermore, because in a capitalist system the never-ending search for new markets logically includes weaponry. There develops, therefore, in the classical thesis ably presented by C. W. Mills in *The Power Elite*, a close congruence of class interests between two main sectors of the ruling class—the industrial capitalists and the military brass. The "military-industrial complex," to use Eisenhower's phrase, has an interest in keeping a permanent war machine, and even in stirring up a small war from time to time, in order to convince the citizenry of the need for "military preparedness."

Applied to racism, the class interest theory, presented by O. C. Cox (1948), is equally plausible. Racism developed in order to rationalize first slavery, then colonialism, and now class exploitation. If subject peoples are less than human, or less than fully responsible adults, it is all right to exploit and oppress them, for their own good of course, because left to themselves they would make a terrible shambles of things. In the industrial United States, racism continues to divide the workers, blinding them to their real class interests, which have nothing to do with race. This too is in the interest of the ruling class.

In the two examples we chose, of armaments and racism, the class interest theory has considerable validity. Selling arms *is* good business; it *is* very convenient to define those one wants to exploit as subhuman, and thus undeserving of the consideration one grants one's peers. But the theory is not general enough to provide a complete explanation. First, if inequality, aggression, war, and the general nastiness of man to man were the product of class conflict in capitalist societies, why do they subsist in "people's democracies" where classes have supposedly been abolished? Leftists argue that socialist countries have to defend themselves against the threat of capitalist aggression, and indeed the list of attempts by capitalist countries to squash socialist revolution by subversion or open military intervention is a long one, from fostering counter-revolution in Russia in the 1917-1922 era and in Spain in the 1930s, to the Bay of Pigs in Cuba in the 1960s and the CIA in Chile in the 1970s.

However, the socialist record is scarcely any better. The two socialist countries strong enough to attack their weaker neighbors have shown little restraint in doing so. The Soviet Union crushed revolts in Berlin, Hungary, and Czechoslovakia; Communist China attacked and invaded Tibet, India, and Korea. The capitalist countries pretend to fight in order to keep the world safe for democracy. The socialist countries claim to defend the revolution. In fact, both ideologies are transparent rationalizations for the pursuit of naked power politics.

Another set of facts calling for a more general explanation than the class interest theory of human propensity for aggression and hatred is that man's nastiness greatly antedates the development of capitalist predation, and indeed of earlier forms of class distinction, like feudalism and slavery. Classless societies, as we have seen, are no more peace-loving than the warmongers of the Kremlin or the Pentagon.

These unpleasant facts suggest severe limitations to social science theory premised on the fundamental goodness of human nature, or the perversity of society or any segment thereof to explain man's obvious failure to conform with his supposedly angelic nature. First, the antithesis of man and society is a false one. Since man is by nature a social animal, it makes no sense at all to oppose man and society. Second, instead of treating aggression and violence as problematic products of perverse social institutions, let us accept them as part of human nature, that is, of our biological heritage. Here, I am not suggesting that man is always and purely a bundle of aggressive instincts. For example, it is clearly a part of our biological heritage that most adults feel protective towards children. Within the family, there are obviously "altruistic" forms of behavior that contribute to the survival of the species.

Aggression Again

Sound social engineering must accept aggressiveness as part of human nature, and must consider the control of that aggressiveness and destructiveness as its central problem. Whatever survival value man's aggressiveness had when he was a hunter, it has obviously outlived its utility for the last few thousand years. Man, of course, is not the only aggressive animal. Many other mammals fight members of their own species to defend their territory, assert dominance, or gain access to females. But man's aggressiveness is uniquely frightful for two reasons. First, man, especially the male of the species, seems to get a greater kick out of killing than almost any other animal. Many other animals kill for food, but only man, it seems, kills for the sheer fun of it, and will go to the elaborate expense and ritual of fox hunts, big game safaris, bullfights, and the like, to quench his thirst for blood without *any* material payoff. Obviously, killing provides its own psychic reward.

Second, man is the most lethal animal to his own species (if we forget those lower animals that eat their young for food and without malice aforethought). Man is not only bloodthirsty, but his equipment to deal instant death to members of his own species is far more developed than that of any other mammal or bird. Here, the famous ethologist, Konrad Lorenz (1966), has an interesting theory. He thinks that animals that are biologically equipped easily to kill members of their own species have evolved an inhibitory mechanism that insures that they virtually never kill each other. This typically takes the form of a gesture of submission, which puts the loser at the mercy of the winner, but immediately inhibits the winner's pugnaciousness. Thus, the "underwolf" in a fight admits defeat by exposing his neck to the winner's teeth, and this instantaneously stops the winner dead in his snarl. On the other hand, animals poorly equipped to kill lack, according to Lorenz, this inhibitory mechanism.

Biologically, man is poorly endowed to kill his fellows, with his atrophied canine teeth and his harmless claws and thus, according to Lorenz' theory, lacks the inhibition. Unlike the wolf presenting his neck, the wounded gladiator in the Roman arena was as likely as not to bring forth a thunderous wave of thumbs down. Red-blooded American G.I.'s were as capable of shooting in cold blood Vietnamese women and children, as were their German counterparts with Jews or Russians twenty years earlier. The great tragedy of man is that his technological capacity to kill developed at such breakneck speed that there was no chance for the biological inhibitions to catch up with it, according to the Lorenz theory. Such inhibitions against killing as exist in human societies seem to be cultural, not biological, and how fragile these inhibitions are is seen again and again by the ease with which they disappear. Nearly all war veterans who have seen and dealt with death at close quarters report how quickly they get inured to death, especially that of others.

Whether Lorenz is right or not, we have an immense capacity to destroy, and show little restraint in the use of violence. Seemingly lacking biological restraints on violence, it is all the more imperative that we develop effective cultural ones. To some extent, we have. The repressive power of the state is, among other things, a means of controlling violence within societies. But the price in terms of loss of freedom has been staggering, and, furthermore, the results have often been far short of impressive. The state itself has often enough resorted to terroristic violence, or else been impotent to stamp out banditry, assault, and murder. In short, while the art of killing has now reached its ultimate limit—the destruction of life on our planet—the art of controlling violence is still in its infancy.

If the atomic era has brought any blessing, it is that mankind suddenly came to the realization that our violent game was up. All of a sudden, we came to the collective realization that we were destroying not only each other, but our habitat as well. If *any* of us were to survive at all, we had to develop the capacity to restrain our greed and our violence. There simply was no viable alternative, at least not on *this* planet. In the old army phrase, it was a stark case of ''shape up or ship out.''

The ecology movement has very little to do with the beauty of singing birds and of redwood groves. It is man's cry of anguish on the last curve of the road to ultimate destruction. However selfish its motivation, ''eco-activism'' is probably the best thing that happened to us in a long time. For one thing, it transcends politics, race, and nationality. It makes all human cleavages seem ludicrously stupid. For the first time in human history, man has looked around himself and discovered that the enemy was *all* of us, and not just some of us, as we had thought before. If enough of us learn that lesson fast enough, we may yet survive for a couple of million years more. But then why should we? Perhaps we should let the chimps inherit the earth. They are so much more endearing and so much less polluting than we are.

The Impact of Sociology on Society

Perhaps it would be useful, in conclusion, to examine how the dominant ideology of sociologists has influenced the definition of social problems and the fumbling attempts at their resolution, and then to see if we can do any better. If sociologists have made any appreciable impact on any society, it has been in the United States. In the socialist countries, with the partial exception of Poland, empirical sociology has been almost completely suppressed. In Germany, the promising beginnings in the Weimar Republic were wiped out during the Nazi era, and the postwar reconstruction was in good part destroyed by the assaults of the New Left. In France the Durkheimian tradition became largely fossilized, and much of what empirical sociology there is has become intellectually colonized by American sociology. The same is true of the Netherlands, Denmark, and Sweden, the European countries where sociology is relatively best developed, but generally unimaginative. In Britain, sociology has traditionally been very policy-oriented and intellectually subordinate to anthropology. Italy has perhaps been the most successful of the European countries in preserving its own distinctive tradition, but the medieval character of Italian universities has hindered the development of sociology.

Japanese sociology is well-developed, but since most of us do not read Japanese, it might as well not exist as far as its world influence is concerned. Of the other Asian countries, only India has a reasonably well developed sociological tradition, heavily influenced by British social anthropology. But work conditions for scholars are so miserable that most Indian sociologists seek refuge in the greener pastures of the United States, Canada, or Britain. Canadian sociology is a mere appendage of the U.S. brand, not unlike the whole of Anglo-Canadian society, as a matter of fact. In Latin America some countries, like Mexico, Argentina, Brazil, and Peru, have developed an imaginative neo-Marxian sociology to attempt to deal with the various predicaments of dependence and underdevelopment, but that brand of sociology is only a faint echo on the world scene. In Africa the little sociology there is, is mostly British or French structural anthropology.

North American sociologists have dominated world sociology, not through intellectual achievements, but by the sheer weight of numbers and power of financial resources. This is not the place for a critique of American sociology. It would require another book, and there are several such books in existence. Every few years, a prominent sociologist fires a volley of amusing shots at his profession (Sorokin, 1956; Mills, 1961; Gouldner, 1970; Andreski, 1972). Rather, I shall endeavor to suggest how a few key features of American sociological (and, more generally, academic) ideology have helped define social problems in a way that has hindered rather than promoted their solution. In capsule form, my characterization will have some features of a caricature, and cannot do justice to dissident minorities within the discipline who have not shared the mainstream ideology. However, I believe that good caricature captures the essence of truth, and that is what I shall try to do.

The Left and the Right in Sociology

In the broadest terms, the last two decades of American sociology have been dominated by an ideological debate between the "left" and the "right." A multiplicity of labels and epithets have been affixed to each of the camps. At the "theoretical" level, the two groups have been called the "conflict" versus the "consensus" or "order" theorists, or the "dialecticians" versus the "functionalists." At the political level, lines were drawn between the "radical," "New Left," or "Third World" sociologists, versus the "Establishment," the "liberals," or the "Fascist pigs." The right wing dominated the field, and indeed was largely unchallenged until the early 1960s; during the next decade, the left wing was increasingly on the offensive, but, by the early seventies, it had largely run out of both political and intellectual steam, and had as dismally failed to solve any fundamental problems as the "Establishment" it sought to overthrow. The current ideological mood is one of disorientation, withdrawal from the political arena, cynicism, and disabusement. Most sociologists once more do their academic thing, and for many of them frustration with their inability to deal with the real world has meant, once more, retreat to the empty formalism of quantitative methodology and to the grand playroom of the computer terminal.

What were the basic premises of the two wings of American sociology and why did they fail to make the impact they sought to make on American society? The "right wing" of sociology has not been conservative and certainly not reactionary in any usual sense of these words. Rather, its ideology has been that of bourgeois liberalism dedicated to meliorative reform by constitutional means. Establishment sociologists have, by and large, supported the democratization of access to education (though often shielding their own children from the effects of it by sending them to private schools where some serious learning still went on); social mobility and equalization of opportunity; universalistic tests of achievement based on merit; the abolition of racial prejudice and discrimination (though not being adverse to seeking the security of the white middle-class suburb for themselves); an individualistic view of civil liberties; a pacifist or at least an antimilitaristic and antiinterventionist outlook on foreign relations; an abhorrence of violence; a therapeutic rather than a punitive approach to crime; and even in many cases a vaguely populist ideology of opposition to big government and big business.

The ideology of "left wing" sociology shared most of these values, with slightly different emphases. "Radical" sociologists have been a little more inclined to advocate more revolutionary, unconstitutional, and even (if necessary) violent changes. But put to the test of action, they typically behaved in a way very similar to their liberal colleagues. They usually put a greater stress on civil *rights* than on civil *liberties,* and have proven less concerned about individualism. At the rhetorical level, they have been far more vocal in their support of oppressed groups and in their opposition to big government and big business; but at the behavioral level, their radicalism assumed more the character of mild eccentricities of life style than a genuinely activist revolutionary stance.

Neither liberals nor radicals, then, successfully passed the test of congruence of their own private behavior with their professed ideology. In fact, both groups behaved in ways fully compatible with their narrowly defined class interests as middle-class, academic professionals. Both groups were about equally elitist and withdrawn in the ivory tower. In fact, the "radicals" were perhaps a little more academically elitist and ivory-towerish than the "establishmentarians." The radicals had no place but the campus to go to; the establishment sociologists got their hands dirty dealing with government, business, and the foundations in their frantic pursuit of research money. Generally, the establishmentarians did lavishly supported trivial research; the radicals did no research at all.

In one important respect the two groups differed; namely, in their conception of sociology in general and American society in particular. The liberals generally believed that the social system in which they lived was, if far from perfect, at least basically good. Whatever was wrong about American society could be cured by one of two things:

1. Infusion of vast sums of money into meliorative programs like the Great Society, the New Deal, the War on Poverty, the Peace Corps, the Alliance for Progress, and other lofty-sounding enterprises so dear to Democratic Party rhetoric.
2. Therapy for the misguided individuals who are so wrong-headed as to not to share the ideology of the academic liberals (e.g., those poor, ignorant racists who still look down on their black brethren), or who, because of unfortunate circumstances in their upbringing, commit crimes that make life for academic and other middle-class persons unpleasant and dangerous.

The basic outlook of the liberals, then, has been that social institutions are fundamentally good, though often ineffective, and that most people in positions of power are generally well-meaning, though often blundering. Basically, there was nothing wrong with America that a lot of money and good will could not solve, and both were assumed to be forthcoming if we put our minds to solving social problems as all good, fair-minded liberals should.

The liberals, then, thought kindly both of human nature and of their bourgeois liberal institutions. To be sure, there was also a truly conservative strain in sociology, made up of those who believed man to be fundamentally evil, and thus in need of powerful social institutions to restrain him, but these were distinctly in the minority. Liberal optimism was the dominant *Weltanschauung*.

The "radicals," on the other hand, while they shared the liberal belief in the goodness of man, proclaimed society, or at least capitalism, to be evil. The road to the good society, then, was the overthrow of the capitalist system and the substitution of a new one, which covered the whole gamut from welfare-state socialism to anarchism. With the *détente* of the 1960s, the New Left associated the Soviet Union with authoritarian state capitalism, a system scarcely any better than the American one, but, curiously, it managed to maintain a myth of Communist China or Cuba as a revolutionary Garden of Eden. (The State Department, by denying those radicals passports to visit these workers' paradises, probably did much to keep these myths alive. Conservatives who now visit China often come back far more impressed than radicals.)

The Failure of Revolution and Reform

By now, it is reasonably clear that the Marxian model of revolution has lost its relevance for industrial societies. It was not even a very good model for the industrial societies of the later nineteenth or early twentieth century, and it achieved most practical success in agrarian societies still barely on the threshold of industrialization. Its contemporary relevance is practically nil in Africa (except possibly in South Africa), still considerable in much of Asia and Latin America, and hopelessly dated in all the industrial societies. The New Left efforts to substitute a new model for the revolutionary transformation of industrial societies have not been impressive. The New Left only came credibly close to a real revolution in France in 1968, and that hope was killed when it became apparent that the Communist Party was the petty bourgeois adjunct to the French establishment. Otherwise, it only managed to attract television coverage for a few years on a few campuses.

What of the liberals' efforts at reform? Alas, the liberals were no more successful in bringing about change in the desired direction than the radicals. Let us illustrate that statement by examples drawn from three important areas in which practically all good liberals would agree change would be desirable. One area is international—the enormous economic disparity between the developed industrial countries and the underdeveloped agrarian countries, especially the ones that recently emerged from colonialism. The other two are domestic—the problems of racism and crime.

UNDERDEVELOPMENT IN THE THIRD WORLD

The liberal theory of development and underdevelopment is rather naive and ostensibly apolitical. Some countries, it holds, are backward, poor, and undeveloped because of lack of resources, capital, and "know-how," as well as because of such problems as uncontrolled population growth, "tribal" enmities, waste, corruption, inefficiency, and a host of other ailments. The developed countries must provide the underdeveloped countries with the necessary technical aid, loans, and so on, to help them attain the "take-off" point when their economic growth will become self-sustaining. Foreign aid of the rich countries to the poor ones is not only charitable but makes good sense because, by some kind of optimistic logic, we should all mutually benefit from common prosperity.

By now, several trends have clearly emerged. Many "Third World" countries show no signs of reaching the "take-off" point; the few that are moderately successful in rising out of abject poverty do so through flukes of fortune, such as the sudden discovery of oil deposits; and the contribution of the rich countries to the poor ones is not only infinitesimally small (compared, for example, to the armaments budgets), but tied to political and military strings that perpetuate the dependency of the poor countries on the rich ones.

To be sure, the causes of underdevelopment are many and complex, and include the factors mentioned by liberal social scientists, such as galloping demography, lack of capital, poor communication and transport systems, and lack of political integration. However, the disparity between the poor and the rich countries is *also* in good part the very result of the dependent colonial or neo-colonial relationship between them. All parts of the world were at one time underdeveloped, but when more developed countries conquered or controlled less developed ones, the gap in development between them tended to increase rather than to decrease, as development theorists would have us believe. The poor countries stayed poor or were gradually impoverished through an unequal relationship of political tutelage and economic exploitation. They were forced to sell raw materials cheaply and buy manufactured goods dearly. As colonies, they were prevented from industrializing by the colonial masters for fear of the competition of their cheap labor. In short, they were deliberately sucked of their substance and kept underdeveloped. It is, therefore, the height of naiveté to expect the rich countries (whether capitalist or socialist) to behave altruistically and to show an interest in developing the poor countries, when the interest of the rich is to keep the poor dependent and exploited.

The totally unrealistic expectations of the liberal development theorists, and their failure to take into account the stark political consequences of colonialism and neo-colonialism have invalidated both their analysis of the situation and their meliorative suggestions to bridge the gap. The Communist powers, while attacking capitalist neo-colonialism, engage in as blatantly domineering and self-interested a brand of "foreign aid" as the capitalist countries. The problems of the poor countries remain basically unsolved and unlikely to be solved. In the apt phrase of Frank (1967), capitalism for the Third World has led not to economic development, but to the development of underdevelopment. And Communism has not served them much better. A decade of Soviet tutelage in Cuba, for example, still leaves Cuba at least as badly off economically as it was under the yoke of American capitalism and of corrupt military dictatorships.

Only through genuine independence, both political and economic, has a country any real chance of development, and even then, the task is far from easy because of innumerable internal problems. The Marshall Plan in Europe is always cited as the great success story of foreign aid. There, however, the problem was not one of development but of reconstruction of an economy where all the basic social, political, economic, educational, and organizational conditions for growth were favorable. The few countries that successfully emerged from poverty (e.g., Mexico, Brazil, and oil-rich Arab countries) have grown by gaining political independence, controlling their natural resources, and fostering industrialization. Foreign aid seldom achieved anything more than building mercenary armies, fostering prestige projects of dubious value (like airports, conference halls, and hydroelectric dams), and filling the pockets of the local elite friendly to the donor power.

Did the liberal ideology of American social scientists achieve greater success domestically? Let us answer the question by examining the impact of social scientists on two of the most massive social problems in contemporary America—crime and racism. Practically everybody (laymen and social scientists) agrees that both are bad and costly. Hundreds of sociologists claim specialized expertise in one or both of these areas and make a career out of pretending that they have solutions. Yet crime rates climb steadily and racism shows few signs of abating.

CRIME

First, let us examine the liberal theory of crime. Liberal social scientists took exception to the earlier view of the criminal as a depraved individual who must be punished, and substituted the notion of a misguided victim of improper socialization who must be reformed. Thus, for instance, the influential "differential association" theory explains crime in terms of individuals being socialized in groups whose norms deviate from those of the general society (Sutherland and Cressey, 1966). Society, whatever that means, is responsible for failing to motivate individuals to behave as good citizens should, and therefore the criminal is a socially diseased victim of an inadequate social environment. Incarceration is no longer justified as a form of punishment or social retribution, or even as a means of keeping the streets safe for law-abiding citizens, but as a form of social therapy.

Criminologists broadly share this ideology, and broadly regard it as a vast moral improvement over a vengeful conception of law enforcement. What a nice Christian thing it is to treat the criminal as a victim! The only trouble with the ideology is that it bears no demonstrable relationship to social reality. Crimes in America, especially murder and other crimes of violence, are much more frequent than in most other countries, with the exception of South Africa, and their incidence tends to increase. Criminal homicide rates in the United States, for example, increased 30.4 percent between 1956 and 1966. Americans kill each other at the rate of some 22,000 a year, a rate far higher than in Japan, Germany, Austria, Australia, Canada, Belgium, Switzerland, Denmark, Norway, England, France, or Italy. Two hundred million Americans produce some 6500 gun murders a year, compared to 135 for the combined population of 214 millions in England, Japan, and West Germany. The rate of criminal homicide with firearms in the United States is over 50 times higher than in these other three large industrialized countries. Similarly, American crime rates for forcible rape, robbery, and aggravated assault are all several times higher than in Great Britain, Canada, and Denmark (Radzinowicz and Wolfgang, 1971).

The apparatus of police, courts, parole boards, and prisons is both expensive and inefficient. It has some limited ability in hunting criminals down and in apprehending, convicting, and incarcerating them, but the evidence for "rehabilitiation" is scanty indeed. In fact, many criminologists and prison officials admit that rehabilitation policies generally fail, and that prisons, far from being schools for civism, are crime academies. The 1967 FBI Uniform Crime Reports gives a 65 percent *rearrest* rate within four years for all offenders released from custody. The overall *reconviction* rate was only 23 percent. This discrepancy between those two indices of recidivism is interpreted by the liberals in terms of the propensity of the police to arrest innocents, but it could equally be seen as resulting from the courts' proclivity to acquit the guilty. The truth is obviously somewhere in-between. There is no denying the fact, however, that a large amount of certain categories of crime, especially property crimes, such as burglary, larceny over $50, and auto theft are accounted for by a relatively small number of recidivists.

Much controversy surrounds what constitutes success or failure of a penal and legal system (Tittle, 1974), but the simple facts are that, in the United States, crime rates are on the increase, crimes of violence are much more frequent than in most comparably industrialized societies, and an unknown but probably very substantial proportion of certain categories of crime is accounted for by recidivists. Clearly, the legal, police, and penal systems do not succeed in either suppressing or "curing" crime down to the level of other comparably urbanized and industrialized societies. This suggests that perhaps the entire view of crime as deviant behavior, and of the criminal as a patient in need of therapy, is a liberal fantasy unrelated to the behavior it seeks to explain.

There is an alternative theory of crime associated with radical sociology that bears a much closer resemblance to reality. The radical theory of crime says in effect: crime is whatever those in power define as such. If it pleases a hundred moralistic bourgeois in the state legislature to declare that smoking marijuana, drinking beer on Sunday, or copulating with your neighbor's spouse is a crime, then so it is by definition. The crucial element in the radical theory of crime is that crime, the law, the judicial process, and the entire apparatus of prevention, apprehension, and detention are largely defined as the product of differential relations of power. (Quinney, 1969; Chambliss and Seidman, 1971). While conceding that certain crimes, like raping five-year-old girls, or throwing bombs in Sunday-school classrooms, or hanging people from the nearest lamp post because you disapprove of their skin color, are frowned upon by practically everyone and are indeed pathological acts, it is evident that much "criminal" behavior and "justice" are *heavily* determined by class factors.

If commission of a crime were to secure one a stay in one of our "correctional establishments," then the running of the police, the courts, the jails, and indeed the state itself would be left by default to children under 10 years of age. Practically all of us commit crimes daily, yet relatively few of us get caught, fewer yet come to trial, and only a small select group enters the portals of our "reformatories." Looking at the chosen few, it is immediately apparent that they are hardly a cross-section of the population. They are overwhelmingly male, because males are much more prone to crimes of violence, and good middle-class liberals hate violence. They disproportionately belong to racial pariah groups like blacks and Puerto Ricans, because the police keep an especially sharp lookout for those groups, in the belief that they are especially crime-prone. They are typically a generation younger than those who put them there, in part because violence is age-linked and in part because ideas of what is criminal vary greatly with age. They belong principally to the lower classes, especially to the urban *Lumpenproletariat* of derelicts, unemployed, prostitutes, vagrants, alcoholics, and, of course, those who consciously chose certain profitable lines of crime as a career.

This selective process, which ends in admission to a prison, is extraordinarily complex, involves many different steps, and implicates the police, the courts, the electoral process, and the criminal underworld in a complicated web of intrigue and corruption, but the basic forces at work are starkly simple. The well-to-do and the well-placed have little incentive to engage in crimes of violence, and little chance of being caught in so-called white-collar crimes. The reverse is true of the poor, the outcasts, and the powerless. White-collar criminals, on the rare occasions when their indiscretion makes it too embarrassing to overlook their criminality, receive preferential treatment at every step of the legal process because they understand the process better, can hire the legal talent to bail them out, and, perhaps most importantly, because those in charge of enforcing the law are themselves white-collar criminals with much the same social profile as their clients. Even when the vice-president of the Republic is convicted of criminality, resignation from office and a nominal fine are considered punishment enough. As to Richard Nixon, only the presidential pardon of his hand-picked successor saved him from criminal prosecution. He too was deemed to have suffered enough by having resigned his ill-gotten office in order to avoid conviction and to retain his pension rights.

RACE AND ETHNIC RELATIONS

Liberal social science ideology concerning crime, thus, has been miserable sociology, because it largely insisted on viewing the problem in moralistic and therapeutic terms instead of as a power relationship. Another glaring instance of the failure of liberal sociology is the field of "race and ethnic relations," also one of the main areas of

specialization in sociology. I have criticized the field in detail elsewhere (van den Berghe, 1967, 1970, 1972), but a few comments are in
order here. As we have seen, many social scientists until the 1920s
were racists; that is, they believed that various human groups represented different stages of evolution, and were endowed with different levels of innate abilities such as intelligence. Then, when the
absurdity of racism was exposed for what it was; namely, a pseudo-
scientific ideology to justify slavery, colonialism, and racial discrimination, social scientists atoned for their sins by proclaiming the dogma
that human behavior was totally unrelated to anything biological.
Racism, like crime, was now proclaimed a social or psychological
disease. Individuals were racists because they had picked up the virus
from their sick racist society, and some individuals were more racist
than others because they found it satisfying to vent their frustrations in
the form of aggression against harmless scapegoats (Allport, 1958;
Adorno *et al.*, 1950). America was afflicted by a moral dilemma: how
to reconcile the inhumane treatment of blacks with the ideals of liberty
and equality for all (Myrdal, 1944). The problem was, to reeducate
whites to be nice to blacks, by making them see that racial prejudice
was unfair.

To a limited extent the reeducation strategy worked: some well-
meaning people could be made to see that racism was not only nasty
but stupid. The main gains of the 1950s and the early 1960s, however,
were achieved by repealing racially discriminatory laws and by out-
lawing the institution of racial segregation, especially in education—
not by telling whites to stop being racists. To the extent that integration
was a success, it was a result not of applying the liberal social
interpretation of the situation as a social disease, but through the
federal government forcing change, at the point of bayonets if necessary.

Then, in the late 1960s came Black Power, with its demands for
black studies programs, quotas, preferential treatment, and even re-
newed racial segregation. The liberal academics were at first greatly

surprised, disoriented and even hurt by these "militant" black demands. After all, blacks were the good guys, so how come they too were racist? Or were they really? Soon, liberal thinking reoriented its paternalism to the new black "militancy." Blacks were not racist; they just had to go through a phase of rejection of whites in order to achieve a "positive identity" (like growing up, perhaps, because, as we all know, blacks are "childish"?) Previously, the virtues of racial integration were sung because it would upgrade blacks educationally to the level of the white middle class, and because whites and blacks would learn to like each other by getting to know each other as individuals. Now, black demands for segregation were supported by white liberals on the grounds that it was damaging to the fragile egos of blacks to compete with whites (who were, of course, assumed to be superior). Blacks therefore needed "role models" of their own pigmentation so that they could "find their own identity."

All this psychologistic nonsense once more misplaces the locus of the problem, which is not in the minds of people, but in the politics of power groups. The stark reality of the situation of American blacks is that as a group they lack all the ingredients of a viable nationalist or separatist movement: they are too small a minority to matter much in politics; they are too poor and not educated enough to have a major economic impact; they are territorially dispersed; and they do not have a separate and distinct language and culture (except in the most minimal sense of minor dialectical differences). Therefore, for blacks to seek the attainment of real power (as opposed to make-believe power as racial middlemen) by organizing as a racial group against whites is a self-defeating strategy. The alternatives are either the reinstallment of a Jim Crow society with blacks in a perpetually subordinate position, or the incorporation of blacks into the "mainstream" of American society as individuals and on the basis of universalistic criteria. The modest gains of the 1950s and early 1960s in the direction of integration are now being casually reversed with liberal support for separate treatment for blacks. Even a casual reading of the current sociological literature on this topic shows an extraordinary degree of incomprehension of the dynamics of power involved and a naively optimistic faith that everything will turn out for the better in the end. *Historia magister vitae*, said the Romans, which loosely translates: history teaches us to live. If so, why must American sociologists fail to learn from history?

Part of the answer is that, in common with many of their compatriots, they know precious little history. They also fail to learn from the mistakes of other societies, because they do not know much about them either. Finally, they fail to understand the present in their own society because their ideology incapacitates them to deal with power. Power is nasty and it corrupts, therefore academic liberals prefer to hold their moral nostrils shut and pretend that power does not exist, or that it is not important, or that it has to be legitimized, or that it is only sought by evil people, or that its exercise is generally benevolent, or that it is subject to the consent of the governed, or some such pious nonsense.

By now, it should be clear to most sociologists that America, like Humpty Dumpty, had a great fall, and that all the President's men cannot put it together again. Overseas, the American empire is crumbling fast since the mid-1960s, and this might cause some optimism for world peace, were it not that other bellicose powers like China and potentially Japan are quickly filling in the vacuum. At home, the American economy is increasingly showing the symptoms of "stagflation" (inflation, stagnation, unemployment), which we once thought was a Latin American monopoly. Corruption, incompetence, and arrogance in high government circles, and thievery and rapaciousness in high business circles, although hardly novelties on the American scene, have assumed monumental proportions. The entire constitutional fabric of government is punctured full of moth holes. Cynicism, egoism, anomie, and hedonism, the classic symptoms of decadence, are widespread individual reactions to collective disarray. Violence and crime are endemic and increasing, and the police, courts, and prisons seem less and less capable of controlling them. Things, in short, seem to fall apart, much like they have in other periods of decadence in other societies, though, probably faster and on an unprecedented scale.

Sociology as Alienation

Can sociology save us? Collectively, as a society, I believe not, but individually it has something to offer. Periods of decadence are often times of great intellectual creativity. When nothing seems to work any more, necessity becomes the mother of thinking. Periods of decadence also tend to be very private periods. Withdrawal into little private worlds (counter-cultures, messianistic sects, drugs, eroticism, de-schooling, and a multitude of other escapes) seems a logical step when the social fabric comes apart at the seams. I suggested at the outset that I conceived of sociology as a tool for the critical alienation of an individual from his society and its constraints and conventions. Alienation by itself leads to anger and disarray; but a disciplined, reasoned, critical alienation is enormously liberating. In a society that works smoothly, the rewards for conformity often lull the mind into an uncritical stance. When things come unstuck, individual liberation from social constraints becomes an appealing alternative. Insofar as sociology can and should sharpen our awareness of these constraints and of their arbitrariness, it should be liberating. Its failure to have been liberating is not intrinsic to the discipline, but results from the intellectual mediocrity or venality of its practitioners. The great opportunity that a decadent society like ours offers us is to sharpen our wits against the grindstone of collective absurdity, and to become free of spirit. More than ever, we have a chance to go through life asking fundamental questions and rejecting pat answers, especially the ones that so obviously serve the interests of organized groups. Things have come to such a pass that the search for a better way is of compelling urgency.

A sociology worth its salt must *demystify* all brands of social order, as a modest first step in discovering the basic parameters for the construction of a new and better society, or, failing that, the necessary conditions for a tolerable individual *modus vivendi* within an existing society. My view of sociology is that it cannot provide solutions, but merely expose nonsolutions. A sociology that proposes a solution to social problems becomes an ideology, and an ideology, insofar as it invariably serves group interests, is by definition false. If I leave my readers with a gnawing and lingering sense of dissatisfaction with their society, their place in it, and my own irreverent and impertinent remarks about it, I shall consider that I have accomplished my purpose. The rest is up to them.

ADDITIONAL READING

Most of the stark problems of underdevelopment in Africa, Latin America, and Asia are dealt with in Myrdal (1968), Dumont (1969), Worsley (1970), Frank (1967), and Rhodes (1970). Indeed, they were already foreseen by Lenin (1969) more than half a century ago. The sociological literature on criminology is enormous and most of it is in the liberal tradition (Sutherland and Cressey, 1966; Johnson, 1974; Bloch and Geis, 1970). Quinney (1969) and Chambliss and Seidman (1971) articulate the radical perspective, which views crime not as "deviance," but as an expression of conflicting group interests. Race and ethnic relations have also spawned an immense bibliography, likewise mostly in the liberal tradition (Allport, 1958; Adorno *et al.*, 1950; Myrdal, 1944). More recently, Blauner (1972) has sought to provide scholarly legitimation for the "radical" position on race. For attempts to deal with race in a wide comparative perspective, see van den Berghe (1967) and Schermerhorn (1970). The reader seeking intelligent reflections on the role of sociology in both capitalist and socialist countries, and on what a humanistic, "reflexive" sociology should do, would do well to read Gouldner (1970). For a radically different view on the role of social science from a behaviorist slant, see Skinner (1971). Much closer to my own viewpoint are the melancholy musings of Moore (1972). Moynihan (1970) gives a good account of the failure of applied social science in the "war on poverty" in the United States.

Bibliography

NOTE: *To enhance the usefulness of this bibliography for the English-speaking layman, I have referred to recent English-language editions of the works that follow, in paperback if available. Where appropriate, the date of original publication appears in parentheses at the end of the reference.*

ADAM, HERIBERT. *Modernizing Racial Domination.* Berkeley: University of California Press, 1971.

ADORNO, T. W., et al. *The Authoritarian Personality.* New York: Harper, 1950.

ALEXANDER, R. D. "The Search for an Evolutionary Philosophy of Man." *Proceedings of the Royal Society of Victoria,* 84, pp. 99–120, 1971.

ALLPORT, GORDON W. *The Nature of Prejudice.* Garden City: Doubleday, 1958.

ANDRESKI, STANISLAV. *Military Organization and Society.* Berkeley: University of California Press, 1968.

———. *Social Sciences As Sorcery.* London: André Deutsch, 1972.

———. *The Uses of Comparative Sociology.* Berkeley: University of California Press, 1964.

ARDREY, ROBERT. *African Genesis.* New York: Atheneum, 1961.

———. *The Territorial Imperative.* New York: Atheneum, 1966.

ASHBY, ERIC. *Universities, British, Indian and African.* Cambridge: Harvard University Press, 1966.

BANDURA, ALBERT. *Aggression: A Social Learning Analysis.* Englewood Cliffs: Prentice-Hall, 1973.

BELL, NORMAN W., and VOGEL, EZRA, eds. *A Modern Introduction to the Family.* Glencoe: The Free Press, 1960.

BEN-DAVID, JOSEPH. *The Scientist's Role in Society.* Englewood Cliffs: Prentice-Hall, 1971.

BENDIX, REINHARD, and LIPSET, S. M. eds. *Class, Status and Power.* New York: The Free Press, 1966.

BENEDICT, RUTH. *Patterns of Culture.* Boston: Houghton Mifflin, 1934.

279

BERNARDI, B. "The Age-System of the Masai." *Annali Lateranensi,* 18, pp. 257–318, 1955.

BÉTEILLE, ANDRÉ, ed. *Social Inequality.* Baltimore: Penguin Books, 1969.

BIGELOW, ROBERT. *The Dawn Warriors.* Boston: Little, Brown, 1969.

BLAUNER, ROBERT. *Racial Oppression in America.* New York: Harper & Row, 1972.

BLOCH, HERBERT A., and GEIS, GILBERT. *Man, Crime and Society.* New York: Random House, 1970.

BOHANNAN, PAUL. *Social Anthropology.* New York: Holt, Rinehart & Winston, 1963.

———, and DALTON, GEORGE. Markets in Africa. Evanston: Northwestern University Press, 1962.

BRINTON, CRANE. *Anatomy of Revolution.* New York: Random House, 1957.

BROOM, LEONARD, and SELZNICK, PHILIP. *Sociology.* New York: Harper & Row, 1973.

BURN, BARBARA, ed. *Higher Education in Nine Countries.* New York: McGraw-Hill, 1971.

CAILLOIS, R. *Man, Play and Games.* New York: The Free Press, 1961.

CANCIAN, FRANK. *Economics and Prestige in a Maya Community.* Stanford: Stanford University Press, 1965.

CHAMBLISS, WILLIAM J., and SEIDMAN, ROBERT B. *Law, Order and Power.* Reading, Mass.: Addison-Wesley, 1971.

CHAPPLE, ELLIOT D. *Culture and Biological Man.* New York: Holt, Rinehart & Winston, 1970.

CHOMSKY, NOAM. *Language and Mind.* New York: Harcourt, Brace & World, 1968.

COHEN, JOHN. *Chance, Skill and Luck: The Psychology of Guessing and Gambling.* Baltimore: Penguin Books, 1960.

COLBY, BENJAMIN N., and VAN DEN BERGHE, PIERRE. *Ixil Country.* Berkeley: University of California Press, 1969.

COLLIAS, N. E. "Aggressive Behavior among Vertebrate Animals." *Physiological Zoology,* 17, pp. 83–123, 1973.

COOK, SCOTT. "Economic Anthropology," in John J. Honigmann, ed., *Handbook of Social and Cultural Anthropology.* Chicago: Rand McNally, 1973.

COSER, LEWIS A., ed. *Sociology Through Literature.* Englewood Cliffs: Prentice-Hall, 1963.

COSER, ROSE L., ed. *The Family: Its Structures and Functions.* New York: St. Martin's Press, 1964.

COULBORN, RUSHTON, ed. *Feudalism in History.* Princeton: Princeton University Press, 1956.

Cox, Oliver C. *Caste, Class, and Race*. New York: Doubleday, 1948.

Dahrendorf, Ralf. *Class and Class Conflict in Industrial Society*. Stanford: Stanford University Press, 1959.

Dalton, George. "Theoretical Issues in Economic Anthropology." *Current Anthropology*, 10, pp. 63–102, 1969.

Davis, Kingsley, and Moore, Wilbert. "Some Principles of Stratification." *American Sociological Review*, 10, pp. 242–249, 1945.

De Vore, Irven, ed. *Primate Behavior*. New York: Holt, Rinehart & Winston, 1965.

Djilas, Milovan. *The New Class: An Analysis of the Communist System*. New York: Praeger, 1959.

Dollard, J., et al. *Frustration and Aggression*. New Haven: Yale University Press, 1939.

Dore, R. P. *City Life in Japan*. Berkeley: University of California Press, 1965.

———— ed. *Aspects of Social Life in Modern Japan*. Princeton: Princeton University Press, 1967.

Dumont, Louis. *Homo Hierarchicus*. London: Weidenfeld and Nicolson, 1970.

Dumont, René. *False Start in Africa*. New York: Praeger, 1969.

Durkheim, Emile. *The Elementary Forms of Religious Life*. London: Allen & Unwin, 1915 (1912).

————. *The Division of Labor in Society*. New York: Macmillan, 1933 (1893).

————. *The Rules of Sociological Method*. Chicago: University of Chicago Press, 1938 (1895).

————. *Suicide*. Glencoe: The Free Press, 1951 (1897).

Eberhard, Wolfram. *A History of China*. London: Routledge and Kegan Paul, 1960.

Edwards, Harry. *Sociology of Sport*. Homewood: The Dorsey Press.

Eisenstadt, S. N., ed. *Political Sociology*. New York: Basic Books, 1971.

Engels, Friedrich. *The Origin of the Family, Private Property and the State*. New York: International Publishers, 1942 (1884).

Evans-Pritchard, E. E. *The Nuer*. London: Oxford University Press, 1940.

Firth, Raymond, ed. *Themes in Economic Anthropology*. London: Tavistock, 1967.

Flores Ochoa, Jorge. *Los Pastores de Paratía*. México: Instituto Indigenista Interamericano, 1968.

Fortes, Meyer, and Evans-Pritchard, E. E., eds. *African Political Systems*. London: Oxford University Press, 1940.

FRANK, ANDRÉ GUNDER. *Capitalism and Underdevelopment in Latin America*. New York: Monthly Review Press, 1967.

FRAZER, JAMES GEORGE. *The Golden Bough*. London: Macmillan, 1890.

FRAZIER, E. FRANKLIN. "Sociological Theory and Race Relations." *American Sociological Review*, 12, pp. 265–71.

GHURYE, G. S. *Caste and Race in India*. New York: Philosophical Library, 1952.

GOFFMAN, ERVING. *The Presentation of Self in Everyday Life*. Garden City: Doubleday, 1959.

———. *Behavior in Public Places*. New York: The Free Press, 1963.

———. *Relations in Public*. New York: Basic Books, 1971.

GOLDTHORPE, JOHN H. "Social Stratification in Industrial Society," in Reinhard Bendix and S. M. Lipset, eds., *Class, Status and Power*. New York: The Free Press, 1966.

GOODE, WILLIAM J. *World Revolution and Family Patterns*. New York: The Free Press, 1963.

GOUGH, KATHLEEN. "The Origin of the Family." *Journal of Marriage and the Family*, 33, No. 4, pp. 760–70.

HARLOW, HARRY F., and HARLOW, MARGARET K. "The Effect of Rearing Conditions on Behavior," in John Money, ed., *Sex Research: New Developments*. New York: Holt, Rinehart & Winston, 1965.

HERMAN, ROBERT D., ed. *Gambling*. New York: Harper & Row, 1967.

HERSKOVITS, MELVILLE J. *Man and His Works*. New York: Alfred A. Knopf, 1950.

HUIZINGA, JOHAN. *Homo Ludens: The Play Element in Culture*. Boston: Beacon Press, 1955.

HUTTON, J. H. *Caste in India*. Cambridge: Cambridge University Press, 1946.

HUXLEY, ALDOUS. *Brave New World*. New York: Doubleday, 1932.

INKELES, ALEX. "Social Stratification and Mobility in the Soviet Union: 1940–1950." *American Sociological Review*, 15, No. 4, pp. 465–79.

JENCKS, CHRISTOPHER, and RIESMAN, DAVID. *The Academic Revolution*. Garden City: Doubleday, 1968.

JENSEN, ARTHUR. *Environment, Heredity and Intelligence*. Harvard Educational Review Reprint Series, No. 2.

JOHNSON, ELMER H. *Crime, Correction and Society*. Homewood: Dorsey Press, 1974.

KROEBER, A. L. *Anthropology*. New York: Harcourt, Brace, 1948.

KUHN, THOMAS S. *The Structure of Scientific Revolutions*. Chicago: University of Chicago Press, 1962.

KUMMER, HANS. *Primate Societies*. Chicago: Aldine-Atherton, 1971.

KUPER, LEO. *An African Bourgeoisie*. New Haven: Yale University Press, 1965.

LENIN, VLADIMIR I. *Imperialism: The Highest Stage of Capitalism*. Peking: Foreign Languages Press, 1969 (1916).

LENNEBERG, ERIC H. *Biological Foundations of Language*. New York: John Wiley and Sons, 1967.

LENSKI, GERHARD E. *Power and Privilege*. New York: McGraw-Hill, 1966.

———. *Human Societies*. New York: McGraw-Hill, 1970.

LÉVI-STRAUSS, CLAUDE. *The Savage Mind*. London: Weidenfeld and Nicolson, 1966.

———. *The Elementary Structures of Kinship*. Boston: Beacon Press, 1969.

———. *Tristes Tropiques*. New York: Atheneum, 1970.

LÉVY-BRUHL, LUCIEN. *Primitive Mentality*. Boston: Beacon Press, 1966.

LIPSET, S. M., and BENDIX, R. *Social Mobility in Industrial Society*. Berkeley: University of California Press, 1959.

LORENZ, KONRAD Z. *On Aggression*. New York: Harcourt, Brace & World, 1966.

LUNDBERG, GEORGE A., SCHRAG, CLARENCE C., and LARSEN, OTTO N. *Sociology*. New York: Harper & Row, 1963.

MAGALHÃES DE GANDAVO, PEDRO. *The Histories of Brazil*. New York: The Cortes Society, 1922 (1575).

MALINOWSKI, BRONISLAW. *Magic, Science and Religion*. Boston: Beacon Press, 1948.

MANNHEIM, KARL. *Ideology and Utopia*. London: Routledge and Kegan Paul, 1946.

MARCUSE, HERBERT. *One-Dimensional Man*. Boston: Beacon Press, 1964.

MARSH, ROBERT M. "Values, Demand and Social Mobility." *American Sociological Review*, 28, pp. 565–75.

MASON, PHILIP. *Patterns of Dominance*. London: Oxford University Press, 1971.

MAUSS, MARCEL. *The Gift*. London: Cohen and West, 1954 (1923–24).

MICHELS, ROBERT. *Political Parties*. Glencoe: The Free Press, 1949 (1911).

MILLAR, SUSANNA. *The Psychology of Play*. London: Cox and Syman, 1968.

MILLER, STEPHAN. "Ends, Means and Galumpling: Some Leitmotifs of Play." *American Anthropologist*, 75, No. 1, pp. 87–98, 1973.

MILLS, C. WRIGHT. *White Collar*. New York: Oxford University Press, 1951.

———. *The Power Elite*. New York: Oxford University Press, 1959.

———. *The Sociological Imagination*. New York: Grove Press.

MONTAGU, ASHLEY. *Anthropology and Human Nature*. New York: McGraw-Hill, 1957.

MOORE, BARRINGTON. *Soviet Politics: The Dilemma of Power.* Cambridge: Harvard University Press, 1950.

———. *Social Origins of Dictatorship and Democracy.* Boston: Beacon Press, 1967.

———. *Reflections on the Causes of Human Misery.* Boston: Beacon Press, 1972.

MORGAN, LEWIS HENRY. *Ancient Society.* New York: Holt, 1877.

MORRIS, DESMOND. *Primate Ethology.* London: Weidenfeld and Nicolson, 1967(a).

———. *The Naked Ape.* London: Jonathan Cape, 1967(b).

———. *The Human Zoo.* London, Jonathan Cape, 1969.

MOSCA, GAETANO. *The Ruling Class.* New York: McGraw-Hill, 1939 (1896).

MOYNIHAN, DANIEL P. *Maximum Feasible Misunderstanding.* New York: The Free Press, 1970.

MURDOCK, G. P. *Social Structure.* New York: Macmillan, 1949.

MYRDAL, GUNNAR. *An American Dilemma.* New York: Harper, 1944.

———. *Asian Drama: An Inquiry into the Poverty of Nations.* New York: Twentieth Century Fund, 1968.

NADEL, S. F. *A Black Byzantium.* Oxford: Oxford University Press, 1942.

OGBURN, WILLIAM. *Social Change. New York: Viking, 1950.*

ORTEGA Y GASSET, JOSÉ. *The Revolt of the Masses.* New York: Norton, 1932.

ORWELL, GEORGE. *Animal Farm.* New York: Harcourt, Brace & World, 1946.

———. *1984.* New York: Harcourt, Brace & World, 1949.

PARETO, VILFREDO. *The Mind and Society.* New York: Dover Publications, 1963 (1917–19).

PARSONS, TALCOTT, and BALES, ROBERT F. *Family Socialization and Interaction Process.* New York: The Free Press, 1955.

PARSONS, TALCOTT, and SMELSER, NEIL J. *Economy and Society.* Glencoe: The Free Press, 1956.

PIAGET, J. *Play, Dreams and Imitations in Childhood.* New York: Norton, 1951.

POLANYI, KARL, et al., eds. *Trade and Market in the Early Empires.* Glencoe: The Free Press, 1957.

QUINNEY, RICHARD, ed. *Crime and Justice in Society.* Boston: Little, Brown, 1969.

RADCLIFFE-BROWN, A. R., and FORDE, DARYLL. *African Systems of Kinship and Marriage.* London: Oxford University Press, 1950.

RADZINOWICZ, LEON, and WOLFGANG, MARVIN E., eds.. *Crime and Justice.* New York: Basic Books, 1971.

RHODES, ROBERT, ed. *Imperialism and Underdevelopment*. New York: Monthly Review Press, 1970.

ROBBINS, F. G. *The Sociology of Play, Recreation and Leisure Time*. Dubuque, Wm. C. Brown, 1955.

SAPIR, EDWARD. *Language*. New York: Harcourt, 1921.

SCHERMERHORN, RICHARD A. *Comparative Ethnic Relations*. New York: Random House, 1970.

SCOTT, J. P. *Aggression*. Chicago: University of Chicago Press, 1958.

SILBERBAUER, G. B., and KUPER, ADAM J. "Kgalagari Masters and Bushman Serfs." *African Studies*, No. 4, pp. 171–79, 1966.

SIMMEL, GEORG. *The Sociology of Georg Simmel*. Glencoe: The Free Press, 1950.

SIPES, RICHARD G. "War, Sports and Aggression." *American Anthropologist*, 75, No. 1, pp. 64–86, 1973.

SKINNER, B. F. *Beyond Freedom and Dignity*. New York: Alfred A. Knopf, 1971.

SMELSER, NEIL J. *The Sociology of Economic Life*. Englewood Cliffs: Prentice-Hall, 1963.

SOROKIN, PITIRIM A. *Social and Cultural Dynamics*. New York: American Book Company, 1937–41.

———. *Fads and Foibles in Modern Sociology*. Chicago: Regnery, 1956.

SPENCER, HERBERT. *The Evolution of Society,* Chicago: University of Chicago Press, 1967.

SRINIVAS, M. N. *Social Change in Modern India*. Berkeley: University of California Press, 1966.

SUNDKLER, BENGT G. M. *Bantu Prophets in South Africa*. London: Lutterworth, 1948.

SUTHERLAND, EDWIN H., and CRESSEY, DONALD R. *Principles of Sociology*. Philadelphia: Lippincott, 1966.

TIGER, LIONEL. *Men in Groups*. New York: Random House, 1969.

———, and FOX, ROBIN. *The Imperial Animal*. New York: Holt, Rinehart & Winston, 1971.

TITTLE, CHARLES R. "Prisons and Rehabilitation." *Social Problems*, 21, pp. 385–95, 1974.

TOURAINE, ALAIN. *The Academic System in American Society*. New York: McGraw-Hill, 1974.

TRUZZI, MARCELLO, ed. *Sociology for Pleasure*. Englewood Cliffs: Prentice-Hall, 1974.

TUDEN, ARTHUR, and PLOTNICOV, LEONARD. *Social Stratification in Africa*. New York: The Free Press, 1970.

TUMIN, MELVIN. "Some Principles of Stratification: A Critical Analysis." *American Sociological Review*, 18, pp. 387–94, 1953.

TURNBULL, COLIN. *The Forest People*. New York: Simon & Schuster, 1961.

———. *Wayward Servants*. London: Eyre and Spottiswoode, 1965.

VAN DEN BERGHE, PIERRE. "Hypergamy, Hypergenation and Miscegenation." *Human Relations*, 13, pp. 83–91, 1960.

———. *South Africa: A Study in Conflict*. Middletown: Wesleyan University Press, 1965.

———. *Race and Racism*. New York: John Wiley and Sons, 1967.

———. *Race and Ethnicity*. New York: Basic Books, 1970.

———. *Intergroup Relations*, New York: Basic Books, 1972.

———. *Age and Sex in Human Societies*. Belmont: Wadsworth, 1973.

VAN LAWICK-GOODALL, JANE. *In the Shadow of Man*. Boston: Houghton Mifflin, 1971.

VEBLEN, THORSTEIN. *The Theory of the Leisure Class*. New York: Macmillan, 1899.

VOGEL, EZRA F. *Japan's New Middle Class*. Berkeley: University of California Press, 1963.

VOGT, EVON Z., and HYMAN, R. *Water Witching, USA*. Chicago: University of Chicago Press, 1959.

WALLERSTEIN, IMMANUEL, ed. *Social Change: The Colonial Situation*. New York: John Wiley and Sons, 1966.

WASHBURN, S. L., and DE VORE, I. "Social Behavior of Baboons and Early Man." *Viking Fund Publications in Anthropology*, 31, pp. 91–105, 1961.

———, and HAMBURG, D. A. "Aggressive Behavior in Old World Monkeys and Apes," in Phyllis C. Jay, ed., *Primates: Studies in Adaptation and Variability*. New York: Holt, Rinehart & Winston, 1968.

WEBER, MAX. *The Protestant Ethic and the Spirit of Capitalism*. London: Allen & Unwin, 1930 (1920–21).

———. *The Religion of China*. Glencoe, Ill.: The Free Press, 1951 (1920–21).

———. *Ancient Judaism*. Glencoe, Ill.: The Free Press, 1952 (1920–21).

———. *The Religion of India*. Glencoe, Ill.: The Free Press, 1958 (1920–21).

———. *Economy and Society*. New York: Bedminster Press, 1968 (1922).

WHORF, BENJAMIN L. *Language, Thought and Reality*. Cambridge: M.I.T. Press, 1956.

WITTFOGEL, KARL A. *Oriental Despotism*. New Haven: Yale University Press, 1957.

WORSLEY, PETER. *The Trumpet Shall Sound*. London: MacGibbon and Kee, 1957.

————. *The Third World*. Chicago: University of Chicago Press, 1970.

WYNNE-EDWARDS, V. C. "Self-Regulating Systems in Populations of Animals." *Science*, 147, pp. 1543–48.

YOUNG, MICHAEL. *The Rise of the Meritocracy*. Baltimore: Penguin Books, 1961.

————, and WILLMOTT, PETER. *Family and Kinship in East London*. Glencoe, Ill.: The Free Press, 1957.

ZINSSER, HANS. *Rats, Lice and History*. Boston: Little, Brown, 1935.

ZURCHER, LOUIS A. "The 'Friendly' Poker Game," in Marcello Truzzi, ed., *Sociology for Pleasure*. Englewood Cliffs: Prentice-Hall, 1974.

————, and MEADOW, ARNOLD. "On Bullfights and Baseball," in Marcello Truzzi, ed., *Sociology for Pleasure*. Englewood Cliffs: Prentice-Hall 1974.

Index

289

97279

301
V227